Ernie Banks

ALSO BY LEW FREEDMAN
AND FROM MCFARLAND

Connie Mack's First Dynasty: The Philadelphia Athletics, 1910–1914 (2017)

Baseball's Funnymen: Twenty-Four Jokers, Screwballs, Pranksters and Storytellers (2017)

The Boyer Brothers of Baseball (2015)

Joe Louis: The Life of a Heavyweight (2013)

DiMaggio's Yankees: A History of the 1936–1944 Dynasty (2011)

The Day All the Stars Came Out: Major League Baseball's First All-Star Game, 1933 (2010)

Hard-Luck Harvey Haddix and the Greatest Game Ever Lost (2009)

Early Wynn, the Go-Go White Sox and the 1959 World Series (2009)

Ernie Banks

The Life and Career of "Mr. Cub"

LEW FREEDMAN

McFarland & Company, Inc., Publishers
Jefferson, North Carolina

LIBRARY OF CONGRESS CATALOGUING-IN-PUBLICATION DATA

Names: Freedman, Lew, author.
Title: Ernie Banks : the life and career of "Mr. Cub" / Lew Freedman.
Description: Jefferson, North Carolina : McFarland & Company, Inc., Publishers, 2019 | Includes bibliographical references and index.
Identifiers: LCCN 2019017087 | ISBN 9781476667119 (paperback : acid free paper) ♾
Subjects: LCSH: Banks, Ernie, 1931–2015. | Baseball players—United States—Biography. | African American baseball players—Biography. | Chicago Cubs (Baseball team)—History. | Discrimination in sports—United States—History—20th century.
Classification: LCC GV865.B26 F74 2019 | DDC 796.357092/396073 [B] —dc23
LC record available at https://lccn.loc.gov/2019017087

BRITISH LIBRARY CATALOGUING DATA ARE AVAILABLE

ISBN (print) 978-1-4766-6711-9
ISBN (ebook) 978-1-4766-3513-2

© 2019 Lew Freedman All rights reserved

No part of this book may be reproduced or transmitted in any form or by any means, electronic or mechanical, including photocopying or recording, or by any information storage and retrieval system, without permission in writing from the publisher.

Front cover: Chicago Cubs first baseman Ernie Banks (National Baseball Hall of Fame and Museum/Doug McWilliams)

Printed in the United States of America

McFarland & Company, Inc., Publishers
 Box 611, Jefferson, North Carolina 28640
 www.mcfarlandpub.com

Table of Contents

Preface 1
Introduction 3

1. Ernie Banks Day 7
2. Growing Up 10
3. Moving On 18
4. From Kansas City to Chicago 26
5. The Majors 32
6. Race 39
7. Banks and Baker 49
8. 1955–1957 57
9. 1958–1959: Most Valuable Player 65
10. Ron Santo: A Sidekick 73
11. Coach O'Neil and a Whole Bunch of Other Coaches 80
12. Downs and Ups 88
13. The Strangeness of 1965 96
14. Ernie and Leo 103
15. New Look Cubs 111
16. Ready for a Breakthrough 119
17. 1969 127
18. Another Highlight 139
19. Retirement 146

20. A New Life Begins	153
21. A Hall of Famer	160
22. Living to the Fullest	168
23. The End	175
Chapter Notes	181
Bibliography	187
Index	189

Preface

Ernie Banks is the heart and soul of the Chicago Cubs franchise. I always considered him to be the best player in the history of the ballclub as well.

I never had occasion to meet or interview the Hall of Fame shortstop, first baseman and slugger before I moved to Chicago to work for the *Chicago Tribune* in 2001. For most of the time I resided in Chicago, Banks lived in California. But he routinely visited Chicago and made special appearances at Wrigley Field.

At other times, I interviewed Banks via telephone for book research on projects that related to Chicago Cubs history. He unfailingly picked up the telephone and answered with the phrase "Ernie Banks here. And how are you feeling?"

Some of my most humorous talks with Banks involved topics somewhat removed from baseball, although that was the reason I had dialed him. Ernie realized that almost everybody who got in touch with him wanted to discuss baseball in one form or another, but he never wanted to simply dive in.

Whether it was a personal rule or his natural manner, Ernie always chose to ease into the subject, prefacing baseball chatter with personal chatter. Of course, this was the most polite way to begin anyway.

First and foremost, Banks, someone who was often married and sometimes between relationships, wanted to know if the love lives of his acquaintance were humming along acceptably. When we spoke one-on-one on the phone, this seemed to be the No. 1 thing on his mind. I was always able to assure him I was happily married.

For those who saw Ernie later in person in his life, or saw photographs of him as an older gentleman, chances were he was wearing a bow-tie. When and how he became partial to them as an accouterment of his more formal attire, I cannot say. He did look dapper in them, however. Once, seemingly out of nowhere, he began quizzing me on whether I ever wore bow-ties (no) and began urging me to start. I had to reply, "Ernie, bow-ties look good on you, but they wouldn't look good on me."

At the start of another phone interview (it must have taken place in early February), Ernie peppered me with questions about what I was going to get my wife for Valentine's Day. Whether or not he had a sponsor connection with Hershey, Godiva, or Mars, he pushed hard for a present of chocolate. I tried to slip in a sentence here or there about my wife not liking chocolate, but I am not sure that clicked.

My wife Debra has long been the transcriber of my tapes for book projects, and more than any other interview subjects, she always got a kick out of listening to Ernie conversations. She was struck by his upbeat demeanor and just how often he worked the phrase "That's wonderful!" into his answers.

To this day, when she hears Ernie Banks' name, the first thing she is likely to say is "That's wonderful!"

Surely, Ernie Banks met 100,000 people during his long life, and I'm willing to bet that for the vast majority it was a wonderful experience. He was a warm man with an ever-ready smile who was the proudest and best ambassador the Chicago Cubs ever had. No one is perfect, but it was hard to hang up the phone or walk away from an encounter with Banks without him leaving a smile on your face.

Introduction

Ernie Banks' primary nickname during his Major League career—and beyond—was "Mr. Cub."

He was thoroughly and completely identified with the Chicago Cubs, from his earliest days on the playing field to his death in 2015. Banks represented the franchise with class and enthusiasm, and once he achieved stardom, and long into retirement, he was the one person most closely identified with the franchise.

Born in 1931 in Dallas, Texas, Banks grew up a black man during the South's Jim Crow era, when no advantages were accorded to someone with a darker skin color. It would have been easy to become soured, but one of Banks' trademarks was always being cheerful.

From his rookie year of 1953, when he broke into the majors at the age of 22 as the first African American player in Cubs history, throughout his 19 seasons in the bigs, ending in 1971, Banks was an optimist. Every player plays to win. Banks came to play harboring the dream of making the Cubs a winner. He never could pull off that achievement. Banks never played in a World Series game, never competed in a post-season game.

For most of Banks' big-league career, the Cubs were one of the weakest teams in the National League. When the sportswriters surrounded Banks in spring training, he always predicted the Cubs would be a winner that year, but by autumn all of his hopes had been dampened by sad reality.

"I always believe," Banks said. "Some people think I don't. Some people think I should be in a lunatic asylum. But I say it every year and I believe it every year."[1]

Between 1953 and 1966, the Cubs never finished higher than fifth (twice) in the National League. One year, after the league expanded from eight teams to ten, the Cubs finished tenth. Twice, near the end of Banks' playing years, the Cubs finished second in the National League East under a new divisional format. The one that really hurt was 1969, when Chicago seemed to have the Mets beat, but couldn't hold on.

Still, Banks never spoke a discouraging word. One of Banks' other nicknames was "Mr. Sunshine" because of his unceasing optimism. He saw sunshine through the clouds, and most reporters couldn't even get Banks to bash bad weather.

The epitome of Banks' positive outlook was encapsulated in his trademark, often repeated phrase "Let's play two!" If someone remarked that it was a beautiful day for a ballgame, Banks upped the bidding. To him it was so nice out, why not play a doubleheader?

Supposedly, Banks first uttered his "Let's play two" signature comment for the first time in the clubhouse before a July game when the temperature was about 105 degrees. Banks was like the postman, not deterred by snow, rain or hail, or even extreme heat.

In 2013, when Banks was presented the Presidential Medal of Freedom by President Barack Obama, he explained the origin of "Let's play two."

"It was a very bad day in Chicago," Banks said. "I came into the locker room, and I was feeling great. And I said to all my teammates, 'It's a beautiful day—let's play two!' That was a time in my life that I was really excited about going to Wrigley Field."[2]

When wasn't he?

Banks told more than one story about when "Let's play two" got started. It should be noted that Banks did not mention a year to Obama. Of course, he did say it many times, and most assuredly the sentence stuck to him. There was romance in the statement. What American in love with baseball, who got paid to play it for a career, wouldn't love to see the fairy tale go on and on, and instead of playing ball every day play two games a day? There was that kind of appeal in Banks' comment.

Another time, Banks provided an explanation for why playing two sounded great to him. While saying he was happiest at a ballpark, the Banks who was always concerned about others' love lives sounded less than romantic when linking his wife at the time to playing a doubleheader. "I was married and that was the only place I could make my own decisions, when I came to the ballpark—when to swing, when not to swing, when to run," he said. "I couldn't do that at home. That's why I said let's play two. I didn't want to go home because I couldn't make those decisions."[3]

The marriage didn't last. Banks' love of baseball did. Chicago's love affair with Ernie Banks never waned either.

The "Let's play two" phrase is the most famous one-liner attributed to Banks. However, he was also the Cub who began calling Wrigley Field "the Friendly Confines." That too has become part of Cubs lexicon, frequently employed as a description for the venerable park over the last half-century. Banks made the comment after the team returned from a long road trip. He was noting how good it felt to be home again for the Cubs' next games.

As a player, Banks began as a shortstop and switched to first base midway through his career. He won two Most Valuable Player Awards and is a member of the 500-home-run club, those long shots products of his supple wrists. Banks was an All-Star in 11 seasons, but was chosen for 14 All-Star games because he was active during the brief period (1959–1962) when two All-Star games per season were played. Banks won one Gold Glove Award, in 1960 as a shortstop. Before the really big money spread through the sport, according to baseball-reference.com, he made a maximum salary of $60,000 in 1969.

Banks was inducted into the Baseball Hall of Fame in Cooperstown, New York, in 1977, and he was chosen as a member of baseball's All-Century team in 1999.

Banks became closely identified with the number 14 during his playing days, and in 1982 the Cubs retired that number.

On March 31, 2008, the Chicago Cubs unveiled a statue of Ernie Banks outside Wrigley Field. Banks spoke at the event while wearing a Cubs cap. The statue portrayed him in his right-handed batting stance. In addition to his name, the black sturdy base had two phrases carved into it. One read, "Mr. Cub." The other read, "Let's play two."

During the later years of his life, Banks spoke of trying to make a greater contribution to mankind. He felt more people needed to help the world's poor and humanity in general. He said his last remaining goal in life was to win the Nobel Prize for Peace.

Some may have thought Ernie Banks had done enough already to gain a Nobel Prize. Certainly, if there was such an award, he would have already claimed a Nobel Prize for Baseball.

1

Ernie Banks Day

One of the greatest days in Ernie Banks' Major League baseball career did not involve a meaningful Chicago Cubs victory, a big day at bat, or a hot play made with the glove. He was in uniform and stood on the field at Wrigley Field, but what he remembered best about this baseball day was how it represented all of his baseball days in Chicago for more than a decade.

August 15, 1964, was proclaimed "Ernie Banks Day" at Wrigley and throughout Chicago. This day of honor was special to Banks. Many thousands turned out to show their appreciation for what his feats on the field meant to them and what he as a man meant to them. Any athlete would be grateful for such attention, although the practice of so honoring a baseball star with gifts has become antiquated.

During Banks' heyday on the diamond, when many greats became especially identified with a city for the duration of their careers, the players may have been in the limelight, but they mostly did not make outrageous salaries that dwarfed the average working man's paydays. When a team and a city gave presents to a ballplayer and his family, it really was significant. The items were bonuses well beyond the typical take-home salary. In 2018, the top-earning baseball players in the majors made upwards of $25 million a year. Only CEOs of Fortune 500 companies make comparable money. No fans want to see such a player further enriched. If the centerfielder wants a fishing boat, let him go buy one, or buy a fleet. He can afford it. He doesn't need a free vacation. He can purchase his own jet to fly to an island where he can afford to operate his own hotel.

The highest-paid player in the big leagues in 1964 was Willie Mays with the San Francisco Giants. His salary was $105,000. Banks made $57,500 with the Cubs that year. The average American worker's salary was $4,576, so Ernie was doing fine compared to the rest of the country.

Banks was 11 years into his Major League career and 33 years old. He was already a beloved figure in Chicago, a status he never relinquished. The Cubs were closing in on one of their typical hapless finishes. Manager Bob

Kennedy steered them to a 76–86 record and an eighth- and last-place National League finish. In those days, all Cubs home contests were still played during the day.

As Mayor Richard J. Daley made sure the rest of Chicagoans took note of the occasion due to his proclamation, the paid attendance was listed as 23,003 for the game between the Cubs and the Pittsburgh Pirates. As they did quite often that summer, the Cubs lost, 5–4. Banks played first base and went 0-for-3 at the plate. He walked once and scored a run. But there was nothing particularly notable to distinguish this game in his memory among the 2,528 games he played.

Lindy McDaniel took the loss in relief for the Cubs—no one offered him any gifts that day. Roberto Clemente, one of Banks' contemporary greats, and Manny Mota, had big days for the Pirates.

At the time, Banks, who was married four times in his life, was wedded to Eloyce. She, his father Eddie, and twin five-year-old sons Joel and Jerome, who wore mini Cubs outfits adorned with dad's number 14, were present for the on-field ceremony. Apparently nervous being in front of the large Wrigley crowd, which was supplemented by thousands of Little League players, at one point in a cute scene, the boys each grabbed on to one of their father's legs.

The master of ceremonies that day (which lasted 22 minutes) was the famed Cubs broadcaster, Jack Brickhouse. Charlie Grimm, who over the decades was as ubiquitous at Wrigley Field as the ivy in a variety of Cubs roles, was the team's representative as vice-president. National League president Warren Giles was present.

Among the goodies given to Banks and his family were a diamond ring, a nine-passenger station wagon, a transistor radio, a silver serving tray, a hi-fi record player, and savings bonds for his three children (a two-year-old daughter stayed home). The tray was engraved "Mr. Cub."

Banks was lauded as a player and a person. Philip R. Clarke, the chairman of the event organizing committee, made that clear immediately in his talk about Banks. "We are saluting Ernie Banks with stirring words as not only one of the all-time greats of baseball, but as a great American."[1]

Giles echoed those words, referring to Banks as not only a great player (he had won the Most Valuable Player Award twice by then), but as "a great man."[2] He handed over a plaque which represented a tribute from the other National League clubs. *The Sporting News* got in on the action, too. A framed copy of a cover of the publication announcing Ernie Banks Day was given to the player, and representative Bob Inserra called Banks "everybody's All-American."[3]

Banks got his turn to say thank you and made his own speech. "First, I want to thank God for making me an American and giving me the ability to be a Major League baseball player," Banks said.[4] He thanked his wife, children and parents, the fans, the Cubs organization, and owner Philip K. Wrigley. "I will never forget this day," he said. "I thank you all from the bottom of my heart."[5]

There was one different type of gift on display at Wrigley. The Rehabilitation Institute of Chicago ordered a gigantic cake, five feet long, with a Banks figure on top, with icing decorated with baseball bats and balls. It was accompanied by a thank you note to Banks for being Banks. It was said at the time that he had visited the center 17 times to cheer up patients, and this was how they acknowledged his gift to them.

Banks said one more thing, another thank you. He used the word "wonderful" for the fans and noted how appreciative he was "for your warmth and acceptance in making this day possible."[6] Those were telling words. In 1953, when Banks first joined the Cubs, he could not have imagined what lay ahead, either on the field or in his relationship with the city.

This was a young man who grew up with segregation, whose first big-time baseball adventure was for the Kansas City Monarchs in the Negro Leagues. When Banks was a youth, it was useless for an African American boy to dream of playing in the majors.

There were many superb, dark-skinned baseball players all over the country, some the greatest of all time, from Satchel Paige and Josh Gibson to Cool Papa Bell and Judy Johnson. White-dominated American society relegated their careers to the hinterlands. The American League and National League had no jobs available, even for such great and talented players. Not yet, at least.

Jackie Robinson broke the modern-day color barrier with the Brooklyn Dodgers in 1947. Ernie Banks was 16 years old that year. Even six years later, when the Cubs brought Banks to Chicago, only marginal gains had been made in the hiring of black ballplayers. Several teams had inched into integration. Others had not taken a single baby step in that direction, and it would be years before they put an African American player into uniform.

Certainly, the Ernie Banks of 1930s and 1940s Dallas, the Ernie Banks of 1947, and even the Ernie Banks of 1953, would not have imagined that in 1964 he would be the toast of the town as the symbol of one of baseball's oldest franchises, treated as a hero by thousands in one of the nation's largest cities.

2

Growing Up

They didn't play baseball at Ernie Banks' high school. The game most comparable to what was referred to as the National Pastime in the United States at his Dallas, Texas, school was softball. Softball. The name implied it was for girls, not teenaged boys, as opposed to hardball.

But that's what was on the menu, and if you wanted to play the sport of Satchel Paige, Josh Gibson and Cool Papa Bell, some of the most famous competitors in the Negro Leagues, you adapted.

Funny thing was, the future Hall of Fame infielder for the Chicago Cubs wasn't much interested in baseball as a youth. His father, Eddie, loved the game and played for all-African American semi-pro teams that competed around Texas. Young Ernie was sports-minded, but his affection drifted to football, basketball and swimming with more passion than it did baseball. That was despite his father's encouragement to take up the game. In a poor family (by Banks' description), spending about $3 for a baseball glove caused a pause because there was little discretionary income. Eddie Banks bought the glove anyway and then discovered he still had to bribe his second-oldest child to play the sport by throwing nickels or dimes at him. In later years it took a lot more cash than that to pay Ernie Banks to wield a mitt.

Ernest Banks was the birth certificate name of the future star when he was born in Dallas on January 31, 1931. Banks' mother's name was Essie, and she and Eddie had 12 children. Eddie worked in construction and did physical labor, loading goods at a warehouse for a grocery-store chain. Essie wasn't as big on sports as her husband and would have preferred seeing Ernie become a minister. The closest he came to that career was his ministerial disposition as a preacher of his own good and kind words to people later in life. He never pretended to be an instrument of God, but only of the Cubs.

As a Major League baseball player, Ernie Banks' personal dimensions were listed as 6-foot-1 and 180 pounds, and he had the power to strike 512 home runs. When he was born, if anyone did any projecting, it was difficult to picture him growing that large and sturdy. "My father always said I was

2. Growing Up

the smallest baby he had ever seen," Banks said of his five-pound, two-ounce initial weigh-in after being delivered to the wide world by a midwife. There was no money for a doctor, and the same circumstances limited everyone else in the neighborhood.[1]

Very early in his Cubs career, Banks developed a good relationship with one of the regular newspaper beat writers, Jim Enright of the *Chicago Evening American* and *Chicago Today*. Enright not only anointed him "Mr. Cub," his enduring nickname, but Banks collaborated on his first book with Enright, delving into painful childhood details of poverty seared into his memory.

Banks recollected that his father worked seven days a week at two jobs to support the family. Dating back to when he was five years old in the mid–1930s, Banks remembered what he called the welfare truck that toured the neighborhood, giving away food and clothing to those in need. Once, as a child, he was so thrilled to receive a new pair of jeans that he did not take them off even to go to bed. He loved those pants so much that he ran out of the house to avoid taking them off when his mom wanted to wash them. "They were new, they were mine and I was determined to wear them all the time," Banks said.[2]

The earliest days of Banks' life played out against the backdrop of the Great Depression, which afflicted all of the American economy and American cities. The poor became poorer, and those who had never experienced poverty went broke from the stock market collapse and its ripple effects, such as massive unemployment. Eddie Banks obtained jobs through President Franklin D. Roosevelt's Works Progress Administration.

Growing up without took many forms, especially in a large family where Banks was the oldest boy in the clan. He walked everywhere, mostly in an eight-block radius, and his recreation came through the YMCA. A Banks chore was keeping the kerosene lamps in the home filled with fuel. He also transported the fuel for the wood-burning stoves in the house. His mother cooked on one of them. He also hauled water from an outside pump for drinking and bathing. He did not explicitly state that there was no running water in the house or no electricity, but his account of carrying out those tasks definitely implied that was so.

How she managed it with limited resources Banks does not say, but his mother made Sunday dinners special. Perhaps she skimped the rest of the week, but the menu for Sunday's hearty meal included chicken, black-eyed peas, red beans, rice, corn bread and dessert, featuring Essie's specialty of the house. Banks called them "T-cakes" and said they resembled cupcakes with syrup and jelly.

Banks had one older sister, three other sisters and seven brothers. Two of them died in young adulthood, one of a gunshot wound in an apparent accident, although complete details of the case were not given to the family.

As Banks aged, the Depression ended and the family finances improved. Prized childhood presents were a bicycle and a BB gun. Banks shot rats with the gun, which says more about the status of the neighborhood than whether or not he could put food on the table with a clear aim. Eventually, Banks joined his father as a part-time cotton picker. Many a Southern biography has been written where the individual talks of picking cotton as the worst days of his life, back-breaking work in 100-degree temperatures, the work in the fields fueling a desire to make something better for himself. Not Banks. "I liked cotton picking," he said.[3]

He rose at 5 a.m. with his father. They ate a quick breakfast, and then, along with other workers, were bussed to the fields about 30 miles away. Banks adopted his own method in the fields, crawling on both knees and picking. The bosses paid $2–3 per hundredweight turned in. A little bit later, Banks and a friend started their own lawn care company. They were paid 25 cents to trim a lawn.

All of what Banks knew and experienced as a youth was in his own segregated neighborhood. No white people lived in his section of Dallas. His playmates, his work partners, and other families around the Banks were all black. The same thing was true at Booker T. Washington High School.

Today, Dallas is a thriving, fast-growing city of 1.3 million people, the economic engine of Texas, home to professional sports teams at the highest levels of play in the world, from the National Football League to Major League Baseball, the National Basketball Association, and the National Hockey League. But Dallas was not considered big-time enough for a franchise in any of those leagues until 1960, when the NFL Cowboys were founded in response to the creation of the American Football League and its Dallas Texans.

The Dallas of 1930, according to census reports from the year before Banks was born, was home to 269,475 people. It was still adjusting, adapting or reacting to being labeled the most racist city in the United States by the crusading *Dallas Morning News* in the 1920s. That may come as a surprise to those who picture Dallas as being more a part of the Old West with its six-guns, rodeos and galloping horses than harboring a kinship with the Deep South and its antebellum mansions, old-world slavery, and the Confederacy.

In the 1920s, Dallas burgeoned into a hotbed of Ku Klux Klan activity. What might be called the ultimate white supremacist organization began gathering memberships in Dallas in 1920, and its rolls increased as the city grew in population over that decade. Klan members were thrust into office by Klan-sympathizer voters. Over a short period of time, whatever latent racism had been resting within the breast of sore losers of the Civil War came to the fore.

A 1921 incident shocked the public. An African American male was kidnapped, driven out of town, whipped with chains and had the initials "KKK" carved into his forehead. When the abductors and torturers set the man free in Dallas, he was ordered to walk bare-chested into the hotel where he worked as an elevator operator. His crime was supposedly a romantic connection with a white woman. While the *Dallas Morning News* railed against the Klan editorially, those running the *Dallas Times Herald* were viewed as Klan supporters. The criminals actually allowed a reporter from that paper to witness their mistreatment of the man. So these men lacking shame actually sought publicity. When asked about punishment, the sheriff said the elevator man no doubt did something to deserve what happened to him, and the man with the badge (later revealed as a member of the Klan) said there would be no investigation.

As Klan membership grew, the *News* battled on editorially despite being the focus of subscription cancellations and advertising boycotts. The Klan went through a downward spiral not long before Banks was born. Still, this was the prejudiced city Banks was born into. He practically never saw white people—even those who would have been on the African American's side in ugly confrontations with the Klan—and did not stray from his all-black neighborhood. As a good boy, he never got in trouble with the law, and as a homeboy essentially, he did not face racial intolerance up close as a youth.

Whatever was truly going through Ernie Banks' mind about race relations in the United States when he was a teenager is not something he talked about. For the most part, throughout his playing career and long years in retirement, Banks was rarely drawn out on the topic. If there were scars left by racism in his youth, they were never overtly apparent. Certainly, he understood the segregated world, but he may have been fortunate to escape direct insults and confrontations based on where he lived within Dallas.

In the early 1960s, long after he was an established star in Chicago, while the country was in the throes of upheaval over African Americans' civil rights, Banks was asked if he experienced racism in baseball. He ducked the question, replying, "The only race we have in baseball is trying to beat the throw to first for a hit, or to second, trying to steal a base," he said.[4]

Banks was an intelligent man. He certainly understood the nature of racism in everyday life and whatever racism existed in baseball. Consistent with his image and approach to the game and his connection with a single team, he chose to keep his thoughts secret. He had no interest in engaging in discussions that would surely prove controversial. This was a man who was widely embraced by all races, and he had no wish to alienate any of his fans.

Eddie Banks, Ernie's father, said he gave that first inexpensive glove to his son when the boy was eight. By then Eddie was retired from baseball after his eight years as a catcher with the Dallas Black Giants in the 1920s. "I was a pretty good hitter, but I couldn't carry Ernie's bat," his father said while attending a 1960 baseball dinner that honored his son.[5]

Eddie Banks said he played catch with Ernie whenever he could after work when Ernie was still a small fellow. He made it sound as if Ernie's hitting skills came naturally when he first began swinging hard a few years later, and he described him as a terror endangering any object situated too close to withstand a blow.

"The bat came later," the elder Banks said, "and that almost wrecked everything. Drives off Ernie's bat broke so many windows in the neighborhood that we were always in trouble. He broke so many windows that I was almost broke trying to pay for them."[6] For a while, Mr. Banks engaged in a gambit in his own home, flattening tin cans to fill holes where glass previously reigned. He took some heat for that from family members, too, who grew tired of trying to gaze outdoors through tin.

Confirming Essie's lack of interest in baseball as a projected career for Ernie, Eddie said she never thought the father-son time investment was worthwhile, and she wanted Ernie to spend his time working instead of playing ball. It may be his mother's encouragement that sent Ernie into that lawn-cutting business, one of her off-the-cuff suggestions.

Banks enrolled at Booker T. Washington, his all-African American high school, in the late 1940s, just as World War II ended. He played some football, ran some track and played formal softball since the school did not have a baseball team. Softball (except for the U.S. national team level, for women), is identified with men in one of two ways. Almost always the players are pictured as out-of-shape, older men, hobby players seeking diversion from their jobs by competing in "soft pitch." There is also "fast pitch," where the best hitters might bat .800 and crash home runs out of play with startling regularity. The rules of the games are instantly identifiable to baseball players, but it is not the same as playing baseball.

Banks did not play organized baseball in his youth, just fast-pitch softball as he grew up. Clearly, he demonstrated the necessary skills in the related game that others thought would translate to baseball, and he was getting pointers from his father. Many years after Eddie retired from the Dallas Black Giants, Ernie became a bat boy for a different local African American team, the Dallas Green Monarchs. According to his dad, Ernie was very slow to grow into his adult physique. "He was still so small his mother had to cut the store uniform we bought for him to about half its original size. He was the most batless batboy you ever saw. For he'd be playing catch with some of the players when he should have been doing his regular chores."[7]

The older Banks said he never tried to steer Ernie towards his position of catcher because he wasn't interested in it, but always tried to keep him away from the mound. He feared pitchers were too fragile, and he had seen too many of their careers snuffed out early because of injuries.

One telling thing Eddie Banks mentioned about his son was his outlook on life that so many millions more people came to see. He said the Green Monarchs never seemed to mind Ernie spending so much time throwing the ball around instead of fulfilling his duties, because of his pleasing personality. "Ernie was such a happy-go-lucky kid, nobody minded too much that he was spending more time playing than working," he said.[8]

Ernie became a high school athlete—he mentioned touch football more than tackle football—as well as dabbling in whatever else was offered, from track to swimming to softball. He had filled out a little bit, topping 150 pounds finally at Booker T. But he was destined to follow a unique route to baseball success. He may be the only Hall of Famer fundamentally schooled in softball instead of baseball. He also never played high school–affiliated baseball or college ball. Banks most definitely did not dream of becoming a Major League player when he began high school.

Jackie Robinson was one of the most famous Americans in the country in 1947, when he made his pioneering big-league debut with the Brooklyn Dodgers, his opportunity facilitated by team president Branch Rickey. Rickey warned him he was entering a hostile environment. Robinson was old enough, experienced enough, and mature enough to realize he was penetrating a previously closed society where racism had thrived for decades. As Robinson began his tour of the nation's large cities, he was met with a mixed reception. Some fans were hostile and shouted invective at him. Simultaneously, he became a hero to the African American population. Banks was 16 that year, mostly sheltered from personal racial trauma, but not unaware.

Late in Banks' Cubs career, he was invited to write a column for the *Chicago Tribune* called "The Wonderful World of Ernie Banks." In one of the articles, he talked of his baseball world view at the time. "When I was in my early teens, I never dreamed of becoming a big-league baseball player," he said.[9] He said he did not even believe he could make a sports team at his high school.

He recalled standing on the sidelines of football practice as a sophomore with an older friend named Bill Blair, who believed in him and felt he could play that sport. Banks, his confidence not the equal of Blair's, said he was too small for the game. But he ended up joining the team. The following summer, acting as if he was Banks' agent, Blair, who had watched Banks star as a softball shortstop for the YMCA, introduced him to a man named Johnny Carter, who was recruiting baseball talent for a team called the Amarillo Colts. Banks told Carter he had never played baseball, only softball. "If you can play softball, you can play baseball," the optimistic Carter informed him.[10]

Amarillo is 365 miles northwest of Dallas. Banks was 17, and his parents had to approve his version of going to summer camp to play games in Texas, Oklahoma, New Mexico, Kansas and Nebraska. In his first game, Banks, who was nervous, timid and wondering what this world was all about, hit a home run. In the old style of underpaid minor leaguers, Banks was urged to dash up into the stands and collect his bonus money—coins contributed by happy home fans. Banks called this early home run a thrill. There are varying reports that when Banks wasn't collecting change, he was paid something between $12.50 and $15 a game. When he gave his mother Essie some money at the end of the season, she was happy and began to see the potential financial value in his playing baseball.

Banks loved every minute of the way he spent his summer between sophomore and junior year in high school, and the next summer he returned to the Colts for a second year of play. Although still anchored in Amarillo, the traveling team was much more often referred to as the Detroit Colts, the way Banks remembered his second year. The Colts did not belong to Detroit, but operators must have felt such an allegiance sounded more sophisticated or big-time. Banks had developed his skills considerably during his first season with the Colts and was an even better player his second season. Others began to take note of his potential.

The comment Eddie Banks made about Ernie being a happy-go-lucky kid might be the perfect characterization of him that followed for a lifetime. It makes it seem as if young Ernie's personable manner was set in stone early. There is no such thing as a perfect person, and after all Banks did cope with several divorces, but there are few people in the world who encountered Banks over his many decades in and around baseball who will not praise him. His father may have thought of it first, but if the way Banks behaved in public from the beginning of his Cubs days on was the same way he behaved on his way up, there would not have been much to criticize.

Ernie Banks of the Chicago Cubs came to the ballpark cheerful, optimistic, smiling and chatting. There was no reason to think he was any different as a youngster and had experienced a personality transplant, even if witnesses of those earliest playing days are not so plentiful. There is little ambiguity in how most people think of Banks.

The late Ron Santo wrote a book in the twilight of his life with some passages on Banks. In part, Santo wrote,

> I have known Ernie for more than 45 years and in all that time I have never heard him say a bad word about anybody (or anything) and I have never heard anybody say a bad word about him. People who meet him for the first time, who hear him expound for the first time on the beauty of baseball, the Cubs, Wrigley Field and life in general, think it's all an act, a façade. They keep waiting for him to drop his guard, but he never does. I have known him for more than 45 years and I, too, have waited for him to drop his guard, to be anything but upbeat, positive and optimistic. I'm still waiting.[11]

Being in a good mood can make a good impression. That might have been especially true when Banks was a teenager breaking in with the Colts, and as he gained notoriety from scouts looking to sign the best players. Scouts might well put a one-liner in a report commenting that a prospect is a surly jerk. In Ernie's case, they probably wrote something like "Good guy. Always smiling. Would be well-liked in the clubhouse."

3

Moving On

Ernie Banks' first and most important patron once he departed the world of softball for hardball was the estimable Buck O'Neil. He nurtured the teenager, taught him, endorsed him and served as the conduit to his place in the majors.

After two years of his slugging with the Amarillo Colts, Banks was much more of a known quantity than he had been as a high school student in Dallas, where he didn't even play baseball. Banks turned 19 in 1950 and was ripe to mix it up with better competition. His old friend Bill Blair had connections to the Kansas City Monarchs of the Negro Leagues, but Banks was also spotted as a future talent by the famous speedster, Cool Papa Bell.

Bell was born in 1903 and was regarded as one of the greatest players in Negro Leagues history. His given name when born in Starkville, Mississippi, was James Thomas. Bell was among the first handful of stars from the days before baseball integration in 1947 elected to the Baseball Hall of Fame. He was regarded as perhaps the fastest man ever to circle the bases. Bell's final on-field appearance with the Homestead Grays occurred in 1946, and he retired to his St. Louis home. Post–Jackie Robinson, he was invited to give the majors a shot, but felt he was too old.

Cool Papa was one of the unfortunate gifted African Americans that Major League baseball snubbed during his prime. When the Hall of Fame developed 20-20 hindsight, Bell was selected for membership under the auspices of a special committee. One of those serving on that body was Eddie Gottlieb, best-known for his pioneering NBA involvement in the early days of that league, but he also was noted for promoting Negro Leagues baseball in Philadelphia. "If Bell had played in the major leagues he would have reminded fans of Willie Keeler as a bunt-and-run, hit 'em-where-they-ain't batter and Ty Cobb as a base runner," Gottlieb said. "And he might have excelled both."[1]

Most talk of Bell revolves around his remarkable speed. No one told a better story about the swift player than Negro Leagues legend Satchel Paige. Of Bell's lightning running, Paige said on many an occasion, especially at baseball dinners, that he "was so fast that when he flipped the wall switch in a hotel, he'd be in bed before the light went out."[2]

For his first four years in retirement, Bell scouted for the St. Louis Browns. But that gig was ending, and in a sense he was a free-agent talent scout when he first saw Banks play.

Bell was an expert on those who had talent in their legs, but he knew baseball and he recognized the young man had the goods.

Bell said he first saw Banks on a field when he was in his late teens, starting his days working out with the Colts. At the time, Bell was running a loosely affiliated farm club belonging to Kansas City called the Little Monarchs. He told Banks, "When you get out of school, kid, we'll pick you up."[3] Bell claimed he tried to sell the Monarchs on going after Banks right then, but O'Neil wasn't biting because he already had a solid shortstop in Gene Baker.

Some of the retelling of the discovery of Ernie Banks has become muddied. In one of his accounts, O'Neil said he welcomed Cool Papa's tip about Banks, whom he had seen playing for the "Black Sheepherders out of San Antonio."[4] There was a team referred to as the Black Sheepherders, but representing San Angelo. Banks did not even mention the Sheepherders in his "Mr. Cub" autobiography.

O'Neil referred to Bell's enthusiasm for Banks occurring in 1949, when Banks was 17. Banks would have been 18 by the end of January, so grabbing him would have taken place very early in the year. As a first baseman, O'Neil, whose given name was John, hit .300 or higher for the Monarchs several times in his playing days (as high as the .390s) and took over as manager in 1948. It was a dream of his to manage that team. However, the Monarchs, like other Negro Leagues clubs, were coming to the end of their existence as a vehicle for black ballplayers who had been blacklisted by the majors. This was the last-hurrah period as one by one, big-league clubs slowly but steadily began integrating.

A young Ernie Banks from the 1950s (National Baseball Hall of Fame).

O'Neil called Banks "our biggest find" during that era of the Monarchs. "Cool had seen him play in several games and loved his power and potential, so that winter I drove to Dallas and signed him up even though I had never seen him swing a bat. Cool's word was good enough for me."[5] This was a transitional time for Banks, who was maturing into a full-grown man, getting used to being away from home and still honing his skills.

O'Neil was a pivotal figure in Negro Leagues history, not only because he was an excellent player teaming with some of the true greats like Paige and Bell. As the baseball world slowly adapted to the arrival of the African American on the biggest stages, O'Neil was a go-between. He hung on to the end of the Negro Leagues, sticking with Kansas City as manager until 1955. However, before that, O'Neil helped shepherd some of the young players with potential into the majors. In 1955, he officially became a scout for the Chicago Cubs, and in 1962 became the majors' first African American coach, again with the Cubs.

Later in life, O'Neil was restored to prominence in the baseball world and in the public mind by documentary film-maker Ken Burns. When Burns filmed his 18½-hour, monumental 1994 baseball epic, he chose O'Neil as a narrator for the Negro Leagues period. O'Neil's grace, charm, distinctive speech and fresh exposure catapulted him into the limelight. He was a bit like a best supporting actor stealing the show. By then, O'Neil had also played a significant role in founding the Negro Leagues Museum in Kansas City, where he lived. Until he died in 2006 at 94, the white-haired O'Neil was sought out for his story-telling and historical knowledge, and in his engaging manner, he kept images of black baseball alive.

One of his many contributions to baseball was O'Neil's guidance of young Ernie Banks. Banks soon recognized that there was a major financial difference between playing for an all-black team in the hinterlands of Texas and for one in a major city like Kansas City. O'Neil, a perpetually cheery man, was blessedly shorted on the bitterness gene when he was born in 1911 in Carrabelle, Florida. The O'Neil family moved more than once in Florida, and he said, "no black family was immune from injustice."[6] Like so many thousands of African Americans of his generation, O'Neil was introduced to the work force in the fields. In his case, it was the celery fields, and he called his experience "miserable work." In fact, the chapter of his autobiography where O'Neil discussed this phase of his life was titled "Damn, There's Got to Be Something Better Than This."[7]

O'Neil worked the celery harvest for three seasons, his pay being $1.25 a day. He was fed up with that work and determined to improve his life. Baseball was his choice and opportunity.

Banks credited the Blair-Bell combination for being the middle men connecting him to O'Neil and the Monarchs. His parents indulged his ball playing, even encouraged it, but did not take it seriously as a career option. They expected Banks to enter the mainstream work force. They were stunned when two Monarchs representatives traveled to Dallas to gain their permission to sign Banks. They nearly fainted when they learned he would be paid $300 a month. To them, that was like winning the lottery.

There was one teeny problem. Banks had not yet graduated from Booker T. Washington High School, and mom and dad told him he had to get his diploma first. Banks completed his senior year and then promptly began his new life. "The day after graduation I was on a bus to Kansas City," Banks said, "arriving just in time for a banquet honoring the Monarchs. All the players were asked to say a few words and when they called on me all I could say was, 'Thank you. I'm happy to be here and I hope to make the team.'"[8]

He made the team. And while he was very much still learning, Banks proved that he fit in. The Monarchs of the early 1950s were not the super power of the Negro Leagues they had been over the years, but they were still a very good team and won pennants. Many of the famous names that had given the club cache amongst all Negro Leagues baseball fans were out of the game, retired, moving on to the next stage of their lives. Satchel Paige was still in the game. The term immortal is used for a great player who is a member of the Hall of Fame. Paige gave the word double meaning because he said that perhaps he would pitch forever, and for a long time it seemed as if he might.

It was hard to keep up with Paige, who was famous for his work in the Negro Leagues, but equally in demand to join barnstorming teams. He frequently jumped one club for another when offered more money. He was affiliated with the Monarchs and hurling for his good friend O'Neil when he finally got his chance at the majors with the Cleveland Indians in 1948 as a 42-year-old rookie. Crowd-pleasing owner Bill Veeck was boss of that team, and the year before he had hired outfielder Larry Doby to integrate the Indians and the American League. In 1948, past his prime, but still owner of stunning control and good speed, Paige became the first black player to pitch in a World Series.

Paige also played for the Indians in 1949, but that year Veeck and his first wife were divorcing and he needed cash for his settlement, so he sold the team. Once Veeck was gone, Paige was jettisoned from the Indians. In 1950, when Banks hooked up with the Monarchs, Paige was free to rejoin his old team, which he did before resurfacing with Veeck and the St. Louis Browns in 1951.

Satchel was certainly an old man by professional baseball standards in 1950, even though his real age was constantly debated and he teased fans and sportswriters relentlessly on the topic. Eventually, a birth date of July 7, 1906, was settled on for Paige. The young Banks was mighty impressed by the old

Paige, however. "I still haven't figured out how anybody could hit his hesitation pitch," Banks said nearly two decades after the men overlapped in Kansas City.[9]

One of Banks' teammates in Kansas City, also on his way up, was Elston Howard, who later starred for the New York Yankees. Curt Roberts, who later played second base for the Pittsburgh Pirates, and Connie Johnson, who threw for the Baltimore Orioles, were other teammates. Another player passing through Kansas City on his way to the majors was Gene Baker, like Banks an infielder. Anyone who walked away from O'Neil recognized him as a genial gentleman, and the same could be true for Banks. How much of Banks' nature was set in concrete or not by then is unclear, but O'Neil was definitely a role model in terms of demeanor. "Ernie has been kind enough over the years to credit me with his positive outlook on life, but I have to say he was a delight right from the start, on the field and off," O'Neil said.[10]

Banks was a shortstop in those days, but he wasn't quite as polished in the field as he needed to be if he was going to make his mark in the majors. O'Neil advised him of such, and Banks listened. He was willing to put in the work to improve, and O'Neil was willing to invest time in him. "Buck used to take me out to the field early and stand behind me while one of the coaches hit grounders to me at short," Banks said. "He'd show me how to go into the hole and get the ball. He's a fine instructor and a tremendous leader. He was always saying nice things about me."[11]

Banks formed a life-long bond with O'Neil, who was always proud of his old shortstop's accomplishments. Banks never forgot O'Neil's kindnesses, but he also viewed his first of two stays with the Monarchs as a kind of finishing school. By the early 1950s, the Negro Leagues were on the verge of extinction. The Brooklyn Dodgers, Cleveland Indians, New York Giants and a few other teams were in the forefront of integration. Some other teams, not so much. Famously, the Boston Red Sox were the last big-league club to integrate, with infielder Pumpsie Green in 1959. That was 12 years after Jackie Robinson first suited up for the Dodgers.

Despite some teams being slow to scout and foolish to ignore black talent, some clubs were very aggressive. The Dodgers did not stop with their signing of Robinson. Dan Bankhead, future Hall of Fame catcher Roy Campanella and Don Newcombe, winner of the first Cy Young Award, soon followed. By 1951, the Indians had hired Doby, Paige, Minnie Minoso, Luke Easter, and Sam Jones. The St. Louis Browns suited up Hank Thompson and Willard Brown. The Giants featured Monte Irvin in the outfield and had a couple of less-famous guys before Willie Mays came along.

Hall of Fame owner Bill Veeck was at the helm of the Indians when they integrated and in charge of the Browns when they integrated. Before running either of those teams, Veeck sought to buy the Philadelphia Phillies, in the 1940s the worst team in baseball. While there are doubts that this really happened, Veeck later insisted his intention was to sign as many stars from the Negro Leagues at once to change the fortunes of the team while integrating baseball. Veeck said that when word spilled this was his plan, he was outmaneuvered and shut out of buying the team. When he had his chance, however, Veeck did bring in black players for his clubs. Although overshadowed, Doby was brought up to the Indians and the majors only months after Robinson made his debut.

So this was a time period when owners and general managers who were forward-thinking recognized that the African American player was here to stay. They recognized that the teams that signed the best players were tapping a new fount of talent and those that remained rooted in an ugly, racist past were going to fall behind as their punishment. The New York Yankees, slow to integrate compared to most other teams, were an exception. The Yankees continued to have success throughout the 1950s. Elston Howard was the first African American on the team, starting in 1955.

Banks was not a worldly young man when he linked up with the Monarchs in 1950 at age 19. His only away-from-home experience had consisted of the two seasons spent with the Colts, a touring team, essentially semi-pro, unaffiliated with a Major League club or a Negro Leagues club.

So Banks was somewhat naïve when joining a famous team which he had heard about since he was young. The city of Kansas City was founded in 1838 and for a time was really part of the Old West. It was a beef town, a cattle destination. The stockyards were second in size and significance only to Chicago. Some called it a Cow Town. But in the 1950s, Kansas City was about to burgeon. The census said 457,000 people lived there, which wasn't much bigger than Dallas, where Banks had his roots, but he had not roamed Dallas, was only associated with a corner of it.

Late in life, when O'Neil was quizzed about what was presumed to be his deprivation because he played only in the Negro Leagues, he responded that his life was grand. He got paid to pay ball and stayed in the finest of hotels in black areas that were black-owned, and enjoyed the finest of black entertainment. He was talking about jazz and the blues at the heartbeat of it all, roughly the clubs located at 18th and Vine—exactly where the Negro Leagues Museum is today.

Banks was still innocent and wide-eyed enough to be impressed by all the sights, and that included Municipal Stadium, which was called Blues Stadium between 1943 and 1954 when Banks played there. Banks' Monarchs coming out party was the team banquet, but he was on the field the next day when Kansas City faced the Indianapolis Clowns. Two years later, a young Hank Aaron would be signed by Indianapolis.

"I had never seen a park as big as that one, much less played in one," Banks said of the ball yard which at the time held around 17,500 people.

"When we reached the clubhouse, O'Neil read us a time schedule for the warm-up. Everything was measured to the minute, so much time for hitting, so much for infield practice, and so on. All I wanted was to look around and get the feel of everything, the well-manicured green grass, the big advertising signs on the outfield fences, the huge dugouts complete with water fountains, and the massive stands."[12]

Banks had tremendous recall of his first day with the Monarchs. He remembered the infield drills, with O'Neil explaining what the grounds crew was accomplishing by watering and dragging the infield into the best possible shape, something that was not done on smaller, older and shabbier fields where the Colts often played. Everything was new to Banks. Having more than 10,000 fans in the building with 10,000 sets of eyes on him was intimidating, and taking the field with a new club made him edgy. You couldn't tell Ernie Banks this wasn't the big-time.

Even with second sacker Curt Roberts shouting at him to relax, Banks was nervous. He could not calm down and was not at his sharpest in the batter's box. He was a right-handed swinger, but he was not his usual self at bat. "The tension, I found out, affected my timing at the plate," he said. "I made contact with the ball all three times, but I was swinging late and flied to right field each time."[13]

Negro Leagues travel was all by bus. The players received either $3 or $5 in meal money, the way Banks remembered it, depending on how long the trip was from Kansas City. The other teams in the league that season besides the Monarchs and Indianapolis were the Baltimore Elite Giants, New York Cubans, Philadelphia Stars, Cleveland Buckeyes, Birmingham Black Barons, Memphis Red Sox, Houston Eagles and Chicago American Giants, although the Buckeyes went kaput midway through the year.

Banks had never visited those big cities and said that one way or another, he was learning at all times—American geography by going to those towns, on tips from O'Neil, experience on the field, life on the road, and, he added, by reading big-city newspaper sports pages that reported on their local Major League clubs. The team may have been close on the field and forced into close quarters for long bus rides, some of them overnight, but when it came to food, Banks reported, it was kind of every man for himself.

The schedule did not call for off-days. When the Monarchs got to some towns, they played the locals ten games straight, but then had to hustle to another city, driving all night. The temptation to sleep was powerful, but sometimes if a player succumbed, choosing rest, he paid for it by learning that his share of the food was scarfed up by a teammate. The fare on those rides, the way Banks described it, today would resemble raiding a 24-hour convenience store of its cold cuts, bread, cookies, candy bars, sodas and crackers. It was obvious no one on the team had majored in nutrition anywhere.

3. Moving On

It sounded a bit like a high school team of decades later on the move. Even worse, sometimes a player who missed the dinner bell would be broke and couldn't afford a snack at the next pause. Many times the fatherly O'Neil would lend out $1, while offering admonition to players to pay better attention to the dining circumstances and his budget.

Banks played well enough, especially for a young guy, and it caught his attention when Elston Howard was signed by the Yankees and left the team before season's end. That was a boost to Monarchs players' spirits. Yes, they could get noticed and picked up by a Major League club.

As the end of the season approached, Banks discovered that he also had been noticed, but not in a way he expected. Buster Hayward, the player-manager of the Indianapolis Clowns, asked Banks to call him following the final game. Banks did so and was surprised to hear that if he wanted to make some bonus money for an extra month of playing, he should head to Jacksonville, Florida, where a Jackie Robinson All-Star team was forming to play exhibitions.

Three years into his pioneering career, Robinson was one of the best-known Americans in the country, an idol to all young African American players, and he wanted Ernie? That was remarkably flattering. When he met Robinson, Jackie gave him the low-down. He would alternate at shortstop between the All-Stars and the Clowns so everybody would get playing time. Banks said it was like stepping into "a dream world."[14]

Banks was mingling with big-leaguers, not only Robinson, but Campanella, Newcombe and Larry Doby. The tour made a stop in Dallas, and Banks' parents showed up to watch. Banks made $400 for the tour, stopped in a clothing store to spiff up his wardrobe, and left with Robinson's praise rattling around in his head. Robinson told him he was a very good hitter and gave him a few pointers on turning the double play quicker, something he improved on almost immediately.

Not yet 20 years old, Banks was welcome to fantasize a little bit more. His season with the Monarchs was a graduate education in baseball, and for the first time he truly could believe he had the potential to become a big-league player.

There was only one problem with his immediate ascension. A higher authority, the United States government, required Banks to put on a different uniform for a while. His swift baseball improvement was interrupted. The Army borrowed Banks for two years, and it was not until early 1953 that he was able to return to Kansas City and again play for the Monarchs.

4

From Kansas City to Chicago

Ernie Banks loved playing for the Monarchs. Much of the goodwill he felt for the team stemmed from Buck O'Neil, who was his manager, teacher, father figure and friend. Although it was reported that Banks was 20 years old in September of 1953, that was a mistake. By then he was actually 22.

He was still a young man, just not as young as some thought. After a somewhat cloistered upbringing in Dallas and touring with the Monarchs, he was not quite worldly, but he seemed to understand how the world worked when a man had dark skin. Unlike some others, Banks had not endured an over-abundance of bitter experiences due to racism. And unlike some older players, being born later gave him a potential opportunity they could never have dreamed of: Being invited to play in the major leagues.

Banks was about to become the beneficiary of the Jackie Robinson effect, Branch Rickey's so-called grand experiment. Robinson unlocked the door to the majors for the African American ballplayer. Others had trickled through in recent years. Although integration was hardly complete across the American and National Leagues, there was no retreat. Most of the 16 ball clubs were now scouting black talent.

Some years later, and after his big-league career ended, Banks reminisced about his year with the Monarchs, looking back on the experience fondly, citing teammates who made him feel comfortable and helped him.

> I enjoyed black baseball very, very much. I played with some outstanding men when I was with the Kansas City Monarchs. Men like Gene Baker, Connie Johnson, who was formerly with the White Sox, Curt Roberts, who played for the Pittsburgh Pirates, Barney Sorrell ... a lot of great players who were playing at that time and in the early fifties, and I remember those days extremely well.[1]

The baseball world itself was less sophisticated in the early 1950s. Still, Major League players stayed in finer hotels, received more meal money, and traveled via higher-class transportation than the players in the Negro Leagues, where money was scarce and there was always the chance a team might be turned away from a restaurant or hotel by a white racist.

4. From Kansas City to Chicago

Typical of Banks' sunny personality, though, he viewed his traveling days with the Monarchs as a blast. It sounded as if his attitude towards the entire experience was that it was somewhat of a lark. His view, divulged long after the occasion, seemed to track that of a college athlete at a low-budget school.

> We had a tremendous love for the game and were happy to be together and represent the Kansas City Monarchs. We traveled by bus. It was tough, but we had a lot of fun. We kind of enjoyed that camaraderie on the bus, in the hotels, in the ballparks. It was an all-around, well-balanced life and a great experience ... an awful lot of fun. I really enjoyed it.[2]

Remember that in the early 1950s, big-league ballplayers did not make much more money than civilian workers doing 9-to-5 jobs, they did not travel by plane, and their lifestyle was more to be envied by young men than thought of as challenging. The Monarchs had to put up with more discrimination than a team in organized baseball, but it made plenty of sense for Banks to look back on that time of his life and regard it only positively.

It definitely offered more enjoyment than being deployed by the Army to Germany. Banks was fortunate he was not sent to the front lines because this was the period of the Korean War.

The great dream of black ballplayers in the 1920s, 1930s and 1940s was just to be treated fairly, to be given an equal shot at the majors rather than being ignored and thrust into the shadows of the game. Although there were rumblings of possible tryouts at times, not even extensive lobbying efforts by sportswriters in the black press for newspapers like the *Chicago Defender* and the *Pittsburgh Courier* led to much happening. It took until after World War II, when myriads of African Americans fought to make the world safe for democracy, just like their white brothers, and the foresight of (at last) a white man with enough authority (Branch Rickey) to break the color barrier.

By 1947 and beyond, many top Negro Leagues stars had aged, were past their primes or retired, apparently forever doomed to be footnotes in the game because of their skin color. Banks was young enough to be in the second wave of African American players, succeeding, though overlapping with, the first wave of pioneers. The Jackie Robinsons, Dan Bankheads, Roy Campanellas, Satchel Paiges and others were the pathfinders. Now it was up to Banks, Willie Mays, and Hank Aaron to further prove the case that greatness had been stifled in the past, and now was ready to be unleashed.

O'Neil could have been selfish about the Monarchs. He was the boss of one team, and his job was to lead it to victory and a championship. He was under no obligation (except perhaps a moral one in the context of the times) to offer up his finest talent to sign elsewhere. But anyone who ever met O'Neil understood that he was too nice a man to keep such secrets, to stand in the way of player advancement. Instead, consistent with his character, he put in the extra time to help his young guys. The handwriting on the wall heralded the imminent death of the last Negro Leagues teams, including the Monarchs.

League play was on the verge of extinction, and even barnstorming all-black teams died out before the end of the 1950s. In 1953, Banks was in Chicago competing in an all-star game at Comiskey Park. O'Neil whispered in Banks' ear that he had a good chance to receive an offer from one of the Chicago teams. Whether his appearance in the game was an unofficial tryout or not was never clear, but he did smack the game-winning hit.

"Buck called me in the [Pershing] hotel that night and said to meet him in the lobby the next morning at seven," Banks said. "I didn't know what it was all about."[3]

The session to follow wasn't quite as clandestine or secretive as it may have sounded, but was more the way things were done in an era of wide-open scouting. Someone having knowledge of a player's talent who was an advocate for him brought him to a ballpark to meet team honchos. Often, an on-field tryout was performed. This short trip didn't even involve a workout. Banks was already in demand.

> So I met him [O'Neil], me and a pitcher on the club named Bill Dickey. Buck hustled us into a cab and said, "Let's go for a little ride." I didn't even know where we were bound for. We ended up at Wrigley Field. Buck took us up to the office where we signed our contracts. I went back and played another week with the Monarchs and then reported to the Cubs in September.[4]

By then, Banks was old enough to sign for himself without the need for his parents to agree. Certainly, in a later era, there would have been more deliberation and haggling, with an agent representing the player, not a manager who took matters in his own hands to deliver a coveted player.

O'Neil developed goodwill with the Cubs by his actions, and O'Neil's entrée to the majors when he departed the Monarchs came through the Cubs. But that did not take place until 1956, when he became a full-time scout for the Chicago club. In 1962, O'Neil became the first African American coach for a Major League team, also with the Cubs.

O'Neil recounted his version of the events in his autobiography, beginning with Banks' play in the all-star game across town at Comiskey Park the day before the signing. O'Neil was in the dugout. Dr. J. B. Martin, the owner of the Memphis Red Sox, was in a box seat next to him and leaned his head in to talk to O'Neil when the score was tied.

"Buck," O'Neil reported Martin saying, "I think we might need another dozen balls." O'Neil shook off the suggestion as Banks came to the plate. He said, "No, Doc, I don't think we're going to need anymore because this kid is going to hit the ball out of the park."[5] Banks promptly hit the game-winning home run. "Doc Martin thought I was a swami," O'Neil said. "What I knew was that Ernie Banks was destined for greatness."[6]

4. From Kansas City to Chicago

After the game and back at the team hotel, O'Neil said he received a telephone call from Tom Baird, owner of the Monarchs. He gave instructions for O'Neil to bring Banks to Wrigley Field the next morning. Wid Matthews, the Cubs' director of player personnel, greeted them. O'Neil said Matthews had informed him Baird was going to put the Monarchs on the market, and once the manager parted ways with the team he had a job waiting for him as a scout with the Cubs.

This sounds a little bit telescoped since Baird did not sell until 1955, and O'Neil joined the Cubs for the scouting job in 1956, but although a couple of years did pass, this is the way things played out for the Monarchs, O'Neil and the Cubs.

In all, some 17 players who competed at least for a little while with the Monarchs played in the majors. Banks outshone everyone else (except Paige, although he was two decades older and at the end of his career), but there were other top-flight players, including Gene Baker, who became Banks' roommate with the Cubs, Elston Howard, Lou Johnson, George Altman and Hank Thompson. Along with Larry Doby and Don Newcombe, Altman is one of only three ballplayers to play in the Negro Leagues, in the majors, and in Japan.

O'Neil said Matthews once showed him a letter from a complaining fan that in part read, "What are you trying to do, make the Cubs look like the Kansas City Monarchs?"[7]

By the time Banks cut his deal with the Cubs, he was known as a promising player. Major League teams that only a few years earlier barely knew the names of the teams in the Negro Leagues were dispatching scouts all over the United States to get a jump on other teams with young African American players. Everyone was searching for another Campanella, Newcombe on the mound, or Willie Mays. It was obvious that not every black player signed would become an all-star or make it to the Hall of Fame, but only the most head-in-the-sand teams refused to look at or seek African American prospects.

Banks said that only after he signed with the Cubs did he realize that some of the people watching him play in 1953 were scouts from other teams. He knew for sure that the St. Louis Cardinals and the Chicago White Sox had interest. The Yankees were said to be in the hunt as well. It did not seem that any clubs made concrete offers to Banks, but he was on their radar. Although Banks was raw in terms of experience in organized ball and had lost time to the service, his talent was apparent.

Once Banks returned to the Kansas City lineup after his military time, he emerged as such a hard hitter, especially for a shortstop, it was clear that it was only a matter of time before he moved on and up. He was batting .388 for the Monarchs when he shifted to the Cubs in early September of 1953.

Author of one of the first stories about Banks joining the Cubs was Jim Enright, who became Banks' friend, anointed him "Mr. Cub," and wrote a biography with Banks. The lead on Enright's story was "The Cubs have landed the season's foremost Negro baseball player. He's Ernie Banks, the Kansas City Monarchs' prize 22-year-old shortstop who was eagerly sought by several Major League teams."[8]

It was noted that Bill Dickey, then 18, and owner of an 8–6 record for the Monarchs, was also signed. This was right when Bill Dickey, the catcher for the New York Yankees who batted .313 lifetime, was about to be inducted into the Hall of Fame. Dickey, the right-handed pitcher, was sent to Cedar Rapids in the Three-I League for the 1954 season, ostensibly to begin his minor-league climb to the Cubs. He never made it all of the way up the ladder.

Banks was ready-made. The Cubs were not shipping him to Cedar Rapids. They were keeping him right in Chicago for the rest of the big-league season. The team finished the year with a 65–89 mark in the National League, so there was no reason to wait till next year for Banks. While only a few weeks remained in the season, Banks was expected to contribute immediately.

At the press conference announcing his signing, Banks said, "Naturally, I'm pleased over becoming a major leaguer and I'll do my best to help the Cubs. I know I can field and I'm confident I can hit Major League pitching."[9] Banks definitely turned out to be right about that skill.

Historically, baseball has always expanded its rosters for September call-ups of minor leaguers. Most minor-league seasons are over, and this way clubs get a sneak preview of young, talented players in the organization who might be ready by spring training of the

Banks joined the Cubs as a shortstop, and he had the glove for it before his switch to first base (National Baseball Hall of Fame).

following season. A typical roster expansion over the decades was from 25 men to 40. Sometimes September call-ups are meaningful and a young player will impress the brass. Sometimes they are inconsequential, with future stars bogged down hitting .172 or pitchers going 0–2 in a handful of games.

Banks was not following that traditional path where he was summoned from Class AAA. He was an outsider coming in, believed to be ahead of all the cultivated talent in the minor-league system.

The signing of Ernie Banks was big news for the Cubs, for more than one reason. Although there were other African American players in the organization, none had yet to take a swing at the plate or throw a ball off the mound for the big team. The Cubs officially had not been integrated. The team did have one other top prospect ready to play who had been with the Cubs' AAA Los Angeles team since 1950.

Especially in the early days of Major League integration and during an era of tightwad business practices, teams hesitated to bring just one African American to the majors, preferring two. It was a bit like Noah's Ark, two-by-two, because players shared hotel rooms on road trips, and there was a fear of discontent and backlash from white players being forced to live with a black player. So the issue was ducked by promoting two black players to the roster at once.

The Cubs had just the guy in mind to fill that role. Gene Baker, another former Kansas City Monarch, may not have had the kind of pop in his bat that Banks did, but he was regarded as a dazzling infield glove man. Baker received his long-awaited summons to the majors following his play in L.A.

Gene Baker and Ernie Banks were going to integrate the Chicago Cubs together.

5

The Majors

Ten days elapsed between Ernie Banks' introduction to Chicago sportswriters and his introduction to Chicago Cubs baseball fans.

When he realized what was happening in Wid Matthews' office, Banks later reflected, hearing that he was Major League material right then, he was stunned. When he was asked to sign his name, he was shaking. "I was so nervous I had to hold my right hand with my left as I scribbled 'Ernest Banks' on a document that seemed to be a mile long," he said.[1]

Humorously, as evidence of how nervous he had been, Banks said he was not even aware of how much he was going to be paid. He discovered his salary was to be $800 a month. Just six months had passed since his Army discharge.

On September 17, 1953, Banks became the first African American to suit up for the Cubs in a game. Chicago lost to the Philadelphia Phillies, 16–4. It was a Thursday at Wrigley Field, an afternoon game, as they all were in the venerable ballpark during that era. The Cubs were on their way to a seventh-place finish in an eight-team National League, and that was neither unexpected nor especially mourned as being out of the ordinary.

Banks was 22 years old, 6-foot-1, 180 pounds, with a grand future in the game predicted. He started at shortstop and batted seventh in the order, although that would change soon enough as his power became evident. There was nothing earth-shattering about the numbers attached to Banks' name that day. He committed an error in the field and went 0-for-3 at the plate with a run scored. The game lasted just 2 hours, 21 minutes, and the debut of Mr. Banks was hardly enough to stir the locals as the team rode out a dismal season. There were just 2,793 paid witnesses who in future years could honestly say, "I was there" when Banks broke in.

Simultaneous with Banks' signing, the Cubs announced the promotion of Gene Baker from the Los Angeles AAA team. Baker, like Banks, was a shortstop, but he ranked behind Banks in the hierarchy. The team informed Baker that he was moving to second base. The regular shortstop for most of the season, playing in 82 games, was veteran Roy Smalley. He was in his sixth season in the job for the Cubs. A decent glove man, Smalley never hit well, and he was playing for Milwaukee by 1954.

Technically, Banks broke the color barrier for the Cubs by himself on September 17. There was a travel day on September 18, and the Cubs resumed play with a series at St. Louis starting September 19. On September 20, Baker made his Major League debut, two games after Banks, becoming the second African American player for the Cubs. Baker pinch-hit in his inaugural game, going 0-for-1.

It was not until September 22, at Cincinnati's Crosley Field, that Banks and Baker started together as the Cubs' keystone combination. Baker held down second base. Baker, six years older than Banks at 28, got into seven games that season and hit .227.

Banks appeared in ten games and hit .314. He made the stronger first impression. In fact, those first ten games of Banks' career jump-started a games played streak of 424 straight, a record for consecutive games starting a career. Banks was one of the rare players who never played in a minor-league game in organized baseball. Of course, he had played professionally with the Monarchs and those other summer teams.

Until Banks came along, Baker may have been victimized by racial considerations. The Cubs paid $6,500 to obtain Baker from the Monarchs in 1950, but he took bus rides through the minors until settling in at shortstop for Los Angeles in the Pacific Coast League.

The Cubs had paid Kansas City $20,000 for Banks and Bill Dickey combined, more of an investment than they made in Baker. Banks was the prize in the deal, a fact made obvious when he was immediately placed on the big-league roster and Dickey was sent to the minors.

Baker, meanwhile, spent parts of four years, 1950–1953, with the Angels, the minor-league forerunner of the Major League Angels. The first was his landing spot after quickly navigating through other Cubs minor-league stops in Springfield, Massachusetts, and Des Moines, Iowa. Baker was a vacuum cleaner in the field, gobbling up grounders, and while he was not a batting title contender at the plate, he had seasons of .280, .278 and .284. He also hit 20 homers with 99 runs batted in during 1953 before the Cubs promoted him at the end of that season.

Baker had his fans and supporters who looked at the numbers or watched him play every day. Bobby Bragan, the long-time manager, was running the competing Hollywood Stars in the PCL, and he raved about Baker, calling him "as good a shortstop as I've ever seen—and that includes PeeWee Reese."[2] Dodgers great Reese is in the Hall of Fame.

Born June 25, 1925, in Davenport, Iowa, Baker was a Midwestern guy who batted and threw right-handed. His height was listed at 6-foot-1 and his weight at 170 pounds. Baker preceded Banks on a similar path to the majors. He paused with the Monarchs and went to the Cubs. Then he waited, doing everything he could to catch the eye of the bigwigs in Chicago, but instead basically being stuck in L.A., unable to do quite enough.

All of a sudden in late 1953, he was Major League material, but not for the position he played best and was most comfortable in. Banks was recruited over his head.

Prior to September, there was agitation in Chicago newspapers in Baker's favor. Baker seemed to have the skills the Cubs needed and could put to better use than rotting in the minor leagues through his prime years. One sportswriter not only expressed his opinion that the Cubs should bring up Baker, he interviewed opposing managers in the Pacific Coast League about Baker.

"Believe the boy is a Major League prospect," said the one-time great hitter and San Diego manager Lefty O'Doul after watching Baker for one series. "Purely on playing ability Los Angeles shortstop Gene Baker is a big-league player," said Bragan, who managed several teams in the majors. "In those games [22 of them], he has been good to sensational," said Sacramento manager Gene Desautel."³

"Despite the fact that the shortstop has leaked like a leaky dike for the Cubs, all through this dismal season," wrote long-time Chicago sportswriter Jim Enright, "there has been no move to see if Baker could help the situation." Elsewhere in the story, this comment was made: "Is it because the 28-year-old Negro isn't ready? Or are there other rea-

Ernie Banks (left) and Gene Baker, a second baseman, integrated the Chicago Cubs together in 1953, though Banks got into his first Major League game a few days before Baker (National Baseball Hall of Fame).

5. The Majors

sons?"[4] No speculation was offered on what any other reason could be, since it was established by all of those other managers' views that Baker was ready for the majors.

In a companion story, Wendell Smith, a legendary African American sportswriter, interviewed Cubs personnel chief Wid Matthews to ask what was the hold-up with Baker being brought up. Matthews said three-plus years of scouting reports indicated that Baker wasn't quite ready for the majors, but he would be given every chance to win the shortstop job in spring training of 1954.

Although racism was not explicitly charged in either *Chicago American* story, Matthews defended himself against overtones of that ilk.

> I think he's probably ready for big-league ball now. We are definitely going to bring him back to our spring camp next February. I think he'll stay up, too. As for people saying that I'm holding him back purposely, that's farthest from the truth. Don't forget that when I was Branch Rickey's assistant at Brooklyn, I had a very important role in Jackie Robinson's case. I was all for him coming up. I think any player who is good enough should get his chance. I think that way about Gene Baker, too.[5]

Just like that, after Ernie Banks was in the fold, the call went out to Gene Baker to fly to Chicago and not to switch planes for an additional stop. Spring 1954 came early for Baker. Unfortunately for Baker, a few days before Banks signed, he injured his back swinging the bat in a game against Oakland, and it was not clear if he would be able to play when he reached Chicago. The Angels were wrapping up their season anyway, and Baker was supposed to report to Chicago healthy or not. He almost missed his long-awaited chance, but he was well enough to play by the time he arrived in Chicago.

Of course, now that the Cubs had Banks at shortstop, Baker had to wonder where he fit in. For that matter, Matthews had similar thoughts. A few years later, he reflected on the timing of having two Major League-ready shortstops joining the team at the same time. "We were grooming Baker as our shortstop," Matthews said. "Then we signed Banks. We suggested to Stan Hack, who was managing Los Angeles at the time, that he try Baker at second base for a few games at the end of the '53 season. Stan wasn't at all sure Baker could make the switch, but he tried it."[6]

When Baker got to Chicago, Matthews met with him to let him know where he stood. It was pretty straightforward. Banks, not Baker, was the shortstop of the future, but there was a place for Baker in the starting lineup if he was agreeable and was willing to adapt. "I told Gene that Banks might be a truly great shortstop, that we couldn't use two shortstops, but that we needed a second baseman," Matthews said. "I explained that we felt that Gene, because of his greater experience, could make the switch to second base more easily. In addition, he could help coach Banks if he was out there alongside of him all the time."[7]

There have been harsher tête-à-tête sessions between management and a player in sports history, where once the office door closed it was apparent the player was going to be cut or traded. Matthews gave Baker a Plan B scenario. He accepted it and worked to make everything go smoothly. During the 1955 season, Baker made the All-Star team and led National League second basemen in putouts and assists.

Matthews was not just talking when he made his comment about Baker mentoring Banks. Baker did take on that role, and Banks appreciated it and later said Baker aided him quite a bit when he was a young player. "Gene has been a tremendous help to me," Banks said. "He's coached me and advised me on lots of things and helped correct my mistakes. Without him, things would have been much more difficult."[8]

Whether Banks realized that he was becoming a symbol for African Americans in Chicago at that stage of his life or not was unclear, although later he did embrace his role as the first Cubs player of his race. To some extent, Banks was aware of racism, whether he had first-hand harsh experience with it or not, but he also seemed somewhat racially naïve. During his Army time, when his only athletic reputation was based on his limited play with the Kansas City Monarchs, Banks was sought out by Abe Saperstein, the promoter who founded the Harlem Globetrotters and, about a decade later, the ill-fated American Basketball League.

Banks was stationed in Texas when famed Globetrotter Goose Tatum requested that he participate in an upcoming Globetrotters exhibition game in El Paso, near Fort Bliss, where he was stationed. Banks met the legendary Marques Haynes for the first time when he showed up for the game and then met Saperstein, who outfitted him for the show. Saperstein also instructed Banks to sit next to him on the bench, so he could provide a crash course on the team plays before being inserted into the game. "I'd never sat next to a white man and I wasn't sure what to do," Banks said of his sitting position.[9] Such was the state of race relations in the United States in 1952. Banks said watching the Globetrotters' routines made him lighten up and relax.

While in the service, Banks also received a letter from Bill Veeck, who had been owner of the Cleveland Indians but now owned the St. Louis Browns, saying he was aware of Banks' talent and that when he got out of the Army, he was welcome in the Browns camp. Still, when Banks was discharged, he went straight back to the Monarchs. Around this time, Veeck was in the midst of trying to move his Browns to Baltimore. When he was turned down by other owners, he disposed of the team. A handful of years later, after Banks was an established superstar and the No. 1 baseball icon in Chicago, Veeck bought the White Sox and operated across town. He would still have loved to have Banks decorating his lineup.

5. The Majors

The North Side of Chicago had first dibs, and years had passed since there was any chance Veeck or anyone else could pry Banks away from the Cubs. He was beloved in Chicago, more closely identified with the Cubs than any player in the history of the team. Of course, he had to work his way to iconic stature. Banks did so by wielding an extremely damaging bat, especially for a shortstop.

For most of Banks' playing days, shortstops were viewed as good-field, no-hit players, most of whom batted low in the order, not far ahead of the pitcher. Some of the best hit for average, but almost none of the shortstops in the 1950s were power hitters like Banks. In Banks' rookie year, the starting American League shortstop in the All-Star Game was Chico Carrasquel. The line of big league star Venezuelan shortstops began with Carrasquel. He batted .279 that year and hit 55 home runs total in his career. The National League starting shortstop was Pee Wee Reese, who hit .271 that season and slugged 126 career homers.

Alvin Dark started at short for the NL All-Star in 1954. Dark batted .293 that year and hit 126 homers in his career. It was Carrasquel again for the AL. By 1955, Banks was starting for the National League. His American League counterpart was Harvey Kuenn, a lifetime .303 hitter, but with just 87 total home runs. Plus, Kuenn moved to the outfield. To demonstrate what an outlier Banks was at short, in 1955 he slugged 44 home runs.

During Banks' rookie year of 1953, when he appeared in just ten games, only four shortstops in the majors reached double figures in home runs for the season: Dark with 23, Solly Hemus with 14, Reese with 13, and Johnny Logan with 11 for the Braves. In Banks' first full season, 1954, he clouted 19 homers. That was the second-highest total in the majors among shortstops to Dark's 20 that season.

As for 1955, fuhgaddaboutit, as was often said on *The Sopranos* or in mobster movies. That 44 was the all-time shortstop single-season record, surpassing Vern Stephens' 39 in 1949 with the Boston Red Sox. For the next 40-plus years, Banks was identified as the most notable slugging shortstop of all time. Only when baseball's steroid era took hold, roughly between 1990 and the early 2000s, did any shortstop exhibit more power than Banks.

Neither Banks nor Cubs fans could foresee his prodigious slamming when he checked in for his brief stay in the clubhouse in 1953. Almost every player remembers his first home run, but not even the best can predict that the first will begat 50, 100, or several hundred. The sport is too unpredictable, and longevity is subject to injury, changing trends, or even changing rules.

Banks launched his first career home run on September 20, 1953, just a few days into his big-league career. It came in the eighth inning in an 11–6 loss to the St. Louis Cardinals at Busch Stadium, off Gerry Staley, a solid pitcher of the time, who won 134 games and saved 61 in his career and who that season finished 18–9.

The blast was not even recorded at Wrigley Field, and it is doubtful if any of the 8,569 fans in the stadium gave a moment's thought to the likelihood of this supple swinger collecting another 511 shots in his just-starting career. Banks had a good game all around that day, going 3-for-4 with three runs batted in. That was the first game in franchise history that two African American players appeared in the same Cubs game. This was Gene Baker's debut day.

At different times over the course of his playing career, and in retirement as well, Banks was often asked his feelings about being the first black player in Cubs history and what he and Baker endured in the way of prejudice. Much of America was a hateful place for a black man to survive in during the early 1950s. The Civil Rights Movement did not begin in earnest until later in the decade, and broad change was not effected through legislation until the first half of the 1960s.

For a man who loved to chatter, who was almost never shy in close company, Banks the young rookie kept his mouth shut. He never issued controversial statements about race. He withheld his candor about any kind of racial incident he encountered. It was not clear, as people got to know the young man, whether he was always naturally sunny or put on a pleasant face regardless of circumstances.

Banks was still getting used to finding his way in the nearly all-white world of the team and the mostly white world of Chicago. He said one lesson Jackie Robinson imparted to him when he toured with Robinson's all-stars in the 1940s was to be quiet and learn. Just listen, Robinson suggested. "The sudden association with so many white people often left me speechless and why they were so kind," Banks said.[10]

A sharecropper in the South would not be so lucky. But baseball fans admired Banks, yes, perhaps because he didn't make waves, but mostly because he could smash the horsehide covering off the ball.

6

Race

For a country founded on the precepts of freedom, the United States was woefully behind in fulfilling the promises it made on equality.

The two greatest, widespread sins in American history are the institutionalized, formally endorsed attempts at annihilating Native-American tribes and the enslavement of African Americans. The North may have won the Civil War, but it did not change Neanderthal minds. Slavery was outlawed, but nearly a century later a sufficient number of attitudes remained rooted in backwards thinking to make life miserable for millions of black Americans.

Baseball was enthusiastically considered to be the national game, The National Pastime, as it was often referred to in print. The 2000s represent a completely different era in sport, where the National Football League is viewed as the king of the heap in team sports, basketball and hockey are embraced by multitudes, and niche sports of many types have their intense followers. Baseball remains incredibly popular, with Major League games witnessed by millions upon millions of fans each season. But it is no longer the societal yardstick it once was.

Crusades to integrate professional ball clubs focused on baseball, not any other sport, because of baseball's designation during the first half of the 20th century as the one game deemed truly national in significance. No one was running around making the case that baseball owed its origins to cricket or rounders, or any other version of a British game. The sport was seen as quintessentially American. Yet it excluded African American players, no matter how great.

The two precipitating events that allowed Ernie Banks to rise above his humble Texas roots to gain notice, to become sought-after, were World War II and Jackie Robinson's barrier-breaking with the Brooklyn Dodgers.

Although it is a story less often told when the glories of victory are revisited from World War II, blacks in the service were discriminated against aboard ship, in the front lines, and throughout a hierarchical system just as much as they were back home in their neighborhoods and communities. Enlisted to battle the worst dictatorships of Germany, Japan and Italy, headed by dangerous men with frightening ideas, there was no ambiguity about the cause. All American ideals were at risk, and America itself was in peril.

As contributors to the critical victories during the first half of the 1940s, African American soldiers who fought for American rights spoke up ever more loudly about any diminishment of their own rights after the war. Concurrent with that, Jackie Robinson became a hero to all blacks for his pioneering role integrating baseball. A genius of Branch Rickey's plan with the Dodgers was his believing other teams would follow suit, signing African American talent rather than let his club corner the market on great African American players and run away with pennant after pennant. Rickey may have been the most astute scout with the broadest mind and the largest amount of courage, but Bill Veeck was right behind. It took him almost no time to add Larry Doby to the Cleveland Indians roster, and Satchel Paige as well.

Some teams moved quickly to seize upon Negro Leagues talent. Some teams moved at glacial speed. The Cubs were in the middle. By 1953, Robinson was six years into his ten-year Major League, Hall of Fame career. Before Robinson's ascent to the Dodgers on April 15, 1947 (following a season with the Dodgers' AAA Montreal Royals team in 1946), there had not been a man of color in the majors since Moses Fleetwood Walker with the Toledo Blue Stockings in 1884. No black man (again Walker) had played in the minors since 1889.

Walker's brother Weldy was a teammate in Toledo during that sole big-league season. William Edward White, who played one game for the Providence Grays in 1879, was said to be a black man passing as white while still at Brown University. The Society for American Baseball Research made the case that if so, White was the first African American Major League player, albeit only briefly.

Records may be searched and paperwork investigated, but baseball never put in writing a policy banning African Americans from the game. It was an understood way of life, a deceitful practice by unwritten rule, abided by the league presidents, Commissioner Kenesaw Mountain Landis, and team owners. Evidence seen by their own eyes of the skills displayed by players in the Negro Leagues, from Satchel Paige and Josh Gibson to Buck Leonard and Cool Papa Bell, was denied.

In that post–World War II environment, bold African American scribes repeatedly challenged team ownerships to give black players a chance. Also, *The Daily Worker*, the newspaper of the American Communist Party, was a loud-voiced, if unexpected ally, banging the drum for equality. Periodically, a tryout was arranged, generally a sham tryout, where baseball people on hand could find some reason not to sign a player.

In 1942, *The Daily Worker* gained a verbal agreement from the Pittsburgh Pirates to offer such a tryout, but the plan disintegrated. In 1945, Wendell Smith won the concession from the Boston Braves and the Boston Red Sox for tryouts of African American players. The Braves tryout never took place. The players at the Red Sox event were Jackie Robinson, Marvin Williams and Sam Jethroe.

Williams played 19 years in the Negro Leagues, Mexico and Venezuela, once batting .401 and accumulating more than 300 home runs during his career. Jethroe became the National League "Rookie of the Year" for the Braves in 1950 and twice won NL stolen base crowns. Robinson, of course, became Robinson, a Hall of Famer and perhaps the most influential player of all time.

Following baseball's poor response to the integration idea, Wendell Smith did link in with Rickey, who hired him as a traveling older brother/guidance counselor for Robinson for the 1946 season.

During 1949, well-wishers repeatedly tried to inform the New York Yankees about a budding star with the Birmingham Black Barons named Willie Mays. They ignored the information offered to them. George Digby scouted the South for the Boston Red Sox and watched Mays play. A conversation with Black Barons team owners made it apparent that the Red Sox could purchase his playing rights for $4,500. Digby telephoned general manager Joe Cronin, and another scout was sent to Alabama. Nothing came of it, to Digby's life-long frustration—and a long life it was, since he died in 2014 at 96.

"I had Willie Mays bought for $4,500," Digby said in 2005. "I called up the Red Sox. I said, 'I got Willie Mays. He'll break the color line.'"[1] As Digby soon realized, the Red Sox were not interested in breaking or bending any color lines. They became the last team to integrate in 1959.

"Cronin sent another scout down to look at him, but [owner Tom] Yawkey and Cronin already had made up their minds they weren't going to take any black players," Digby said.[2]

Digby noted that the Red Sox could have had Willie Mays in center field and Ted Williams in left at the same time. Similarly, the Yankees could have played Willie Mays and Mickey Mantle in the same outfield if they had been more forward-thinking on race. Instead, when Elston Howard first appeared in the Yankees' lineup on April 14, 1955, they were the fourth-to-last team to integrate, ahead of only the Philadelphia Phillies, the Detroit Tigers and the Red Sox. It was nearly eight years to the day after Jackie Robinson's debut with the Dodgers.

The Braves scouted Mays, too, and passed on signing him for the given reason that he could not hit the curveball. Mays of course signed with the New York Giants, and became one of the greatest players ever.

By the time the Cubs inserted Ernie Banks into the lineup in September of 1953, seven other teams had integrated. The Dodgers, Indians and Browns put their first African American players on the field in 1947. The Giants followed in 1949 and the Braves in 1950, with Jethroe. The White Sox fielded Minnie Minoso in 1951. Just four days before Banks made his big-league debut, Bob Trice integrated the Philadelphia Athletics.

Buck O'Neil guided Banks to the Cubs, but before that, Monarchs owner Tom Baird attempted to steer him to the Yankees, another case of a big Yankees personnel misjudgment. Baird was New York's contact when the team first investigated seeking out a black player, by all accounts mostly because of increased criticism the organization was taking by not doing so. Baird seemed flattered even to be in contact with the great Yankees club. He once wrote, "I feel like I am part of the Yankee organization."[3]

Baird was somewhat of a weird duck. He was the owner of a Negro Leagues franchise, the best-known black ball team, yet he was a registered member of the Ku Klux Klan, a fact that surfaced in 2007, long after his death.

During one of his correspondences with the Yankees, Baird wrote, "I signed Ernest Banks, 19-year-old shortstop, and he looks like he will make a hell of a good ballplayer."[4] That was a sales pitch, but the Yankees did not even write back.

It was clear that many teams recognized Banks' ability, but they did not all compete to obtain his signature on a contract. The background of what was going on in the majors with integration team-by-team played a role. Banks was so good and showed so much promise, the Cubs, a team so bad it needed any help it could get, did not waste time sending Banks to the minors for any pretend seasoning, or as a social experiment gauging how well he might get along with white teammates.

Meanwhile, Gene Baker did not stand out as an immediate star and languished in the minors. If born later, Baker probably would have been in the bigs about three years sooner. He more represented a player of solid ability who deserved a roster spot, but was not going to turn around a team's fortunes single-handedly. The Cubs were not in the midst of a pennant race, so one player here or there filling a spot was not going to make much difference. Whether Cubs officials were being disingenuous in their analysis of the limitations of Baker's game, or it was just a cover for a racist outlook, is not known.

However, it should be noted that the Cubs announced Baker would be called up at the end of the Los Angeles Angels' Pacific Coast League season a week before the team announced the signing of Banks. No one seemed happier than sportswriter Jim Enright, who had argued to director of player personnel Wid Matthews regularly that Baker should be promoted to the big club. The headline of the *Chicago American* story of September 1 read, "At Last! Matthews to Bring Up Baker." The proof there was no public indication that Banks was in the wings was Enright's opening sentence: "Gene Baker is going to get an opportunity to become the Cubs' shortstop."[5]

Shortstop had always been Baker's position, but soon enough he was going to be gaining familiarity with second base.

More than a decade ago, when Banks was asked to choose the best game of his career, he did not select a big playoff win (of course the Cubs had none of those during his career) or even a special hitting day. The game of his life, he said, was his first one, his Major League debut, September 17, 1953, the day manager Phil Cavarretta sidled over to him at the batting cage and informed him he was in the starting lineup.

"I didn't think it was that big a deal," Banks said of the moment he got the word. That's because he expected to play, and that's why the Cubs left him on the big-league roster after signing him. "I know some people would say they were nervous, but I didn't have that much time to think about it. Players always remember their first game, though. But as a player you want to continue the journey each day."[6]

Banks had no trouble recounting his 0-fer hitting day, his error, or the Cubs loss. What he did not mention was that his first game made him the first African American player to appear in a Cubs regular-season game. Although many others through the years have taken note of it, Banks never made a big deal of that fact either. When questioned specifically, he always gave a low-key response, indeed even saying that someone had to be that person.

Banks' mentor Buck O'Neil wrote a book titled *I Was Right On Time* about his life. When Banks was asked about being the color barrier breaker for the Cubs, he once responded, "My baseball life started at the right time. I was right on time, Kansas City Monarchs to Cubs."[7]

Over the years, in interviews with different sportswriters, when Banks reminisced about his short stay with the Cubs in September of 1953, he regularly returned to the theme of how he had never before known, interacted with, or shared time with so many white people. He grew up in segregated Dallas and until he joined the Cubs he had played ball only for all-black teams.

> During my half-month stay with the Cubs in September, 1953, I met more white people than I had known in all my 22 years. As a teenager in Dallas, I had lived in an all-black neighborhood, gone to school and associated with other blacks. That was simply our way of life and it was no different with the first two ball teams I played for. The Detroit Colts was a Negro team. So was the Kansas City Monarchs.[8]

In his autobiography written with white sportswriter Jim Enright, Banks listed six white Cubs management personnel—Wid Matthews, Jimmy Gallagher,

Gene Lawing, Phil Cavarretta, Roy Johnson and Bob Lews—with whom he had a "fine relationship" from the get-go, even though his shyness took over in many conversations. Outside of the team, however, Banks did learn quickly that not everyone in the baseball world was in love with African Americans. Two days after his debut against Philadelphia, the Cubs were in St. Louis, the westernmost city in baseball and the southernmost. That latter description was more telling because St. Louis was rough on black ballplayers.

As non-controversial as Banks always tried to be, when recounting his first journey to St. Louis, it was obvious he had learned a bit about the harshness of the world. When the Cubs arrived in St. Louis, the team was split. The white players were all shepherded to the Chase Hotel. Banks and Baker were shipped by cab to the Olive Hotel in the black section of town.

Rather than howl about this, Banks echoed Buck O'Neil's own analysis of how things were on the road for the black player in the Negro Leagues. O'Neil always said the Monarchs stayed in the finest Negro hotels and ate in the best Negro-owned restaurants. Banks' stance about the experiences he and Baker had came across as all positive. "We lived like kings at the Olive," Banks said. "Big beds, a big icebox filled with food, and an insistent manager wanting to know if there was anything he could do to make our stay more enjoyable."[9]

Was this the ever-optimistic, seeing-good-in-all-situations Ernie Banks, the glass-always-half-full Banks? Or was he really stung by the treatment, being exiled from his teammates? Banks was not one to complain. In the American classic song, "Home on the Range," one of the lyrics goes, "Where seldom is heard a discouraging word." In Banks' case, never was heard a discouraging word. Not in 1953, and almost never in all his years in the public eye.

If that was not enough evidence for Banks that life under the surface might not be the same as life on the surface, he said the next day he and Baker went to a movie theater because they had some free time.

> We hopped in a cab and drove around downtown until we finally picked out a show. But as we walked toward the ticket seller's booth we could see her waving us away. Gene caught the significance of the wave and as he turned away, he said, "I hope you enjoyed the show we aren't going to see at this theatre." We took another cab back to the hotel and we went to a show in the black neighborhood.[10]

During that time period, some movie theaters had segregated seating, with African Americans relegated to the balcony. This movie theater did not even allow dark-skinned people in the front door.

This was not Banks' only brush with discrimination that stuck in his mind. He related another story, one that took place a couple of years later, when the Cubs were traveling through the South for exhibition games. He reported riding by bus from New Orleans to Mobile, Alabama, where the game was scheduled. Still the only two African Americans on the team, Banks and Baker were informed that they would change into their uniforms at the ballpark while the white players changed clothes at a prominent Mobile hotel. It was suggested that the two men stay on the bus while the white players went inside.

> I felt like taking a walk. Although Gene suggested I would be better off waiting in the bus, I left anyway. At the downtown bus station I walked into a store to buy a candy bar and a newspaper. Suddenly, the owner rushed out from behind the counter, shouting a string of four-letter words and threatening to call the police if I didn't get out of there, and fast. Needless to say, I left on the fly and hurried back to the Cubs' bus. Noting the expression on my face, Gene laughed overtime. "I see you just learned the facts of life about southern hospitality," Baker said.[11]

This was the world the young, innocent, earnest Ernie Banks walked into when he broke into the majors. This was routine daily life in early 1950s America, a disgraceful period of interracial contact and conflict for a country that never seemed to be able to shake its baseball prejudices over skin color, and where African Americans had few protections against humiliation and little recourse.

Stories like these abound involving early black players in the majors. A common thread was how little team owners and managers seemed to care what happened to their guys when they were separated from the body of the team—and how often they were separated. For every Branch Rickey, who actually paid Wendell Smith to help guide Jackie Robinson and his wife Rachel through the dark shadows and barbed wire awaiting them, ten teams did little to aid black ballplayers except arrange for alternate housing in African American neighborhoods.

Current generations can scarcely believe the stories of the shabby treatment afforded the players, and it is unlikely it can be so smoothly fathomed how many hurts were incurred, all as extra obstacles to on-field performance. At least once, Banks took note of the irony of how segregation played out in reverse fashion when a white Chicago sportswriter joined Banks and Baker for a cab ride at the ballpark in Beaumont, Texas. The scribe learned the hard way what issues the players faced. Their designated African American cab driver recoiled at carrying a white passenger. "I could be arrested if I'm caught with a white passenger in my cab," Banks recalled the driver saying. "I just can't carry that white man."[12]

Banks and Baker talked the driver into taking the chance. When they reached the downtown area, the man insisted that the sportswriter get out of the taxi at the bus station. The man walked back to his hotel. The irony of the entire ludicrous scenario was not lost on Banks.

At the time, Banks and Baker, as the only two African American members of the Chicago Cubs, were partners in these adventures. While they were mostly learning experiences for Banks, Baker was older, more mature, and had been around more. He had a better idea what to expect from situations and served as Banks' advisor—even on those occasions like going for a walk in the wrong part of town—when they were not heeded.

Baker was born in Davenport, Iowa, on June 15, 1925. His father, also Eugene, held some jobs in nearby Moline, Illinois. Both of those communities are part of the Quad Cities area along the Mississippi River. At Davenport High School, the younger Baker played on the basketball team and competed for the track team. Although the school did have a baseball team, no African Americans were on it, so Baker got his start in baseball on area sandlots. Baker and his team excelled in basketball and he was an All-State guard. In one common sign of the times, an item in a newspaper that praised his skills also referred to him as a "dusky guard." That was a regular euphemism for a dark-skinned person in newspapers in the 1940s and later.[13]

After high school, Baker joined the Navy, where he played basketball and baseball. When he was discharged, he continued to develop his baseball talent in semi-pro ball before he joined the Kansas City Monarchs for 1948 and 1949.

All of this took place before Baker's signing with the Cubs organization. His first pro play, though only for a few games, was with Springfield in the International League in 1950. Baker played 49 games in the lower Class A level for Des Moines and batted .321. That earned him his promotion to Los Angeles in the Pacific Coast League, where he stalled until 1953 despite rave reviews of his fielding and signs that he could wield a solid bat.

Although Baker officially became the first African American on the Cubs' roster before Banks signed, Banks made it into a game before he did. And people kept track of those things then.

Some point to outrage associated with "The Martinsville 7" in 1951 as the beginning of the modern Civil Rights Movement. In that Virginia case, seven African Americans were convicted of raping a white woman and sentenced to death. No white man had ever been given the death penalty for rape. The men were convicted by all-white juries. There was nationwide and international response to the verdicts. Some 500 people conducted what they called "a pilgrimage" from Richmond to Martinsville to protest their sentences, to no avail.

That same year, black students went on strike at Moton High, also in Virginia, to protest their segregated educational facilities that even lacked rest rooms for teachers. It was so overcrowded, with some 450 pupils crammed into a school built to house 150, that some classes were taught in old school buses. A tipping point occurred when the state offered money to improve conditions and the local school board turned down the money.

Months before Banks' call-up in 1953, African Americans instituted a boycott of the bus system in Baton Rouge, Louisiana, partially due to a fare increase, but also because bus drivers had the power to force blacks to stand in the back of the bus when seats up front that were ostensibly reserved for white patrons were not being used.

Beginning in 1952, continuing during Banks' shift to the Cubs, and into 1954, was the milestone Brown versus Board of Education lawsuit that consolidated five cases before the Supreme Court. The Court ultimately outlawed the precedent of "separate, but equal" segregation of public school children.

This was the restless world outside of baseball, the changing times swirling around young Ernie Banks, as he ascended to the pinnacle of his sport, and also as he competed during his first several years in the majors. It was no wonder he was asked his opinion on civil rights, no wonder that at various times sportswriters quizzed him about his views on the black man in society. Radicalism did not come naturally to Banks. Yes, he had lived through some discrimination in baseball in those hotels and movie theaters. But he was shy and reticent initially before blossoming into a more gregarious and outgoing individual. He was not unaware, but he was not a boat rocker, not someone given to outbursts, threats, or the like.

Banks did enunciate his thoughts on the issues, but he did not deliver harsh opinions, only thoughtful ones that seem to align with the personality of a gentle man.

> Some people feel that because you are black you will never be treated fairly, and that you should voice your opinions, be militant about them. I don't feel this way. You can't convince a fool against his will. He is still going to hold to his opinions, so why should I tell him, "Look, you are prejudiced. You don't like me because I'm black." If a man doesn't like me because I'm black, that's fine. I'll just go elsewhere, but I'm not going to let him change my life. I don't think it's up to black athletes to get involved in political or racial issues.
> Our main objective should be to play whichever sports we are involved in and play well. We can't use prejudice as an excuse or as a crutch. In athletics, I feel, you are judged on what you can do. If you can play, you will play. If you can't play, you won't play.[14]

Some might say such commentary was naïve, but that was Ernie Banks at the time. In his mind he proved that a poor black man, growing up outside of the mainstream of the baseball world, could get noticed and reach the highest level of the game of baseball by winning a Major League job. Once in place, Banks did not suffer from prejudice in his organization, supporting his original thinking that if he could play, he would play. Likewise, Banks won over a broad swath of fans who gave him his due as a player.

But Banks was not all that innocent. He understood how he might be perceived because of his thoughts, certainly as the Civil Rights Movement expanded and spread through the South and into the 1960s. "As black athletes, if we speak out on various issues, or wear our hair certain ways, we are considered militant," he said, "in opposition to The Establishment, which puts us in a position of being opposed to what gives us our livelihood. If we don't speak up about racial issues, political matters, or the organization itself, we are called Uncle Toms."[15]

For more than 60 years, Ernie Banks was a public figure in Chicago. At no time would anyone have dreamed that he would wear his hair in dreadlocks, preach violent protest over any issue, speak out in disgust about the Cubs, or with any nasty words alienate the millions of friends who loved him. That was just not in his personality.

Rather a statement he made after some years with the Cubs, when he was still a relatively young man, seems a much more natural fit with Banks the man. "As for black versus white, it is my hope and dream that someday men will have more love and understanding for each other," he said. "The color of your skin, the cut of your clothes, the type of automobile you drive, will have absolutely nothing to do with your acceptance by, or your respect for, your fellow man."[16]

If there is anyone Banks sounds like in that statement, it is Martin Luther King, Jr. Banks did not utter many elaborate comments like that one, doing his best to steer away from controversy. The brief statement he responded best with throughout the politically charged times during his two decades playing for the Chicago Cubs was "Play ball!"

7

Banks and Baker

In the earliest days of their shared time in the majors with the Chicago Cubs, Ernie Banks and Gene Baker were regarded together. It was almost as if the organization viewed them as twin brothers. Although Banks was technically first in integrating the Cubs by appearing in a game first, it was almost a tie, and Baker was on the team's radar—and in the local sporting press—longer than Banks before cracking the big-league lineup.

Most obviously, what the men had in common was the color of their skin. They were both African American. In an era when much of America still looked at blacks and referred to the humans as "them," that was a tremendous common bond. Such an observation was as foolish as assuming a 25-year-old white man raised in New York City had more in common with a 25-year-old white man raised on a cotton farm in Alabama.

What Banks and Baker also had in common was a desire to succeed as Major League baseball players. What occurred off the playing field connected them since they were not only the first two African Americans on the team, they were the only two. Naturally, since things were always done that way in the 1950s, Banks and Baker were roommates on road trips. They hung out together for support because if they were going to face discrimination, it was easier to bear it as a pair than as lonely individuals.

Physically, Banks and Baker were structured similarly. Banks was 6-foot-1, and his official playing weight was 180 pounds. Baker was also 6-foot-1 and weighed 170. They were both marvelous middle infielders, but in his coiled body and supple wrists, Banks had a reservoir of power he could unleash on the horsehide that only one in thousands of ballplayers possessed. He was of the always-admired baseball species called a home run hitter.

From the time of Babe Ruth forward, that skill was always prized among scouts and teams. A regular home-run hitter was viewed as someone with almost magical powers. The savviest baseball watchers acknowledged that such a guy had "it." They couldn't always spell out exactly what combination of talents went into the recipe to propel the ball out of the stadium farther than and more frequently than other hitters, but they understood the rarity when they saw it.

Ernie Banks was one of those guys who murdered baseballs. When it came to slugging, results mattered more than style, more than what a player looked like in size and shape. A former Cub, Hack Wilson, stood just 5-foot-6, and his National League record of 56 home runs lasted for decades.

During his ten-game, late-season 1953 stint in Chicago, Banks hit .314. He looked comfortable enough to justify management's decision not to send him to the minors after acquiring him from the Kansas City Monarchs. During Baker's seven-game trial after toiling in the minors for several years, he batted .227. The Cubs wanted them both to succeed and establish a keystone combination (Banks at short, Baker at second) that would last years. There was great confidence in Banks. There was time and hope invested in Baker.

Banks did not come from a wealthy family, and when he made his Major-League debut in September of 1953, no members of the immediate family were present. However, during spring training of 1954, the Cubs scheduled some exhibition games in Dallas. Banks' relatives could take in those games. However, one major team action detracted from those games.

When Ernie Banks connected, he slammed the ball pretty well (National Baseball Hall of Fame).

7. Banks and Baker

The Cubs fired manager Phil Cavarretta. This was a surprise for more than one reason. Cavarretta was a lifetime Cub. He broke in with the team as a 17-year-old and played 22 seasons while batting .293. Although Banks' popularity would exceed Cavarretta's, up until then Cavarretta may have been the Cubs' best-liked player of them all. Also, nobody fires the manager in spring training, the extended period when developing stability and camaraderie are on the front burner.

Cavarretta's sin that spring was being too smart for his own good. He told owner P. K. Wrigley that the way the team was constituted entering the campaign, there was no chance it would record a winning mark. Depending on how one looked at it, Cavarretta was either too much of a pessimist or too much of a realist. Wrigley asked Cavarretta what to expect as the start of the 1954 season loomed. At the time, the Cubs were 5–15 in exhibition games. It was Cavarretta's misjudgment that he thought Wrigley wanted to hear the truth. He said the Cubs had no chance to be winners that summer. "The material just isn't there," Cavarretta said. "What makes it sadder is that the future looks even worse. There just isn't any good new talent coming up."[1]

Cavarretta did provide dispensation for Banks and Baker, who he believed showed promise, plus outfielder Bob Talbot, who managed just two seasons in the majors. "Phil seems to have developed a defeatist attitude," Wrigley said. "We don't believe he should continue in a job where he doesn't believe success is possible."[2]

It was Baker who informed Banks of the change. Banks was startled and asked who the replacement was. No announcement had been made. Baker joked, "Maybe they'll make you the new boss."[3] Banks said he laughed so hard he had to duck into the rest room to avoid attracting attention. Ironically, a couple of decades later there would be widespread speculation about Banks managing the Cubs.

In a less surprising move, the Cubs selected former star third baseman Stan Hack as the new manager. Hack, a .301 lifetime hitter, was a five-time All-Star. To some, Cavarretta was like a football coach. He essentially ordered players to run through a brick wall for him. Hack was what was more commonly referred to as a players' manager. He wanted a loose clubhouse with happy players. Banks knew none of this, but Baker had played for Hack in the minors and filled Banks in on what to expect.

Given the way Hack used them, he certainly seemed to be a believer in Banks' and Baker's skills. In 1954, Banks played in all 154 games, tying for the league high. Baker was used in 135 games. They each recorded more than 600 plate appearances, so they were busy.

This was an important season for both players, officially rookies trying to impress. Baker had scrambled for years to get his chance. Banks' raw talent led him to the majors more swiftly. Baker was 29 in 1954, his first full big-league season. He batted .275 with 13 home runs and 61 runs batted in, smart offensive stats for a middle infielder. He had 32 doubles among his 149 hits.

In July, Baker went on a tear. At one point he had seven hits in 12 at-bats with six RBI. He also helped win two straight extra-inning games. And it was Banks who was supposed to wield the big bat?

After that, Baker had an injury scare in a game against the Pittsburgh Pirates when he and Cubs outfielder Hal Rice had a two-car collision while chasing a foul ball hit by Pirate Preston Ward. Ward's stroke occurred in the first inning of a July 31 game at Forbes Field, and when the fielders ran for the ball, Rice's elbow bashed Baker's face. Baker's sunglasses shattered, and he was cut over his right eye. Baker was knocked out and carried from the field unconscious. He did not appear in a game until August 4—as a pinch-runner—and as a regular not again until August 5.

Banks said he and Baker were players of the watch-and-learn style during their early days in the majors. Jackie Robinson told him to act that way, he said, and it suited him, especially when he was young and everything about the big leagues felt new. "We got on the field and we learned by just watching other people," Banks said. "Watching Monte Irvin. Watching Willie Mays, watching some of your own players—Hank Sauer, Ralph Kiner. Just by watching. I didn't play in the minor leagues."[4]

Banks took note of the Cubs' lousy home attendance at Wrigley Field during the team's fallow play, and it took years for things to change. The Cubs did improve during his career, and more fans came out to Wrigley Field, by far his favorite ballpark.

Given how much the modern ballplayer is paid, such simple gestures have gone by the wayside, but at the end of spring training in 1954, the team gave Banks a Cubs watch proclaiming him the top rookie of the pre-season. He said it made him feel as if he had made the team. There had never been any doubt about that occurring, but the wristwatch was a nice keepsake.

Although Banks in 1954 was like President Teddy Roosevelt, speaking softly and carrying a big stick, that image of Banks did not last long. He is definitely not remembered that way. If he was shy and purposely quiet as a rookie, he was conscious of trying to blend in and fit in. Banks was never flamboyant, but soon after his break-in full season he began making friends by mingling, by being open, friendly and enthusiastic.

Banks swiftly became known for his good attitude in the clubhouse, the dugout, and the ballpark, before and after every game. The phrase "sunny disposition" was practically invented for Banks. Naturally, he was never happy when he struck out or had a bad day at the plate—and everyone has those. And naturally, he was not happy when the Cubs lost games—and they lost more than most for many years, even with a star like Banks on the roster.

7. Banks and Baker

The famous Chicago broadcaster Jack Brickhouse was already on the job with the Cubs when Banks joined the team for that brief appearance in 1953. Brickhouse was born in Peoria, Illinois, in 1916, and at one time or another he seemed to be the voice of everybody in Chicago. He began broadcasting Chicago White Sox games in 1940 and Cubs games in 1941, sticking with the Cubs through 1981. Brickhouse also handled Chicago Bears football games and Chicago Bulls basketball games. It almost seemed that if Brickhouse did not interpret the action, Chicago sports fans would be at a loss to know what really happened.

Over a four-decade period, just about the only time when Brickhouse was not on the air in Chicago was between 1945 and 1948, when he served in the Marines. If it could have been arranged for him to chime in long-distance, he probably would have.

In 1993, 40 years after Banks joined the Cubs, Brickhouse spoke about the occasion at a Cubs winter fan convention. He did note that the White Sox saw Banks first, but he told how Buck O'Neil scooped up Banks for the Cubs. "Ernie was the happiest guy in the world to be in the major leagues," Brickhouse said. "He was just so tickled to be playing baseball. He had a genuine love of the sport. Ernie had the ability to make a little boy or a little girl feel like the reason he came to the park that day was to see them."[5]

Baseball players are not always lumped together with singers and actors as entertainers, but that is a gift every performer wants to possess and the kind of message every one of them wants to impart. The ticket-buying public basically pays the salaries of those entertainers, and part of a professional athlete's job is to sell his image and sell the product. Banks' image was always sterling, and the people loved him.

It did not hurt anything that Banks was a heralded signing, his stature built up from the start, and that even the ten-game taste of Ernie in the autumn of 1953 left people pleased with the tease and wanting more the next season. That first full season, Banks hit 19 home runs, drove in 79 runs, and batted .275. Those were very solid hitting numbers, especially for a shortstop. Not much was expected of shortstops at the plate during that era, so those across-the-board statistics already made Banks a success.

The "Rookie of the Year" Award was still fairly new. In 1947, Jackie Robinson was the first recipient of the award. In 1954, Banks was the National League runner-up. With 20–20 hindsight, baseball fans will chuckle at how the voting went. Fourth that year was some new guy for the Braves named Henry Aaron. The third-place finisher was another Brave, pitcher Gene Conley, who had the distinction of being one of only two ballplayers in history to win a World Series (with the Milwaukee Braves in 1957) and an NBA title (a couple with the Boston Celtics). Catcher Del Rice is the only other one who can make that claim.

The winner of the 1954 NL "Rookie of the Year" Award? Outfielder Wally Moon of the Cardinals—and in a runaway, too.

That year Aaron smacked 13 home runs, drove in 69 runs and batted .280. Conley went 14-9 with a 2.96 earned run average. Moon hit 18 homers, knocked in 76 runs and batted .304. Moon had a 12-year big-league career with a .289 lifetime average. But that was pretty much the last time it was suggested he was better than future Hall of Famers Ernie Banks or Hank Aaron. Whatever Phil Cavarretta was doing poorly to get himself canned in spring training, Stan Hack did not transmit a spark to the Cubs once the regular season began. The Cubs struggled throughout the season, finishing seventh in the eight-team league with a 64-90 record.

In those days, the Major League season did not begin at the crack of April. The ruling partners liked to at least pretend games did not count on the record until it was really spring. The Cubs won the season opener on April 13. They topped the St. Louis Cardinals, 13-4, on the road with Paul Minner the winner. Minner went 9-9 that season as he neared the end of his ten-year career. When he retired the next season, his lifetime record of 69-84 was similar to the team's 1954 mark of 64-90.

Strangely, after that single game, the Cubs went home to Wrigley Field to meet the Cincinnati Reds, again for just one game before a two-game series with the Cardinals in Chicago. The Cubs lost the Reds game and then engaged in one of those Seven-Years-War encounters that periodically break out when the wind is blowing out from home plate at Wrigley. Chicago out-lasted St. Louis, 23-13. It was a welcome-to-Wrigley game for Banks. The Cubs scored ten runs in the fifth inning and banked 20 hits in all. Banks had just one of those hits, although his pal Baker contributed three and scored four times.

Banks spoke of watching Ralph Kiner and Hank Sauer at the plate that season to see how they handled big-league pitching. Kiner, then 31, was just a year away from early retirement, but had led the National League in home runs seven straight years with the Pirates before he was swapped to the Cubs. He once hit 54 homers in a season. Eventually enshrined in the Hall of Fame for his slugging, Kiner went on to an equally memorable broadcasting career with the New York Mets. That Cubs season, Kiner mashed 22 homers, with 73 RBI and a .285 average. He wasn't over the hill yet.

Overall, Sauer's career was not as notable as Kiner's, but in 1952 he led the National League with 37 homers and 121 runs batted in for the Cubs and won the Most Valuable Player Award. Sauer's last great year was 1954, when he blasted a career-high 41 homers with 103 RBI. Kiner and Sauer were both good role models in the batter's box for Banks that season.

There were lessons to be learned from Sauer, for sure. In spring training of 1952, the Cubs had given up on the 6-foot- 3, 198-pound leftfielder, though that did not seem to make much sense. He had struck 30 or more home runs in the previous two seasons. They didn't much like his fielding and put him on waivers. The Cubs seemed schizophrenic about Sauer's talents. Apparently, 14 of the other 15 teams in the bigs had their doubts, too, because only the White Sox put in a bid for him. The Cubs withdrew him from waivers, and general manager Wid Matthews issued an affronted statement.

"It insults the intelligence to believe that we would let a fellow like Sauer go for the $10,000 waiver price," Matthews said. "He has been our best drawing card at the gate for the last few years."[6] Then why put him on waivers? Go figure. It would have been foolish to dump Sauer, who gained so many fans at Wrigley the home crowd began to call him "The Mayor." After the flirtation with the waiver wire, Sauer went out and slammed his 37 homers, won the MVP Award, and was still around two years later to inspire Banks.

Before Wrigley Field morphed into one of the two most beloved ballparks in the majors, along with Fenway Park in Boston, for most players, home and visitors, it was pretty much viewed as just another place to play. That was never true for Banks, however. For him it was love at first sight. If he had been a skilled poet, he would have written rhapsodically about the ivy and the green grass. As it was, he composed love songs in his head about the ballpark, falling for it from the start and virtually imbuing it with the same sentiments a traveler feels upon returning home after a long journey.

Banks felt a strong tie to the park from the start, but it was only decades later, when it was constantly jammed with supporters, when the Cubs grew to a national sensation because of cable television win or lose—that he truly let his feelings out. "The great joy in my life is to come out to Wrigley Field now," he said in the early 2000s. "Coming out here is better than going to a psychiatrist. It's real therapy for me. The other parks are OK, but it's real special coming here. To me, it's just a wonderful place to be and I really love it."[7]

Neither Banks nor the Cubs tore things up in April of 1954. After starting 1–0 and 2–1, the Cubs never got over .500 again all season, though they did hit 9–9 on May 9. It took the first several games for Banks' average to climb over .200. Then he clouted four hits in a 9–2 victory over Cincinnati on April 25 and three more hits against the New York Giants on April 30, and suddenly he was at .282, quite respectable. Meanwhile, Gene Baker was at .351 at the end of his first full month in the majors.

The season played out pretty much as Cavarretta had predicted. Banks and Baker looked good. Talbot hit .333 in limited appearances in 1953, but after hitting .241 in 1954 he was shifted to the Pacific Coast League and never played in the majors again. As for Cavarretta, suddenly without a job because he lost at truth or consequences, he signed to return to the field for the crosstown White Sox, hitting .316 in 71 games that year. He played in just six more games the next season before managing for several years in the minors, scouting for the Detroit Tigers, and serving as a hitting instructor for the Mets. Cavarretta was the last living player who took the field against Babe Ruth in 1935. He lived to 94, passing away in 2010 without ever seeing the Cubs win another pennant.

8

1955–1957

By his second full year in the big leagues, Ernie Banks was an All-Star. It was the first of 11 years he was selected for the National League All-Star team. If Banks was still learning the game in 1954, he was among elite players by 1955, a place he occupied for the rest of his 19-year Major League career with the Cubs.

As he had in 1954, Banks played in every Cubs game during the 1955 campaign, again becoming one of a small number of players who played in all 154 games. From the Cubs' front office to the departed Phil Cavarretta, the team had always seen potential in Banks. He hurried up and fulfilled it in 1955.

The Cubs had not won a pennant since 1945, the year the Billy Goat Curse was slapped on the team. Chicago was facing the Detroit Tigers in the World Series when William Sianis, operator of the Billy Goat Tavern, showed up at the park leading a goat. For some reason, Sianis thought it was a good idea to bring a goat to Wrigley Field as a game companion. The average person might consider that to be a silly, practical joke. The goat, named Murphy, brought along a distinctive smell that other patrons did not appreciate. When told his goat stank, Sianis was insulted.

All would have been fine if Sianis approached the incident with lightheartedness. Instead, when officials turned him and Murphy away, he became indignant, especially so since he had purchased a $7.20 ticket for the animal. In response to being ousted, Sianis leveled a curse on the club. Whatever his exact words, Sianis' meaning was taken to be that the Cubs would never win a pennant or a World Series again while he was alive, or maybe forever.

This pronouncement was likely scoffed at because during that era the Cubs were regular pennant-winners. Even if they had not captured a World Series crown since 1908, they regularly won National League pennants and at least earned the right to play for World Series titles. The Cubs represented the NL in the Series in 1929, 1932, 1935, 1938 and 1945. The Cubs lost to the Tigers in 1945, the year of the goat incident.

Sianis lived until October 22, 1970, and the Cubs did not win another pennant during his lifetime. Believing the Cubs had suffered enough, at times various members of the Sianis family had turned up at Wrigley, making attempts to lift the curse placed by their kin. Nothing they did had any effect. The Cubs kept losing.

Certainly, Ernie Banks' transfer from the Kansas City Monarchs to the Cubs was not contingent on the removal of the curse. In 1953, when he showed up in Chicago, the curse was fairly new. Then Banks hung around for two decades, and the Cubs never won a pennant or a World Series during his stay. It was almost as if the curse was personally aimed at Banks. He became one of the greatest stars in baseball history who never competed in a post-season game.

It was not until 2016, when the Cubs claimed the pennant and won the World Series (interestingly, on October 22, the anniversary of Sianis' death) for the first time in 108 years, that the curse was officially considered kaput. Probably no Cub paid a bigger price for a longer time due to the curse than Banks. But in 1955, nobody could read the future, and the emergence of Banks as a star of the first magnitude that season helped uplift Cubs optimism, if not for that season precisely, then for the immediate future.

The Cubs of 1955 went 32–21 over the first third of the season. There was joy in Wrigleyville. Naturally, it did not last. As the heat of the summer moved in, the Cubs wilted. They finished 72–81, some 26 games out of first place, while residing in sixth place.

While the Cubs muddled along, Banks became Ernie Banks, the shortstop with the keen eye at the plate who possessed hidden and unexpected power. That season, Banks slugged 44 home runs with 117 runs batted in and compiled a .295 average. All of those statistics led the team. At the time, that was the most home runs hit in a single season by a shortstop. Indeed, no shortstop had previously hit as many as 40 in a season. The old record for the position was 39 by Vern Stephens of the Boston Red Sox in 1949.

Banks did come out slugging in 1955, with three home runs in his first four games, then cooled off and hit just one more in 20 games. But he was a pretty busy guy in May. Banks clubbed many of his homers that month off of prominent pitchers, including future Hall of Famer Robin Roberts, Lew Burdette, and Sal Maglie. As the calendar page turned, Banks slugged four-baggers off Curt Simmons, Don Newcombe, Bob Friend and future Hall of Famer Warren Spahn twice.

In typical Cubs fashion, Banks hit two home runs in an April 16 game, but they still lost to the St. Louis Cardinals, 12–11. On May 11, Banks hit the first grand slam of his career off the Dodgers' Russ Meyer. Banks had a proclivity for hitting grand slams and amassed 12 in his career. At the time of his retirement in 1971, Banks ranked behind only a handful of sluggers on the grand slam list, including Lou Gehrig, Babe Ruth, Jimmie Foxx and Joe DiMaggio.

In 1955 alone, Banks hit five grand slams. When Banks talked about that feat, it came off in humorous fashion, just because it sounded as if he had been waiting ages to set some kind of record when in reality he had only been in the majors for a couple of years. "I finally found a way to get myself in the record book in 1955," Banks said. "Five of my 44 homers that season were grand slams that set a major-league record for 154 games."[1] Banks held that big-league record until 1987, when the Yankees' Don Mattingly hit six in a season. But Banks retained the NL mark.

Banks seemed a little in awe of himself with all of those grand slams. "It's the greatest thrill of my life," Banks said after collecting his fifth grand slam. "I still can't believe it's true. Naturally, I knew I needed another one to break the record, but I never dreamed it would happen to me. Then the kid [Lindy McDaniel] gave me a fastball that was a bit outside and I knew it was gone as soon as I hit it. It was one of the best pitches I hit all season, but it's still hard to believe."[2]

When Banks was informed that the Baseball Hall of Fame in Cooperstown, New York, might want the ball that he blasted, he was disappointed. He wanted to hold onto it as a keepsake. "Gee, I hope they don't," Banks said. "I'd like to keep it. I have all four of the other baseballs and this would really be a prize souvenir to add to my collection."[3]

May 12, a day after Banks' first grand slam, the Cubs won by a no-hitter. Sam "Toothpick" Jones, who enjoyed chewing on a toothpick as he pitched, bested the Pittsburgh Pirates, 4–0. The announced attendance was just 2,918 at Wrigley Field. Banks could share the pleasure with Jones since he went three-for-four at the plate.

Banks and Gene Baker were still an entry, linked by the timing of their arrival as Cubs, as well as by race. Baker was a regular in the starting lineup, too, the second baseman complement to Banks' role as shortstop. Baker hit a home run on Opening Day. This was a much less common occurrence for Baker than Banks, although he did crack 11 dingers that season when he drove in 52 runs and batted .268.

Like Banks, Baker played in all 154 games that summer and made his first (and only) All-Star team. Baker and Banks made a good team in the middle of the Cubs' infield, and they were always viewed as a team, perhaps too much so in some instances. There was clearly a feeling that Baker remained in AAA ball at least one season too long because the Cubs were hesitant to stretch the team's color line too boldly. There were sometimes mixed signals from owner Phil Wrigley. When Baker was about to be promoted and Banks was signed, almost simultaneously, some within the Cubs organization wondered if abruptly adding two black players to the roster was too much, too fast. But Wrigley responded, "See if you can find a history book and read the Constitution of the United States."[4]

There had been no editing of the Constitution recently, but baseball owners had ignored some of its provisions for years while keeping African American players out of the big leagues. But no matter about that now as things inched in the right direction.

The friendly, outgoing, smiling, gracious Ernie Banks that everyone came to know brought all of those traits with him to the majors. As part of an early scouting report on him, Cool Papa Bell had said as much. "His conduct was almost as outstanding as his ability," Bell said.[5]

Bell also saw Baker play early in his career, and his observation of what he brought to the table was right on the money. Bell could recognize a future major leaguer, but he could also tell the difference between a big leaguer and a future star. "Baker was good enough to play several years in the bigs," Bell said. "But he was never Banks' equal."[6]

Banks wowed fans with his power at the plate, but (particularly as a rookie when he committed 34 errors) he sometimes made them groan when he was in the field. He was less polished with his glove than his bat early in his career. Baker had him there. This was one area where their partnership paid off for Banks. If he was upset because he made an error, Baker could soothe him. But Baker also offered advice on how to do better next time. This was long before the designated hitter was introduced to the sport, so Banks had to master his position in the field.

"Gene has been a tremendous help to me," Banks said. "He's coached me and advised me on lots of things and helped me correct my mistakes. Without him, things would have been much more difficult."[7] Baker was the big-brother figure who could aid Banks' diamond play, put his mind at ease, and offer useful life observations, at least in part because they were experiencing the same type of social impacts on their lives as black men on a predominantly white stage, working in a realm where "their kind" had previously not been welcome.

Of course, Baker had to take care of personal business, as well. The Cubs were not going to keep him around Chicago just as a personal coach and helpmate for Banks. He had to pull his own weight on the field, and he did. In a May 27 game against the Milwaukee Braves at Wrigley Field, Baker showed how it is done in the field when he recorded 11 putouts in a single game at second base, a National League record. Banks was not about to become a vacuum cleaner overnight in the field, but he could often steer the spotlight in another direction with his hitting.

Two days after Baker performed so admirably in the field, Banks ripped another grand slam. Of all things, about a month later, Baker smacked a grand slam in an 11–7 win over St. Louis. Those muscle-flexing moments

8. 1955–1957

The scene outside of venerable Wrigley Field in 1935 when the team competed in the World Series. This was a scene Banks never experienced during his Cubs career and his 2,528 games (National Baseball Hall of Fame).

were rarer for Baker, though in early August his solo homer gave the Cubs a 1–0 victory over Don Newcombe. Only days prior to that, Banks had a three-homer, seven-RBI game. Chicago needed all of those runs, edging the Pirates, 11–10.

It was on September 19 that Banks powered his record fifth grand slam of the season. St. Louis' Lindy McDaniel was on the mound when Banks sent a pitch into orbit for a 5–0 Cubs lead in the seventh inning. Rather remarkably, the Cardinals came back to win, 6–5, in 12 innings. Banks would have to get used to such developments. Often he did something spectacular for the Cubs in a losing cause.

The July 12 All-Star Game at County Stadium in Milwaukee had to be a proud and satisfying day for both Banks and Baker. Banks played shortstop for the National League (though he went 0-for-2) and Baker pinch-hit (going 0-for-1). The NL won, 6–5, even though the Cubs were not difference-makers.

Banks and Baker were very much regarded as partners in the middle of the Chicago infield. One newspaper story described the relationship this way:

"Banks and Baker today are as much of a team as Burns and Allen [the husband-wife comedy team of George Burns and Gracie Allen], Martin [Dean] and [Jerry] Lewis or Scotch and Soda. They're together off the ball-field as well as on it. And on it they're the best double-play combination in the league."[8]

In the middle of the off-season leading up to 1956 play, an intriguing headline showed up in a Chicago newspaper. Cubs fans had to be curious about what it could mean for the fortunes of their favorite team. The story announced that the Cubs had signed a new player named Benjamin Banks. It was Ernie's 22-year-old younger brother, who had only recently been discharged from Army service.

The article said that Ernie Banks played a role in the signing (not terribly surprising). Banks accompanied team scout Vedie Himsl to the family home in Dallas to seek Ben's autograph. The Cubs did display a bit more caution with Ben than they did with Ernie, however. Ernie was a better-known quantity, recommended by Buck O'Neil and experienced with the Kansas City Monarchs. Ben's deal was with a Class C team in Lafayette, Louisiana. Although Ben Banks was invited to the big club's spring training camp in Arizona, set to begin ten days later, the team was obviously unclear on his potential. "We want to find out just how good he is," said Wid Matthews, director of player personnel. "Maybe he can play in a higher classification than the Evangeline League."[9]

Benjamin Banks never made it big, never played in the majors, and died young, at 37, in 1970.

There were no more questions about Ernie Banks' abilities as the 1956 season got under way, other than how good he could become. He was already setting records and making All-Star teams and was edging into the conversation as one of the best players in the game. Banks' status was established. If not for injuries that limited him to 139 games, his key statistics would likely have been similar to his 1955 totals. Banks hit 28 home runs, knocked in 85 runs, hit .297 and made his second All-Star team.

By the time he was hurt, Banks had played in 424 consecutive games. What sidelined him was an injured finger that grew infected. Football players tape a couple of bruised digits together and play on. But a little thing like that can interfere with a baseball player's hitting. So 95 percent of his body feels fine, and this annoying little tweak puts him on the bench. "The inactivity while waiting for the injury to heal seemed like hell on earth," Banks said. "The Cubs weren't having a very good season, and there I was, out of action, unable to make any kind of contribution. It was one of the few periods in my life I got really discouraged."[10]

That made sense. This was the guy who repeatedly announced to the world, "Let's play two!" as his preferred activity of the day. No one ever heard Ernie Banks say, "Let's play none!"

8. 1955–1957

Baker turned 31 that season, but was still an asset with 12 home runs, 57 RBI and a .258 average. It would not be long, though, before some higher-ups began speculating about encroaching age.

That would be new higher-ups, however. The Cubs were no better in 1956 than they had been the previous year. In fact, they were worse, finishing 60–94 in last place. The organization fired manager Stan Hack and shoved Matthews out the door, too.

Under new general manager John Holland and manager Bob Scheffing, there was optimism in the spring of 1957, as there always is with a change of administration. Banks watched with keen interest as new pitching coach Fred Fitzsimmons labored to teach young pitchers new tricks. The right-handed Fitzsimmons, often referred to as "Fat Freddie Fitzsimmons," was born in 1901 and played in the majors between 1925 and 1943, winning 217 games. He was regarded as a savvy tutor, and the Cubs were trying to grow starting pitching, picking a rotation from among Moe Drabowsky, Dick Drott, Bob Rush, Turk Lown, Don Elston, Dave Hillman and Don Kaiser. Time would show that several of them had shining moments, but not for the Cubs, and were not talented enough to be aces. Banks, the Cubs and Fitzsimmons did not know that yet.

Scheffing guided the Cubs to a 62–92 record. There was no cure for the summertime blues in the Wrigley bleachers that summer. The record tied the Pirates for seventh place, 33 games behind the Braves in the pennant race.

Banks had the blues for part of the season because the Cubs traded away Gene Baker. Baker had appeared in 12 games and was hitting .250 when he was dealt, along with first baseman Dee Fondy, to the Pirates for Lee Walls and Dale Long. Walls and Long were reliable hitters. "I lost my best friend and roommate" was how Banks characterized Baker's departure.[11]

Yet the Cubs made the right call on Baker. He was slowing down, and after the 1957 season he never played more than 33 games in a season again. What has often been overlooked in Baker's baseball career, or forgotten, is that he was a historical footnote on more than one occasion in the coming years as opportunities for African Americans expanded in the sport. A knee injury pretty much finished off Baker in the field a month into the 1959 season, but in acknowledgment of his baseball wisdom, the Pirates hired him as a minor-league instructional assistant, specializing in tutoring fielders. That made Baker the Pirates' first African American employee in front-office administration.

"I feel that he has the experience, personality and intelligence to do a fine job for us," said Pirates general manager Joe Brown. "He will work predominately with our minor league infielders and also help with the analysis of our minor-league clubs and in our scouting program."[12]

Pittsburgh apparently liked what Baker did for them because in 1961 the team made him manager of its Batavia minor-league club. That was nearly 15 years before future Hall of Famer Frank Robinson became the first African

American to manage a Major League team. Robinson was 39 and still active on the field when he was hired as manager of the Cleveland Indians in 1975.

Batavia was a much lower-profile assignment. Batavia was in Class D ball in the New York-Pennsylvania League. Yet bagging that job was still a milestone. Former big-league players who were black were not considered managerial material, even in the minors, at that time. Joe Brown, the GM who brought Baker aboard to scout, was the same man promoting him. "Gene has been most valuable to us as a player and scout," Brown said. "He's a fine gentleman with outstanding baseball experience and knowledge. We know he'll do a fine job in the managerial field."[13]

Everyone talks about the long bus trips taken in the low minors, but Batavia didn't even travel by bus. The squad traveled in a group of automobiles. Baker always drove one of them. Most road trips in the eight-team league were long day-journeys. The team only stayed overnight in the most distant towns in the league. This all very much smacked of low-budget management. Players often did not get home until the middle of the night. There were no pre-dawn wakeup calls following those trips.

As an African American manager, Baker was sure to draw attention. But he thought producing good results was the biggest thing on everybody's minds. "I feel that the fans won't care what color I am as long as the club is scoring runs and winning games," Baker said. "They want a manager who can do the job. Doing the job is my goal."[14]

In 1957, Banks was 26 years old. He and Baker went their separate ways in the game. That season, healthy again, Banks found the same groove he had exploited in 1955. He smashed 43 home runs—28 as a shortstop and 15 as a third baseman—with 102 runs batted in and a .285 average. Banks was about to turn hitting 40 or more homers per year as a shortstop into a habit. Only Alex Rodriguez, who eventually surpassed him with one-season totals, and Rico Petrocelli hit 40 in a year while playing shortstop. A mini-asterisk could be placed next to Banks' total in 1957 because that season the Cubs used him at third base for 58 games.

Banks had some days to remember in September of 1957, even though the team did not as it stumbled to the finish line. On September 4, Moe Drabowsky pitched a two-hitter in a 1–0 win over the Cincinnati Reds. Banks' solo homer accounted for the only run. Ten days later, Banks smacked three homers in one game in a 7–3 victory over Pittsburgh. And on September 29, on the final day of the season, Banks went 5-for-5 in an 8–3 win over St. Louis.

Banks seemed to be getting better and better. Fans may have thought it was a shame the season ended with Banks on fire. As it happened, the winter intermission before the 1958 season began hardly mattered at all. Banks definitely was getting better.

9

1958–1959
Most Valuable Player

Yes, Ernie Banks could get better. He broke into the majors with a bang, and he was the best prospect the Chicago Cubs had in decades. Moreover, he lived up to his promise and his billing almost immediately.

Banks had swiftly become a regular All-Star Game pick. What no one foresaw, as the Cubs continued to founder, was that he would keep improving, becoming the brightest star in the Cubs' galaxy quite quickly. Not that the competition was so stiff. The Cubs pictured Banks as being the cornerstone of a new breed of Cubs, a budding contender that would make annual runs at the National League pennant. Alas, both for Cubs fans and for Banks himself, they were pretty much the same old Cubs, albeit with a jewel of a shortstop that every pitcher in the league grew to fear and respect in the batter's box.

While one superstar has a better chance of uplifting a basketball team than in any other pro sport, it is less likely for even the best hitter on the planet to carry a baseball team. There are nine guys in the batting order, and there is such a thing called pitching. What those guys do on the mound matters a lot.

So no, Banks could not be a one-man savior. The Cubs hoped he would be a trend-setter and they could build around him. That was definitely a laudable goal, but five years into his tour of the majors, there was little indication this plan was working. Banks stood out because he was great, but he stood out because for enemy pitchers he was often the only stick wielder on the roster to worry about.

By 1958, Banks was established. He had set some hitting marks and was already a three-time All-Star. Between 1953, when Banks moved into the lineup for those September wrap-up games, and 1957, the Cubs had only once finished within nine games of a .500 winning percentage. Other years they were 30 or more games under .500. It was fun to be in the big leagues, but it was not fun to play for a perennial loser.

Of course, Banks always took his eggs sunny side-up, so he did not complain. But even the most optimistic fellow in the world (and Banks was a contender for that title every year, if not an NL pennant) has feelings, even if he does not show them. It is doubtful that anyone else could have dreamt up as many explanations and rationalizations for the Cubs' failures than Banks. Recalling that Banks began each spring training get-together proclaiming it was Chicago's turn to win it all, Pete Rose, the all-time Major League hits leader for the Cincinnati Reds, recounted how Banks sounded in conversation each time around the league as the season wore on and the Cubs fell farther behind.

> The first time around, all Ernie talks about is the Chicago Cubs winning the pennant and roaring right through the World Series. Nobody else has a chance. The second time around he sadly laments injuries and bad luck blighting the Cubs' chances, but they'll still end up the spoiler, helping to decide who is going to win the pennant. The third time he's once again bubbling with recharged confidence, telling how the Cubs are building for the future and will win it all next year, including the World Series. I've never known a player with greater loyalty to his team—win or lose.[1]

In 1958, the Cubs flashed a glimmer of hope. They finished 72–82 and in fifth place, just 20 games arrears of the pennant-winning Milwaukee Braves. By Cubs standards, this qualified as good news. Good news was graded on a curve when it came to the team, but Ernie Banks' hitting set a very high bar for everyone else in the game.

Chicago got off to a respectable start with some April games on the road in new locations. The New York Giants had relocated to San Francisco during the off-season, and the Brooklyn Dodgers fled to Los Angeles, as for the first time Major League Baseball was bi-coastal. The Dodgers settled into temporary quarters at the Memorial Coliseum, which was more often used for college football. Wrigley Field was regarded as an unpredictable ballpark, and definitely a hitter's paradise on days the wind was blowing out. The Coliseum had a very short porch in left field that represented a right-handed hitter's target.

The wall was only 250 feet from home plate, making that side of the diamond more closely resemble a woman's softball field. Management erected a 40-foot-tall screen above the wall, but that did not cure pitchers of nightmares. On April 24, 1958, the Cubs feasted on LA pitching, trouncing the Dodgers, 15–2. Lee Walls belted three home runs and collected eight runs batted in. Banks went 0-for-3.

Banks' turn would come early and often during this spectacular season. For him, not the team, though the Cubs did raise hopes when they were 13–7 on May 7 and 46–42 on July 18 before going into a slide. The last time they were at .500 was three days later at 46–45. Banks did not slide, except into bases when stroking doubles and triples.

9. 1958–1959

Banks' highlight reel was longer than the team's highlight reel. On July 14, the Cubs eked out an 11–10 victory over the Philadelphia Phillies and Banks slashed three hits, scored twice and drove in two runs. On August 21, Banks knocked in all five runs in a 5–3 win over the Pittsburgh Pirates. Banks never hit more than two homers in a game that season, but he accumulated 47 of them, breaking his own shortstop record and leading the National League. Banks' 129 runs batted in also led the league, as did his .614 slugging percentage. His batting average was .313, his highest since his autumn ten-game stint of 1953 when he hit .313. It would also be the highest average of his career.

Banks was retired and much older when Alex Rodriguez came along and broke his home run record for a shortstop, but one fan Rodriguez impressed was his predecessor. "To me, he is," Banks said of Rodriguez being the best ever shortstop. "To see this young man play that position with power and his defensive ability, it's really, really impressive. All the MVP candidates [including Cal Ripken Jr., Honus Wagner, Derek Jeter and Nomar Garciaparra, among others] are great players, having great careers and great seasons. But the slight edge with Alex is his power and defense over everything else. Playing shortstop is so exceptional. It's the main position. You've got to make special plays at that position."[2]

Of course, it wasn't until later that Rodriquez was nabbed for taking performance enhancing drugs and was suspended by Major League Baseball. That skewed his status as an all-time great.

Some years, the most dominant player in the National League and American League plays for the pennant-winner, or in more recent years a division champion. The definition of Most Valuable is assuredly different from Most Outstanding Player. A Most Valuable Player's worth does not simply measure statistics, as a Most Outstanding Player review might. It is supposed to include intangibles. Often, the best player on the winningest team is the MVP. The case to be made is often obvious.

However, in a season when the best player is not clear-cut or if he does not play for the best team, debate can ensue. After all, if a team is lousy and finished far down in the standings, what has the great statistical season produced? Surely some voters harbor enough prejudice on that front to withhold a ballot favoring a player who put up a tremendous season for a losing team.

Nonetheless, in 1958, Banks won the National League Most Valuable Player Award while competing for the lowly Cubs with their 72–82 record. That was the first time a player from a losing team won the award in either league. It has happened since. Banks, of course, was a repeat winner in 1959. In 1987, Andre Dawson, another future Hall of Famer, also playing for a losing Cubs club, won the award. In 1991, Cal Ripken, Jr., of the Baltimore Orioles won the AL MVP Award, and in 2003, Alex Rodriguez, then of the Texas

Rangers, won the American League trophy. He also hit 47 home runs playing for a 71–91 team. By then, Rodriguez had eclipsed Banks' single-season mark for a shortstop twice with home run totals of 52 and 57.

During this 1950s Cubs era, someone asked the often comedic and sarcastic manager Jimmie Dykes where the Cubs would finish if they didn't have Ernie Banks to count on. "In Albuquerque, that's where," he said.[3] He was probably right—somewhere in the Pacific Coast League standings—but lower than anywhere the National League measured.

Banks was not a scientific hitter. In the 2000s, he would probably be annoyed by analytics and the dissection of every pitcher's repertoire and tendencies on what he might be thrown in a given situation. Banks was an instinct hitter with good eyesight. If he saw a pitch he liked, he swung. It did not matter to him if the pitcher was left-handed or right-handed, specialized in a fastball or curve. The Banks philosophy was to swing at an incoming pitch if he could see it well and if he believed he could smack it. There will always be both types of hitters in this world, those who operate based on feel and those who operate by ingesting mountains of information that they process, digest, and evaluate.

"Just hit the ball, catch the ball, run to first," is how Banks once defined the elemental approach he brought to baseball. "It didn't matter to me who was pitching. I guess ignorance is bliss. I didn't want to know who was pitching. It was just somebody throwing a ball."[4] He also said, "I know pitchers threw curves, change-ups, all that kind of stuff. I didn't pay attention to it. All I wanted to do was hit the ball."[5]

Could it really have been as simple as that for Banks in the batter's box? Maybe it was. Maybe he told a white lie and he was holding tight to trade secrets. There was no disputing what Banks did and how he thought his method worked for him. At least when Banks was playing, it seemed, most managers and coaches were content to let a hitter be if the results were there. More than anything else, observers seemed to admire the way Banks powdered the ball while appearing to be just an average-sized guy, rather than a behemoth.

There were probably a few reasons why Babe Ruth acquired the nickname "The Bambino," but one was because he looked like a large guy. Banks was lithe and athletic, but he could swat with the best of them. His secret weapon, much like Hank Aaron, a contemporary and another big bopper, was all in the wrists. There was actually foreshadowing to Banks' big 1958 season. Although many dismiss what happens in spring training as inconsequential, Banks was hitting so well, indiscriminately off the best pitchers with the best stuff, to any field, that it was noticed.

The one Banks recalled blasting was a Warren Spahn screwball to left field. Spahn came up to him after the game, marveling at the stroke. "What are you doing?" Spahn asked. "To hit a pitch like that to left field?" Banks shrugged and did not offer an explanation. "I just had quick hands. My hands were just quick, naturally quick, from picking cotton."[6]

Such an explanatory phrase would not be used by Banks or anyone else 60 years later, less an Internet riot occur referring to it as unnecessary racial commentary. Some may have considered Banks' 1958 season a once-in-a-lifetime occurrence with such stellar numbers leading to the Most Valuable Player win for a player on a losing team. But in 1959, Banks did it all over again.

"His swing was so smooth, almost effortless, that you didn't notice the last movement of his wrists just before he hit the ball, how quick it was," said Jim Brosnan, a pitching teammate from the time period. "Ernie's swing was both a long swing and a very compact swing, all in the same swing. 'Cause it was a looping swing, and then bang. The ball would fly off his bat."[7]

Banks agreed that he didn't look much like a home run hitter and didn't figure he would be one at first. "During the early stages of my career I didn't regard myself as a home-run hitter," he said. "Nor was I alone in my thinking."[8]

Richie Ashburn, the Phillies' star outfielder, said he thought Banks would be a "Punch and Judy" hitter, a phrase commonly used for a singles hitter placing the ball elsewhere on the field besides over the fence. Banks said several top hitters, including Ralph Kiner, Monte Irvin, Jackie Robinson and Hank Thompson, recommended that he employ a smaller and lighter bat. Irvin loaned Banks some bats. Banks had used bats weighing between 34 and 36 ounces, but when he switched to a 31-ounce bat it helped keep his swing level and allowed him to whip the wood around more fiercely. That changed the whole picture for Banks.

When the 1958 National League Most Valuable Player voting was tabulated, Banks led the field by a comfortable margin. Willie Mays of the Giants was second and Hank Aaron was third. The points differential was 283–185–166. Although Mays batted .347 and Aaron .326, Banks had far more home runs and runs batted in.

The season was over when the honor was announced, and Banks was just getting ready to go to a public appearance at a Boys Club football banquet when his phone rang with a call from someone he did not know. It was Hy Hurwitz, the secretary of the Baseball Writers' Association of America. "We just finished counting a stack of ballots and I have some good news for you," Hurwitz said. "You have just been elected the National League's Most Valuable Player." Congratulations followed. Banks was nearly at a loss for words, replying simply and straightforwardly, "Thank you very much. That is certainly good news."[9]

Although he made the comment much later when referring to Alex Rodriguez, the same observation applied to Banks himself when he was the

Ernie standing with contemporary superstar Henry Aaron of the Braves, the first to break Babe Ruth's career home run record (National Baseball Hall of Fame).

recipient of MVP Awards with losing teams: "It's the playing that really counts. It's the performance that really counts. It's the commitment to the game, playing the position, the love for the game. That's what it's all about."[10]

Banks did not set a home run record for shortstops in 1959. But he did slam 45 more shots while leading the National League with 143 runs batted in. He added a .304 average. The 143 RBIs was extraordinary for a team that did not win much. And, as usual, the Cubs did not excel in that category. They finished 74–80 (within shouting distance of .500, at least) but no better than fifth in the standings once more. Although Mickey Mantle had just become the fourth man to do so in the American League, Banks was the first

National League player to capture the MVP Award two years in a row. The voting that year ran Banks-Eddie Mathews-Aaron-Wally Moon.

One element of Banks' game that differed from other years was his marked improvement in the field. He no longer made many errors, and he did not brood over the ones he committed, perhaps because they were so much rarer. He set a Major League record for fewest errors by a shortstop with 12 (down from 32) and for fielding percentage at .985.

There was one fielding play involving Banks in 1959 that boggled fans. It was a Cardinals-Cubs game at Wrigley Field, Bob Anderson on the mound for Chicago and Stan Musial at the plate for St. Louis. The count was 3–1 when Anderson uncorked a wild toss nowhere close to the batter and headed for the backstop. Cubs catcher Sammy Taylor did not react because he thought the pitch hit Musial's bat and was a foul ball. The bat boy ran onto the field and picked up the ball, handing it to field announcer Pat Pieper. Musial knew it was ball four, so he trotted to first base. Also realizing the ball was not foul but in action, he kept running to second base. Third baseman Alvin Dark realized what was happening and retrieved the original ball from Pieper. At the same time, Taylor was arguing with umpire Vic Delmore over the walk ruling, and in the midst of this heated conservation, Delmore gave a fresh baseball to Anderson.

So now both Anderson and Dark had baseballs in their hands as they watched Musial run to second base. Anderson threw to second baseman Tony Taylor, but his heave flew into center field. Musial watched that development and figured he had an easy steal of third base. But Dark threw his baseball to Banks, who tagged Musial. After the umpires huddled for discussion, Musial was awarded the walk, bringing him to first base, yet was called out trying to steal second. The Cardinals announced that they intended to protest, but after they won the game, that idea became moot.

This was not emblematic of the type of fielding plays Banks shone with that season, but his sparkling glove work, combined with his high level of slugging, enhanced his MVP candidacy. As Cubs administrators John Holland and Charlie Grimm said, Banks was the only genuine candidate for the trophy. "Nobody ever deserved the honor any more than Banks," said Holland, the team president.[11]

One guy who very much appreciated Banks' performance on the field was manager Bob Scheffing. Scheffing could have used a few more Ernie Banks–like players (who couldn't have?).

During my first 26 years in baseball, Joe DiMaggio is the only player I'd ever consider rating ahead of Ernie Banks after the year Ernie had for me in 1959. He batted fourth behind three hitters who didn't come even close to averaging .260 and still he batted in 143 runs. He also hit 45 homers, and I figured out that his bat was directly responsible for 27 of our 74 victories that season. Afield he was the equal of any shortstop I've ever seen.[12]

Scheffing may have loved watching Banks every minute of the season and admired what he did on the field, but it did not help him that much. Scheffing was fired and replaced by Charlie Grimm for 1960. This was the third time Grimm, the organization's all-time utility man, was summoned to the dugout since 1932. Not that he lasted long this time, with Lou Boudreau, who had led the Cleveland Indians to a World Series crown in 1948 as a player-manager, trading off from the broadcast booth for most of the season.

Banks became famous for his phrase, "Let's play two." He apparently never said, "Let's win two" about his Most Valuable Player Awards, but it was a remarkable achievement, magnified by his playing on losing teams in both 1958 and 1959.

Banks stood out so much on offense for the Cubs, compared to his numbers, his teammates' stats were blurs in the distance. Banks' 143 RBIs was 91 ahead of the second-highest contribution of 52 from Bobby Thomson. Dale Long and Walt Moyrn were next in line behind his 45 with 14 homers apiece. Banks batted .304. Second baseman Tony Taylor's .280 was the next highest on the team.

10

Ron Santo
A Sidekick

The ever-hopeful Cubs were almost always disappointed, especially in the 1950s. Ernie Banks was the gem in the lineup, but he was so much better than anyone else he glittered ever more brightly. The batting order needed more pop, more steady hitting. It was almost miraculous that Banks was able to win two straight Most Valuable Player Awards in 1958 and 1959 with such weak teams.

A new face who arrived part-time in the lineup in 1960, and who made nearly as strong a mark in Chicago as Banks, provided much-needed assistance. As beloved as Banks was by Cubs fans, Ron Santo was not far behind. He too would become a Cubs legend, first on the field and later off it as a broadcaster.

Santo was born in Seattle in 1940 when that was considered a distant outpost in the baseball world, long before first the Seattle Pilots showed up in the majors for a single, lonely 1969 season, and then the Seattle Mariners came along as a replacement. Seattle did have a team in the Pacific Coast League for decades, however, starting in 1903. At different times the club was called the Angels and Indians, but was best-known as the Rainiers.

While situated out of the mainstream, the scouts found Santo. He was such a hot prospect that many teams wanted him. Through the magic of television, though, Santo fell in love with the Cubs and Wrigley Field, and that's where he wanted to play. He also became an Ernie Banks fan before ever meeting him.

Santo was six feet tall and weighed 190 pounds. He was an extremely adept fielder and a power hitter who could complement Banks in the heart of the order. Santo stood out as a marvelous prospect as a high school player competing in local leagues around Seattle. In a 2006 interview reviewing his early life, he explained the challenges of his upbringing after his parents split up when he was six. For a while, his mother supported him and his sister by working two jobs. Things got better when she remarried, but Santo's family was far from wealthy. He said every team in the American League and National League contacted him expressing interest, and in 1959 the Cleveland Indians offered him $50,000 to sign. The New York Yankees and the Cincinnati Reds offered contracts calling for even more money, about $75,000.

Yet something did not feel right. Santo said his reaction to the big-money discussions left his mouth dry while he outwardly played it cool. However, Santo's fondness for the Cubs, something he could not really explain well, ruled his decision-making. The images formed in his head through television were powerful ones. It was not a sufficient rationale to make a life-changing decision in this matter, but when the Cubs came up with an offer of $20,000—same currency—it felt better.

> For some reason I always loved the National League. I have no reason why, other than maybe I was just able to watch the National League more. And when I saw the Cubs and I saw Wrigley Field, right there and then it was something special. I don't know why, but there was something I loved about that ballpark. And that was just through television. And Ernie Banks was special to me, just the way he conducted himself.[1]

Santo was only 20 years old when the Cubs brought him to the majors during the 1960 season. He appeared in 95 games, came to the plate 382 times, and showed enough stuff to convince the organization he was a keeper. In his limited season, Santo hit nine home runs and drove in 44 runs while batting .251.

After the Cubs sent him to the minors following spring training, Santo was recalled and was inserted into the lineup on June 26 for a game against the Pittsburgh Pirates at Forbes Field. It was a contest Santo later described as his favorite game of the 2,243 he played in the majors over a 15-year career. He got the word he was going to start for the first time and left the clubhouse to sit down in the visitors' dugout.

Banks, recognizing that the rookie might need a pep talk, joined him on the bench and offered a little boost. "Are you nervous, kid?" Banks asked. "Oh yeah, Ernie," Santo replied. "Well, look at those guys as if they're AAA pitchers," Banks added.[2]

Santo appreciated the reassurance at the time, but laughed later when he recalled that the Pirates pitchers he was watching were Vernon Law and Bob Friend. The Pirates won the National League pennant that year and defeated the Yankees in one of the greatest World Series of all time. Law was the NL Cy Young Award winner with a 20–9 mark, and Friend won 18 games. "That's easy for you to say," Santo told Banks.[3]

The two aces were warming up because it was a doubleheader. The last time anyone had mistaken Law and Friend for AAA pitchers was about a decade earlier. Whether the words were soothing or not, Santo went out and

10. Ron Santo

played like a Major League All-Star, not a minor-league swinger. The Cubs won both games, and Santo showed he belonged at this level of play. Santo went 2-for-4 with three runs batted in against Friend in the opener. He went 1-for-3 with a run scored and two RBI off Law. Friend and Law took losses that day.

Santo was almost too anxious to hit in batting practice and was so thoroughly fooled by one Friend pitch that Pirates veteran catcher Smoky Burgess said, "That's a major-league curveball, kid." But overall, Santo's debut was memorably successful, or as he put it, "It was a good way to start."[4]

Santo became a nine-time All-Star who hit 342 homers lifetime, knocked in 1,331 runs, batted .277 and won five Gold Gloves at third base.

One of the remarkable things about Santo's career was his behind-the-scenes secret. He was an 18-year-old when diagnosed with Type 1 juvenile diabetes. Less was known about the chronic illness at the time, about how to control and treat it. Santo feared that if it became known he suffered from diabetes, no major-league team would take a chance on him. He knew he could play, but he was sure others would lose faith in his ability if they knew about this problem.

For years, Santo maintained his secret, even when sharing a room with another Cubs player on the road in hotels and he had to inject insulin to remain healthy. Once, roommate Glenn Beckert caught Santo shooting up and mistakenly believed he was using some illegal boosting substance to help his game. Santo made him promise to remain silent about his illness.

Much later, in 1971, in connection with a Cubs "Ron Santo Day," in one of the most valuable services Santo performed in his life, he revealed his own struggle with the disease. He lent his name to the Ron Santo Walk To Cure Diabetes, and the Chicago event raised $65 million for research. Banks was as surprised as the rest of Santo's teammates and the public when Santo told the world about coping with diabetes most of his life. Long after his playing days and well into his long broadcasting career, Santo had numerous visible health battles wearing on his body. He underwent amputations of the lower half of both of his legs and battled cancer. When he asked Banks to write a foreword for a volume on Cubs players which Santo co-wrote, Banks seemed prepared to hand over his personal crown as "Mr. Cub," that title long before bestowed upon him by Jim Enright.

Enright, who knew Banks from the moment he signed with the Cubs in 1953 and covered his career for local sports pages for years, was the creative source for calling Banks "Mr. Cub." Once anointed, the nickname stuck and stayed forever. Banks is Mr. Cub. Period. While always expressing his gratitude for the appellation, at times it sounded as if Banks was prepared to at least share it with Santo. It is generally conceded that if Banks did not already have possession of the Mr. Cub name, it would probably have been affixed to Santo.

Banks noted "there should be a different Mr. Cub every year," but nominated Santo as another long-term Mr. Cub. "Ronnie had, and still has, all the qualities you look for in someone you would want to carry the name 'Mr. Cub,'" Banks wrote. "As a player, he was a great competitor, a hard worker, and a leader. He had intensity. He was determined and ambitious. He wanted to win more than anybody I've ever known. He had spirit and he still does."[5]

When he learned that a friend of his was diagnosed with diabetes, Banks told Santo and Santo insisted on calling the person to cheer him up. After learning of Santo's clandestine illness, Banks was astounded how much Santo was able to accomplish. "Ronnie has handled his own ailment like the true champion he is," Banks said. "He's a very positive person, the most courageous person I've ever been around. I'm inspired by him and by his spirit. Ron Santo is one of my idols, one of my heroes. He's almost like an alien. He's so special it's as if he's not real."[6]

Those words were clearly heartfelt and while written unconsciously or not, most of the same words ironically could have been penned about Banks by the millions of baseball people who thought of him as a great player and a great person, who was always identified as being in a fine mood, and who was very much a public role model for many.

The always smiling Ernie Banks, whose famous saying was "Let's play two!" He autographed this photograph with the word "Hope" (National Baseball Hall of Fame).

Santo may have offered promise for the future when he moved onto the roster in 1960, but that was hardly one of the Cubs' better years. The team finished 60–94, seventh in the league. Banks slugged 41 home runs, drove in 117 runs and batted .271. The 41 home runs was tops in the NL, Banks' second time as a league leader in that category.

Richie Ashburn, the former Phillies star and a future Hall of Famer now with the Cubs, was nearing the end of his career, but batted .291. The "other" Frank Thomas, a good power hitter in the 1950s and 1960s who was not to be confused with the later Frank Thomas of the Chicago White Sox, hit 21 homers for the Cubs that year.

George Altman, who had one of the most interesting of baseball careers, playing in the Negro Leagues and Japan as well as in the majors, saw action for the Cubs in 119 games and hit 13 homers with 51 runs batted in. Buck O'Neil had also been his mentor with the Kansas City Monarchs. Taken as a whole, that group, including Banks, Santo, Thomas, Ashburn and Altman, could hit. Pitching was not a strong point. Glen Hobbie finished 16–20 but had little mound aid.

Altman and Banks became good friends while teammates and often dined at one another's homes. Altman also enjoyed being a member of the Cubs because the fans were so enthusiastic. "It was good to be a Chicago Cub when I played," Altman said. "And that was because of Chicago Cubs fans. The Cubs were not very good on the field, but they had a loyal following, really strong, keen fans. It's not like it is now where everywhere you go fans would recognize you if you were walking down the street."[7]

Altman always felt the Cubs were working hard to improve, but could just not acquire enough top players to move up in the standings. The hitters came through more frequently than the pitchers. "No matter what we did, or no matter what P. K. Wrigley did, the Cubs always seemed to end up near the bottom of the league."[8]

The Cubs made a flurry of trades over the winter and right up until the start of the season in 1960, moving players like chess pieces, but not necessarily improving with the shifts. Ashburn was already 33. Other outgoing players included pitchers John Buzhardt and Ron Perranoski and infielder Alvin Dark. Don Zimmer, the former Dodger and later a long-time coach and manager, joined the club as a 29-year-old. He had been a third baseman, though soon enough Santo locked up that job.

Banks, who once again carried the offense on his shoulders, hit a grand slam on April 14. A couple of weeks later he knocked in all six runs with two three-run homers, yet the Cubs lost to the Cardinals. The Cubs were 6–11 under Charlie Grimm when Wrigley had him and announcer Lou Boudreau trade jobs, with Grimm going to the broadcast booth. Boudreau's guidance didn't help. These were not the 1948 Indians.

One trade that seemed to work out pretty well was for pitcher Don Cardwell. In his first Chicago start in the second game of a doubleheader on May 15, Cardwell pitched a no-hitter to beat the Cardinals, 4–0. Cardwell walked a batter in the first inning and then retired 26 in a row. The game took just 1 hour, 46 minutes to complete. Banks drove in two of the four runs. Cardwell finished 8–14 that season, and the no-hitter was the high point of his Cubs career.

Upon reading Banks' foreword for the Santo book, there is little doubt that Banks and Santo had a mutual admiration society. While Banks was touting his friend as an alternative Mr. Cub, Santo was writing that Banks was indisputably that guy. "He's Mr. Cub and deservedly so," Santo said, "the most popular player in the team's 100-plus-year history. Nobody else is even close. He's No. 1. There is no No. 2." Besides Banks' daunting career statistics, Santo seized on his personality as the other reason Banks was referred to as Mr. Cub. "He's Mr. Cub for his warmth, his loyalty, his sunny disposition, and his perpetual smile. He's Mr. Cub because he is a one-man advertisement for Wrigley Field, day baseball, and the city of Chicago. And because he makes you feel good just being around him."[9]

That was the consensus on Banks from just about his first minute in the majors. He lit up a room and he never got discouraged. He was a pleasure to be around, and he wanted to win as much as anyone else, but did not show the pain of losing with the kind of facial expressions, tantrums or grumpiness others might. When he spoke about Banks' demeanor, Santo had known Banks for 45 years and said he was the same way in private as he was in public, the same in disappointment as he was when things went his way.

> I have never heard him say a bad word about anybody [or anything], and I have never heard anybody say a bad word about him. People who meet him for the first time, who hear him expound for the first time on the beauty of baseball, the Cubs, Wrigley Field, and life in general, think it's all an act, a façade. They keep waiting for him to drop his guard, but he never does.

Santo said that in four and a half decades he had never seen Banks "be anything but upbeat, positive and optimistic. I'm still waiting."[10]

Maybe some pitchers cursed when they heard Banks' name mentioned, since he had taken them yard or beat them with doubles or some other muscle-flexing. On July 9, 1960, Banks gave the Cubs a 7–6 victory over the San Francisco Giants in 12 innings. The blow was Banks' 231st home run with the team, the new club record. Hall of Fame catcher Gabby Hartnett was the previous record-holder. Banks held the team mark for 44 years before being surpassed by Sammy Sosa in 2004.

As usual, Banks was selected to represent the Cubs on the National League side in the All-Star Game. The game was played in Kansas City's Municipal Stadium, an American League ballpark. Banks smacked a home run and a double to lift the NL to a 5–3 win. Later in the season, on August 17, Banks provided a walk-off homer to beat the Dodgers and Don Drysdale, 1–0, at Wrigley Field. Highlights always seemed to break out around Banks, even if his heroics did not always carry the day for the Cubs as a team.

Although the Cubs' scouts could not find pitchers of commensurate talent, at the very end of the season a new face appeared in the lineup. After a cameo in 1959 and another short stint in 1960, from then on Billy Williams of Whistler, Alabama, was in Chicago for good. With the addition of Williams, the Cubs had three everyday players who were bound for the Hall of Fame. During the 1960 season, Banks made a startling announcement. He planned to enroll in college in the off-season. He had devoted his formative years to baseball, moving up the ladder and becoming a star. But he knew he still would be a young man when he retired from the game. What then? He wondered.

Yet even as he tossed out this fresh idea about taking control of his future, Banks uttered the same type of comments he always did about being blessed as a baseball player and a very lucky man to get to do what he did. "This whole thing is so great," he said of his stature in Chicago, "it scares me sometimes. When you're a baseball player, people are kind to you. They recognize you. They call your name. They ask for your autograph. They ask you out. Youngsters admire you. They think the world of a ballplayer."[11]

A sportswriter asked Banks if he believed people wouldn't like him if he wasn't a baseball player. "I wouldn't be here," he said, "here" at the time being spring training in Mesa, Arizona. "I wouldn't be where I am, but you don't have to necessarily be a ballplayer. Being one makes it easier, but being a person who likes people and is liked by them is what makes it the important thing."[12]

Whether or not some of that was the sound of a little bit of insecurity as motivation for Banks' perpetual nice-guy image wasn't really clear. Just as much, he made it sound as if he would have been a nice guy wherever he landed in life. It was just that if he wasn't in the public eye, not nearly as many people would have known it.

11

Coach O'Neil and a Whole Bunch of Other Coaches

As Ernie Banks' manager with the Kansas City Monarchs, Buck O'Neil was in a position to deliver his star to the Chicago Cubs when he was ready to make his switch to the majors. O'Neil was the middle man. Those were the waning days of the Negro Leagues, and soon enough O'Neil would be looking for a job.

By 1955, O'Neil was a scout for the Cubs. He stuck it out with Kansas City until the team was sold. By that point, he had a standing offer from Cubs front office maven Wid Matthews to come aboard as a scout, and Matthews made good.

"It was my job to scour the country for the untapped talent in the predominantly black high schools and colleges," O'Neil said.[1]

> Here is what a scout lives for: I'm driving in my Plymouth Fury down a dirt road outside of Montgomery, Alabama. The road is so narrow that I'm thinking I must have taken the wrong fork a few miles back. Then, suddenly, I hear the crack of the bat and the noise of the crowd. Or is that my car back-firing and my engine whining? No, it's a ball game, sure enough, because when I round the turn, there's a diamond cut out of the woods.[2]

O'Neil had spotted a ballplayer he thought had potential and asked his manager when and where his next game was. This was the follow-up and what led O'Neil to sign outfielder Oscar Gamble, he of the massive Afro hairdo and a .265 average in 17 Major League seasons.

O'Neil understood that the Cubs hired him as much for his skin color as his baseball acumen so he could link the team up with African American players who otherwise might be overlooked. He knew the Cubs were just being smart in choosing him instead of bringing aboard another white coach who might not be comfortable or welcome entering neighborhoods or school areas that were almost all black. O'Neil said Gamble was the best prospect he had seen since steering Banks to the Cubs.

11. Coach O'Neil and a Whole Bunch of Other Coaches

Often, players are local heroes, guys who could hit better or throw faster than anyone else in town or the region. Some don't realize they are big fish in a small pond and their talents won't translate. It takes the knowledgeable scout to sort out the pretenders from the contenders. That is a gift, and O'Neil had it.

> If scouting were just a matter of signing the guys who hit the home runs and pitch the no-hitters, anybody could do it. But the major-league prospect just might be the guy who has something special, even though he struck out swinging, or overthrew the third baseman from right field, or walked nine batters. Tools we call them: Speed, arm strength, range, hands, bat speed. Sometimes you can tell more about a player in one infield or batting practice than you can in nine innings. And give me the flame thrower with control problems over the off-speed pitcher with accuracy every time. You can teach certain aspects of the game. You can't just give a player ability.[3]

O'Neil blended in with the crowd at those mostly African American schools, going incognito compared to white scouts who happened upon the same prospect. He also got to know a kid's parents and said he showed up in church to schmooze with them a day after a game.

Perhaps O'Neil's greatest scouting coup was identifying Lou Brock as big-league material when he was playing for predominantly black Southern University in Louisiana and not quite hitting his weight. Brock became a Hall of Fame outfielder, though he blossomed only after the Cubs made the colossal error of trading him to the St. Louis Cardinals. That was a development called "a sad ending" because Brock's stardom played out with another team.[4]

In 1962, O'Neil became the first African American coach in the majors, putting him back in the same dugout as Banks and George Altman once again. This was a great distinction, though there was not nearly as much attention paid to it as came later when Frank Robinson became Major League baseball's first African American manager.

One reason for that may have been the cockamamie situation O'Neil found himself in the middle of as the Cubs tried out a never-before, never-again experiment with no full-time manager, instead with a rotating so-called "College of Coaches." This offbeat idea came from high in the front office. Perhaps Phil Wrigley's thinking was that he had tried everything and everybody, so why not shared responsibility?

The system was implemented in spring training of 1961 with a board of directors running the team. The original group included Elvin Tappe, Charlie Grimm, Dick Cole, Verlon Walker, Rip Collins, Fred Martin, Bobby Adams, Goldie Holt, Vedie Himsl, Lou Klein and Harry Craft. Coaches were scheduled to take turns as head coach for part of the season.

Wrigley introduced the system to journalists at a January 1961 luncheon. Wrigley, who was apparently reading a different dictionary from what others present knew, said the definition of a manager was a dictator. "Anyway, the job is just too much for one man," he said. "It's like the presidency. No one man can possibly do all the things required of a manager or the president of the United States." Wrigley was asked if this was the structure he had in place to run his chewing gum company, and he said, "I've always run the gum business this way. No man is indispensable. I've resigned twice myself. It's like hiring a man to run a bulldozer. If the man gets sick that doesn't mean the bulldozer has broken down. You simply have another driver step in."[5]

This was surely one of the more bizarre press conferences in the Cubs' long history. It was also announced that Ernie Banks had signed a new contract for $55,000, an estimated $5,000 raise. But after Wrigley's bombshell, not many paid attention to that.

Nothing occurred during the 1961 season to demonstrate that this was a good idea. At 64–90, the Cubs were as bad as usual, indeed in the same rut.

Still, Chicago stuck with this plan for the 1962 season, though some of the faces changed. O'Neil came in. While it was a milestone to become a coach, O'Neil never got a turn as manager and never coached on the field. He felt slighted when he was not permitted to coach third base and realized the team would never give him tasks that would take him beyond the dugout. O'Neil believed he would be part of the rotation, but when he was bypassed for coaching third in a game against the Houston Astros, that was a blow. "I would have been the natural choice and I could sense the buzzing up and down the bench," he said. "After 40 years in baseball and 10 years as a manager, I was pretty sure I knew when to wave somebody home and when to make him put on the brakes."[6]

The College of Coaches was a miserable failure, though the Cubs were slow to concede that. After two seasons, it was phased out. The plan did not get rave reviews. "It was Mr. Wrigley's idea so we had to live with it," recalled Don Elston, the Cubs' ace relief pitcher. "I can't remember much that was good about it. There was jealousy among the coaches. They didn't see eye to eye. When one guy was the head coach, some, but not all, of the other coaches did nothing to help him. They sat there waiting for their turn. It was an unhappy time."[7]

Tommy Lasorda, a Hall of Fame manager for the Los Angeles Dodgers, turned up his nose at the idea. "What are you going to do, have four chefs make the soup?" he said. "Every one of them would make it different."[8] For many of the players, what Lasorda described was exactly the problem. As each new coach took charge, he was likely to change the starting lineup. It drove the players nuts, and they did not achieve.

There were other strange doings surrounding the ball club, all ideas born in P. K. Wrigley's brain that he wanted to try. If the staff was going to be the College of Coaches, then it apparently made sense to hire an athletic director. This was probably the only time the job label was used in the history of Major League Baseball. Robert Whitlow, a retired colonel and former athletic director at the Air Force Academy, was brought in to oversee some workout programs. "We sure did do a lot of calisthenics," Banks said.[9]

Certainly, baseball has been slow to embrace change, but the programs instituted did not feel right to the players. Banks was in the trainer's room being attended to as he stretched his hamstring muscles. There are tried and true methods for stretching, but one day when lying on a training table, Banks began shouting, "Ow, Ow!" He thought he was being mistreated by the trainer, although it was a false alarm and he had merely suffered a cramp. But that did not build confidence in the trainer.[10]

Cubs scouts had been successful signing significant talent. In recent years, the team added Ron Santo, Billy Williams, Lou Brock and a budding star second baseman named Ken Hubbs. Hubbs had one of those late-season cameo appearances of ten games in 1961. In 1962, at 20 years old, he played in 160 games, batting .260. He dazzled in the field, winning a Gold Glove Award and the National League "Rookie of the Year" Award. The Cubs were definitely building a core of talent which, if pitching was added, could become a serious pennant contender.

Williams was emerging as a special player, but not before a scare when it seemed possible he would quit the sport. Playing in AA San Antonio in 1959, Williams was homesick for Alabama and despairing over the constant racial slights he felt. As a player, Williams earned a lifetime nickname paying homage to his hitting. He became known as "Sweet Swinging Billy Williams." That was on the field. Off the field, he was insulted because he was an African American. Pleased with the game, he was disturbed by his surroundings. So he jumped the team and headed home to Alabama. "I was not accustomed to being treated like an animal away from the baseball diamond," Williams said. "I couldn't take the bigotry, the discrimination and the overt racism."[11]

Williams talked his roommate into driving him to the train station and was planning to leave baseball for good. Manager Grady Hatton noticed Williams' absence, and when he found out, Hatton telephoned the Cubs' front office. Williams rode the train to Mobile feeling a weight had lifted, but also beset by uncertainty over his future. He was going to surprise his family (except for one brother in the know), yet wasn't sure how he was going to explain himself.

Although he was not the scout who signed Williams, Buck O'Neil knew about him, had met him and gotten to know his family. Team president John Holland dispatched O'Neil to Alabama on a rescue mission. O'Neil showed up but did not pressure Williams. Nor did he respond strongly when Williams said he was not going back to San Antonio. Instead, he chatted with him, drove around the community with him, and stopped at a local ball field where semi-pros were revving up. They flooded him with questions and compliments about being a pro. The atmosphere rekindled Williams' passion and made him think about the opportunities in the game stretching ahead. Williams went back to San Antonio for a few more weeks and then was promoted to AAA Denver before joining the Cubs. Score another one for Buck O'Neil's savvy in handling and understanding young men. Score another one for the Cubs for not letting a Hall of Famer get away by showing some sensitivity and by not overreacting.

When Williams joined the Cubs, Banks was his first roommate. He said Banks was a fountain of great information, clueing him in about pitchers around the league, but could otherwise drive him batty by uttering his numerous silly sayings. "Do you have change for three cents?" Banks sometimes spouted. Another time, Banks said, "The weather will be cold. The weather will be hot. There will be weather, whether or not."[12] Williams said just a few weeks of Banks' hotel-room company wore thin because of his constant chatter and offbeat commentary. He was a great player and a very nice man, but Williams thought he overdid it with this type of stuff. "Ernie has always made up those strange rhymes and slogans that we have all heard him recite over the years," Williams said.[13]

Banks' most famous ditties almost passed for poetry in predicting how the Cubs would fare in a given season, and the very first one was uttered for 1962. Banks teased the Cubs sportswriters in spring training with his well-read one-liners, explaining to the fans that the team was going to win it all that season, or at least the pennant.

"The Cubs are due in '62," Banks proclaimed about that season. It seemed to be almost a spontaneous contribution to the literature of baseball. Periodically Banks issued another hopeful remark that fans glommed on to and repeated during the season. The only disappointing aspect was that the optimistic Banks' quickie predictions never came true while he was playing. "The Cubs will come alive in '65" had a nice ring to it in 1965. Sometimes Banks knew he was stretching his words to make the thought fit. "The Cubs will be heavenly in '67-ly." Well.... "The Cubs will shine in '69." Almost, almost. "The Cubs will glow in '7-0." Not bad. After he retired, Banks gave it another whirl in 1988. "The Cubs will be illuminated in '88." Even Banks knew that line did not belong on his greatest hits list. "That's a little weak. I'll have to do better."[14]

Banks may have been correct in theory that the Cubs were due in 1962, but in the second year under the College of Coaches operation they were actually worse, finishing 59–103.

Since the National League expanded from eight teams to ten, adding the Houston Colt .45s (who became the Astros) and the New York Mets, the Cubs were able to finish even lower in the standings, in ninth place. The Mets launched their heyday of horribleness and managed to finish behind the Cubs.

Roommate issues aside, Williams became a close friend of Banks and sometimes saw a deeper version of the man up close than Banks ever let the public see. While Williams nearly let racism drive him away from the sport he loved, Banks absorbed such incidents quietly. He did not forget them, however, Williams said. The men commuted together back and forth to games at Wrigley and often talked about more serious issues than who was playing third base that day. "Ernie was raised in the south and endured at least as much racism as I did during the late 1940s and the early '50s," Williams said. "The racism bothered him, but I never heard him say anything publicly. There would be times we would have a conversation and he would talk about racist things that happened to him."15

When he wrote his memoir, Williams mentioned that Banks believed one former San Francisco Giants pitcher was racist because he always seemed to be throwing inside at him, more often than seemed warranted. Williams said the reason may well have been because Banks hit a lot of home runs off Sanford, and it could have amounted to retaliation. Most of the time, in public, in the dugout, in the clubhouse, during games, when Banks talked—and he did a lot of talking—he made his teammates chuckle.

When we come to the big leagues, we don't say much. But once he started, man, you couldn't shut him up. But he was a guy who was one of the most positive guys I've ever known. That was always real. A lot of people ask was he like this all the time and I don't hesitate to say he was. He was all chatter, all the time. I used to say, "I've got to get some rest." During our ride from the South Side to Wrigley Field that was great. I'd learn a lot about Ernie and of course the Negro Leagues. He gave me the history of all the players who played and what they did.16

On May 2, 1961, with San Antonio distantly in his rearview mirror, Williams had a

The always happy to oblige Banks signing an autograph on a baseball. (National Baseball Hall of Fame/Doug McWilliams.

game that truly announced his presence in the bigs. He smashed four hits, including a grand slam, in a 9–4 win over the Giants. On May 28, Banks hit a grand slam against the Giants, too, but the Cubs lost this game. Setting an odd record, Banks collected three sacrifice flies in one game as the Cubs edged Cincinnati, 7–6, on June 2.

Two weeks later, a Banks career note was catalogued, though no one knew how significant it would be. The Cubs were in San Francisco on June 16, when Banks played first base for the first time in his Major League career. As the rotating managers threw out new ideas, Banks had been situated in the outfield for 23 games before the first base shift. He played seven games at first base that season, but starting in 1962, Banks was a former shortstop, stationed at first the rest of his career.

By June 23, Banks had played in 717 consecutive games. But on this occasion in Milwaukee, Banks did not play. A knee injury flared up and he rested. In 1961, Banks hit 29 home runs, down from 41 the year before, and drove in 80 runs, far off his usual production. He still batted .278 and made the All-Star team, but this was the first time Banks had seen a dramatic drop-off in his stats while also appearing in just 138 games instead of his usual 150-something.

On September 10, both Ken Hubbs and Lou Brock made their Major League debuts in the same game, a 14–6 loss to the Philadelphia Phillies. Of the two, following early returns, more fans would have bet on Hubbs as a future Hall of Famer than on Brock. Early in the next season, Hubbs, who was a sterling fielder, bashed out five hits in a game against the Pittsburgh Pirates. He definitely made a good early impression on Wrigley fans.

May 29, 1962, Buck O'Neil's first day as coach, Banks clubbed three home runs and a double. As a shortstop, Banks had been more productive than most who ever played the position. As a first baseman, Banks was now a regular at a position where power was expected. He obliged with 37 home runs and 104 runs batted in.

Although there were mixed feelings inside the organization about Brock's potential, he gave hints of what he was capable of at his best. During a June 24 doubleheader against the Pirates, Brock reached base nine times in one day, with five hits and four walks. As a team, though, the Cubs were sunk long before the schedule ran out. When the Cubs lost to the Phillies on September 26, there were only 930 paid fans in the park. Two days later, attendance was even worse, with just 595 people present for a 3–2 Cubs victory over the Mets, the only team in baseball that year who won fewer games than the Cubs.

On September 30, the last day of the season, the Cubs bested the Mets, 5–1. It was New York's 120th loss of the season, a modern record that still stands. Chicago committed a triple play in the eighth inning on a ball hit by catcher Joe Pignatano. He popped it towards right field. Hubbs chased it down, caught the ball with his back to the infield, threw the ball to Banks at first, catching a runner off base, and saw Banks fire to second base to catch the runner off second. In its own way, that may have been the most fun Banks and the Cubs had all season.

12

Downs and Ups

After nearly a decade with the Cubs, Ernie Banks was about as well-known as anyone in Chicago except for the mayor. And all of a sudden, as 1962 turned to 1963, Banks was about to test that theory. He announced that he was going to run for alderman to represent Chicago's South Side.

Banks said an official of the Republican Party approached him to determine his interest in running for office, and after giving it some thought he decided he wanted to do so. He checked with Cubs owner Philip Wrigley and got his OK. It was just two months to the primary when Banks' intention became public. A Democrat was the incumbent in a Democratic city on the Board of Aldermen, which is Chicago's city council.

This was Banks' home year-round. He was married with three young children, while also taking courses of a sociological nature at the University of Chicago. Banks had no plans to retire from baseball if he won the position, so it would be intriguing to see how that all played out. Banks said this was the advantage of playing all day games at Wrigley Field during that era before lights were installed.

Banks said he was motivated by a desire to help disadvantaged and troubled youth in the community. "There has been some trouble in our community," he said. "It's the kind that happens in any community. But I just think many people don't pay much attention to teenagers. I just love boys. I don't know what I could do if I couldn't lend advice to boys."[1] He had twin young boys of his own at that time.

This was an early indication to many people of Banks' social consciousness, that things besides being able to tell the difference between a curveball and fastball were important to him. Decades later, Banks would reveal that he wanted to win the Nobel Prize for peace for doing something worthwhile for humanity.

Banks was a resident of the ward, but was on vacation in California when he was recruited to try out the electoral process by a member of former U.S. Senator Everett Dirksen's staff. Intrigued by the opportunity, Banks pursued it, but there were other factions at work in the district who preferred other candidates, and the incumbent was not ready for retirement.

The baseball-player-turned-politician did campaign on the needs of youths in the district, but had to overcome the disadvantage of being a professional in another profession while coping with professionals in this profession. He did employ a neat campaign motto of "Put A Slugger In City Hall,"[2] but only a minority of voters in the ward liked it enough to vote for him. Banks finished third in a four-candidate race and then went off to spring training to prepare to try to bring a pennant to the Cubs. Some might say both of his goals were quixotic. "Politics is a strange business," Banks said. "They can strike you out before you get a turn at-bat."[3]

Around that time, Banks was having enough difficulty with his primary job. He had some injury problems in 1961, bounced back strongly in 1962 to hit like his own self, but in 1963 endured the first long-term slump of his career. Banks had a terrible year at the same time there were other positive Cubs developments. The team phased out the College of Coaches and in 1963 recorded a winning record. While the Cubs finished 82–80, the first year above .500 since 1946, for the first time in Banks' career, he batted a miserable .227 with just 18 home runs and 64 runs batted in. After eight straight years of being selected to the National League All-Star team, Banks missed out. At 32 years of age, some wondered if he hadn't begun the downslide of his career on the diamond.

In 1961, Banks struggled at the plate compared to his first years in the bigs and concluded that he was having eye troubles. Those problems were treated successfully, and he returned to his normal hitting form.

This time everything coincided with Banks becoming a full-time first baseman and ended the first half of his career as a shortstop. Whether Banks actually initially embraced the move as permanent or not, not long after testing himself on that part of the field, he began telling everyone he liked his new glove job.

"Fine, fine," Banks said when quizzed about occupying his new real estate.

> I still have things to learn at first base, but I know it's not nearly as strenuous a position to play as shortstop. It could be that I'll be able to carry on there for two or three more years than I could if I stayed at shortstop. There are a lot more balls hit through the shortstop area. You're on the move all the time. There is just no comparison between the positions insofar as the work involved is concerned. You burn up a lot more energy playing shortstop.[4]

Banks did take a hard grounder off his shin and showed up in the field wearing protective gear for a while. But he boasted that he now had a bigger glove to grab those shots than when he was playing shortstop. Sometimes Banks joked with sportswriters about his adjustment to the different position.

"This presents many problems," he said once. "Not the least of them is what to do with my feet. Sometimes I seem to have too many and sometimes not enough." Banks gave an example of how in one game against the Giants when he was taking a throw from the shortstop and keeping his eye on the ball. He stepped back to touch the first-base bag—and he couldn't locate it. "It was embarrassing. I never did find it until I was standing smack on top of it. This violated a fundamental rule. Any first baseman who wants to keep healthy only uses a corner of the bag and leaves the rest of it to the base runner. And here I was hogging it." He gave a few other examples of his learning curve and said, "All clubs should take out more insurance on first basemen, especially those like me."[5]

Whether it was a routine question about how Banks liked his new spot or someone fishing for an expression of discontent, it was no surprise that Banks replied in the affirmative that everything was A-OK with his new role. The only problem was, in 1963, after years of hitting like a first baseman while playing short, he was now hitting like a shortstop while playing first.

On May 1, Banks did produce a fabulous day at the plate, hitting two home runs and notching a single for seven runs batted in, but that was a rare day for him that season. By June, team officials were openly worrying about what had happened to their star. Veteran baseball writer Jerome Holtzman, who years later would become Major League Baseball's official historian, said there were definitely matters for concern. "There have been nonetheless some rather unmistakable signs that Banks, at 32, may be reaching the twilight of his outstanding career. This is said with regret, of course."[6]

In this season, Banks would play in just 130 games, absences mostly chalked up to minor injuries, though he experienced more than one of those, including a knee bruise and a heel bruise. It would have been uncharacteristic of the ever-optimistic Banks to give up on himself, and he did not do so, assuming he would break out with a passel of hits any day. At the time of Holtzman's story, Banks was batting .205. "I can see the ball OK," Banks said, immediately putting the kibosh on the notion that his vision woes had returned. He said it was all about his timing being off.[7]

Right around that time, in a June 9 game against the Dodgers, Banks smacked three home runs, taking future Hall of Famer Sandy Koufax yard twice. Yet somehow the Cubs lost, 11–8.

Ironically, although he was having a very inconsistent hitting season, Banks had reached the point in his career where he was establishing milestones and moving up all-time National League hitting lists. In late June he knocked in his 1,000th Major League run. In early July, he collected his 3,000th total base, and in late July, when he clubbed his 352nd career home run, he surpassed Ralph Kiner for seventh place on the NL list.

For once, Banks was not the Cubs' statistical leader on the field. The

12. Downs and Ups

team could have used Banks' power. The Cubs batted just .238 as a group, but Ron Santo and Billy Williams each belted 25 home runs. Lou Brock showed flashes in the outfield. New shortstop Andre Rogers was good-field, no-hit. Newcomer Ellis Burton hit 12 homers with 41 RBI in 93 games. Ken Hubbs was still around, but hit just .235. The bench was very weak.

However, there were sparks of life on the pitching staff. Southpaw Dick Ellsworth blossomed in his fourth season, going 22–10 with a 2.11 earned run average. He was clearly the staff ace that season. Larry Jackson won 14 games with a 2.55 ERA (although he lost 18 because of poor run support), Lindy McDaniel won 13, and Bob Buhl, over from the Braves, won 11.

The pitching was more of an asset than it had been in a long time, and although the hitters were distributed through the lineup, Banks' bat was missing in action more often than not. Could this really be the end of Ernie Banks the star at such a young age? Nobody had a good explanation for so many swings and misses.

"In 1963, I thought my career was over," Banks said. He wondered if his balky knee was undoing him. He wondered if there were residual effects from being hit in the head by a pitch. Wrigley took charge and directed that Banks leave the team and undergo medical testing in Chicago. "He had personally arranged for the best medical talent available and ordered me to take some time out and relax."[8]

Some of the regularly acquired but curable diseases school-age children contract are measles, chicken pox and mumps. They all can produce high fevers and other specific symptoms. One symptom of the mumps virus is swollen glands. However, another variation of the illness does not produce swollen glands. A blood test administered to Banks late in the 1963 season indicated he was suffering from the mumps virus in his bloodstream without the swollen glands. This meant Banks was playing at sub-par health and had been weakened by the illness. The diagnosis provided a logical reason for Banks' poor performance on the field.

It also offered relief not only to Banks, but to those in the Cubs front office. Yes, their star had just battled through a depressing season, but at least there was a specific reason and reason to believe he could bounce back for a fresh start in 1964. So many other young players on the team seemed likely to keep on improving and hey, the team just topped .500! Things were looking up for 1964, even if the nation as a whole had just endured one of the most wrenchingly traumatic experiences in its history with the assassination of President John F. Kennedy on November 22, 1963.

This was not a baseball tragedy, not a Chicago Cubs tragedy, but a national one, affecting all Americans. The event did not take place during the baseball season, either, but did occur during the National Football League's regular season. The assassination took place on a Friday, and NFL

Commissioner Pete Rozelle ruled that teams would play that Sunday. Later, in retirement, Rozelle said he considered that to be the worst decision he made in his position of leadership. When the September 11, 2001, terrorist attacks occurred during the Major League Baseball season, all play was suspended for a week.

Cubs players were scattered at the time of Kennedy's death. Yet just as they were regrouping for spring training of 1964, the team experienced its own shocking tragedy. Young Ken Hubbs was killed in a plane crash on February 13 while piloting the plane in Utah, at age 22, not long after obtaining a pilot's license. The Cubs went into mourning well before their season began.

Not long before his death, Hubbs showed his new pilot's license to teammate Ron Santo, who wondered where Hubbs had been going evenings. Hubbs had been quiet about his lessons, but was now proud of his accomplishment. This astonished Santo because the Hubbs he knew was scared of flying. "I couldn't believe it," Santo said.[9]

Santo, who had become particularly close to the young player after rooming together, visited Hubbs during the off-season and said Hubbs was like a little kid with a new toy, wanting to show it off and insisting he take to the skies with him for a ride. Santo did so, had a great time, and said Hubbs was "Charles Lindbergh" for an hour. Santo asked Hubbs what he liked about flying and he said, "Ron, it's so great, it's like being closer to God every time I take the plane up. It's wonderful."[10]

The day after his ride, Santo departed for Seattle and Hubbs was heading to Salt Lake City. Less than 24 hours after Santo flew with Hubbs, the young player's plane was reported missing. Hubbs had picked up a long-time friend, but after a brief report to the control tower about stalling, the plane disappeared. The bodies of Hubbs and his friend were not found for two days. "I cannot relay in words the sense of loss felt by his family, his friends, the Cubs' organization and the baseball world," Santo said.[11]

It was an abrupt end before a true beginning. Hubbs had been a great athlete, recruited to play football for Notre Dame and to play basketball for UCLA under John Wooden. He signed with the Cubs for a $50,000 bonus to play baseball instead. He figured to be a big part of the Cubs' future. Instead, in 1964, the Cubs' immediate future once again more resembled its immediate past. The entire team attended Hubbs' funeral, and Santo, Banks and Billy Williams served as pallbearers.

There were plenty of times when things happened around the Chicago Cubs baseball team that seemed to make little sense, but the death of Ken Hubbs and his precocious talent was perhaps the most inexplicable. This terrible event was beyond front office ken. The next blow to the Cubs' fortunes was of a different nature, but self-inflicted by erroneous judgment.

Lou Brock was discovered by Buck O'Neil as a college player at Southern

12. Downs and Ups

University. Brock was bursting with enthusiasm and raw talent. During his early days with the Cubs, his speed was evident, but his overall hitting and game play was average. He needed to work out kinks, stop pressing, gain confidence and comfort at the big-league level. In other words, management needed patience. Brock was 22 in 1961 when he appeared in four Cubs games. The next season he was a regular, in 123 games stealing 16 bases and batting .263. He stole 24 bases with a .258 average in 1963.

In 1964, 52 games into the season, with Brock batting .251 with 10 stolen bases, the Cubs gave up on him. Officials must have thought he had reached a plateau and at age 25 would never get any better. Viewing him as expendable, Chicago traded Brock to the St. Louis Cardinals. The deal sent Brock, Paul Toth and Jack Spring to the Cardinals. The Cubs obtained pitcher Ernie Broglio, the centerpiece for them, one-time star hurler Bobby Shantz, and Doug Clemens.

At that very moment, the average Cubs fan was not the least bit disturbed. Brock was living on the potential label. Right-hander Broglio led the National League with 21 wins in 1960 and only the year before went 18–8 for the Cards. Only past was not prologue. What no one realized was that Broglio, who went 4–7 for the Cubs in 1964 and won just three more games before retiring in 1966, was virtually washed-up because of arm problems.

Brock was on the verge of exploding into one of the best players in baseball, a transformation that was almost instantaneous. Over the rest of the 1964 season, Brock batted .348 in 103 games, stole 33 more bases, and was one of the reasons the Cardinals won the pennant and the World Series. It was the true jump-start to his Hall of Fame career. When he retired, Brock's 938 stolen bases were the most ever, and nearly 40 years later he remains second on the all-time list behind Rickey Henderson.

The trade of Brock for Broglio is considered by most to be the Cubs' worst deal, and some call it the worst in Major League history. Combined with the death of Hubbs in 1964, the repercussions were immediate, and Chicago dropped back down below .500, finishing with a 76–86 record, 17 games behind St. Louis.

Naturally, Buck O'Neil opposed the trade. He was the one who identified Brock as worth signing, and he knew Brock could still make it big. He wanted that to occur with the Cubs. When he told general manager John Holland he was making a mistake by trading Brock, Holland showed O'Neil letters from Cubs season ticket holders suggesting that the Cubs, who had played five African Americans regularly the preceding season, were getting too black. Specifically, O'Neil recalled one letter that said, "What are you turning the Chicago Cubs into? The Kansas City Monarchs?"[12]

The Cubs, it should have been noted, had done pretty well with acquisitions connected to the Kansas City Monarchs, from O'Neil, Kansas City's old manager, as a scout and coach, to Ernie Banks and George Altman. That was not the point of the irksome letter, of course, but it is unlikely Holland heard from the same pen pal later when Broglio flamed out, Brock excelled, and the Cubs returned to being a losing team.

For Ernie Banks, the spring of 1964 was a new beginning after his awful 1963. During the off-season, after his health had rebounded, he invited his old mentor O'Neil to his home for dinner. The men ate and smoked cigars, and then Banks pulled out a projector showing his batting. He asked O'Neil what he was doing wrong and what he needed to do to fix his swing and get back in the groove in the new season.

O'Neil watched the ugly swings for a while and then asked Banks to "put on the 58–59 reels again."[13] Those were the seasons when Banks was chosen National League Most Valuable Player. Banks handed O'Neil a bat, and he began demonstrating what his pupil needed to do to fix his swing. Nothing like a little bit of home schooling. "He not only told me, he took that bat and showed me," Banks said. "He demonstrated, right there on the living room rug, how I had hit from a wide stance when I was going good, with my arms away from my body. But in '63 I had brought my feet closer together and brought my arms in."[14]

One of the fondest memories of Banks' time spent with the Cubs occurred on August 15, 1964, when the team proclaimed it "Ernie Banks Day" at Wrigley Field for a game against the Pittsburgh Pirates. A special ceremony was held honoring Banks, and he was joined on the field by his then-wife Eloyce and his little five-year-old twin sons, Joel and Jerome, both of whom wore appropriately-sized Cubs uniforms with the same No. 14 on the backs as their dad.

In the 1960s, when baseball players had not begun earning outsized salaries (Banks would have been paid millions of dollars per season if he had come along later), the not-yet-thought-of-as-a-quaint-tradition of presenting a player with gifts was still in vogue. And Banks was given many presents that day, including a diamond ring with 14 diamonds representing his uniform number. Other gifts included $50 savings bonds for Banks' children (his two-year-old daughter Jane did not attend), a radio (which naturally came from WGN Broadcasting), a nine-passenger station wagon, a special edition of *The Sporting News* commemorating his career, a sterling silver tray from teammates that was engraved "Mr. Cub," and a five-foot-tall cake. The cake came from the Rehabilitation Institute of Chicago, where it was said Banks had visited patients 17 times. The cake was topped with a figure of Banks, plus flowers, and a handmade card with 216 signatures came with it.

After the presentations, the microphone on the field was turned over to Banks. He delivered the kind of knock-it-out-of-the-park speech that might have aided him in his alderman's race.

12. Downs and Ups

"First, I want to thank God for making me an American," Banks said, "and giving me the ability to be a Major League baseball player. Next, I want to thank my wife and children and parents for their love and devotion. And, of course, all the wonderful Chicago Cubs fans for your warmth and acceptance in making this day possible."[15]

The crowd at Wrigley Field was 20,003 that day (plus 2,000 youngsters who yelled louder for Banks than the others), although it seemed symbolic that the team lost the game, 5–4.

"I will be forever grateful to the fine Cub organization, the committee [that arranged the day], teammates, here and beyond, and especially to Mr. Wrigley, who has been more than just an employer. I will never forget this day. I thank you all from the bottom of my heart."[16]

It was a special day for Banks overall, but not at the plate, where he went 0-for-3 in the defeat.

Banks' bounce-back season did not match those 1958–1959 years of his prime, but he batted 37 points higher, hit 23 home runs and drove home 95 runs. The losing season was not his fault.

13

The Strangeness of 1965

A rejuvenated Ernie Banks showed off the big stick again during the 1965 season, hitting the 400th home run of his career as he amassed 28 dingers while topping 100 runs batted in. He played in 163 games and was selected for the National League All-Star team for the first time in three seasons.

For all of those concerned about Banks' advancing athletic age earlier in the 1960s, he seemed as good as new at 34 in 1965. He made 680 plate appearances, definitely an indicator of a healthy player. Mr. Cub was the elder statesman of the team, but it was a turn-back-the-clock year for him. The common cliché in daily life is that a person has nothing if he doesn't have his health, and it could be applied to Banks in this year after some woebegone moments in recent seasons.

For Banks, that was all forgotten. Based on his public persona, it seemed he never let bad news stick, never let unfortunate tidings linger. He was one of the most public happy people in the United States. It was Dodgers great Roy Campanella who said that there had to be some little boy inside a player to make baseball a profession, and Banks personified that image.

By the 1960s, Banks had coined his most memorable phrases. He was credited with calling Wrigley Field "the Friendly Confines" because of his embrace of the old ballpark. But his always-on-display good nature was summed up by his use of the enthusiastic sentence, "Let's play two!" That was taken to mean that Banks was forever ready and able to suit up for a doubleheader whatever the weather or circumstances.

The origin of the "Let's play two!" motto stemmed from a scorching hot summer July day—some say it was 105 degrees outside the clubhouse in Chicago. Banks recounted his thinking at the moment. "It was a very bad day in Chicago," Banks said. "I came into the locker room and I was feeling great. And I said to all my teammates, 'It's a beautiful day—let's play two.' That was a time in my life that I was really excited about going to Wrigley Field."[1]

You mean there was a time he wasn't? But that was typical Banks in the locker room, taking the optimist's route when his teammates were probably toweling off the sweat before even taking the field. Sportswriters in the clubhouse overheard Banks' declaration and reported the phrase in their newspapers. After that, it stuck to Banks more rigidly than glue. In its own way, it was Banks' Gettysburg Address, although certainly of less import to a nation. That was Banks' version of how the phrase came to him, told to President Barack Obama in 2013.

Banks repeated his personal phrase uncounted thousands of times over the years. Sometimes it was slightly modified to "It's a great day for a ballgame, let's play two." Nonetheless, the meaning was clear, and the irresistible nature of the comment seemed a perfect fit with its originator's pleasant personality.

As teammate Ron Santo (and others) said, it seemed impossible that Ernie Banks could be upbeat 100 percent of the time in public, but he really never did slip up. Cynics could never trap him. Perhaps once established in the public consciousness in that manner, everyone wanted Ernie just to keep on being Ernie. There was no pressure for him to change, and life was pretty darned good being viewed the way he had been since introducing himself to Chicago in 1953. What was the incentive to show a more complicated side? What benefit was there in issuing controversial statements?

Keen, up-close observers of Banks detected that there was more beneath the surface, but Banks just chose not to reveal himself to the public more than superficially. They never heard Banks discussing racial issues the way he did with teammate Billy Williams in the privacy of the car going back and forth to the park. Yes, Banks was genuine in his enthusiasm about baseball, the Cubs, Wrigley Field and the city of Chicago. But maybe, some suggested, that was the icing, hiding the cake.

Jim Brosnan, a perceptive writer as well as a solid Major League reliever, was a Banks teammate who believed the public did not get the full picture of Banks. Keeping personal things quiet is everyone's right, of course, and in this modern era with ubiquitous social media and instant postings of any slightly unusual comment, and with relationships dissected online, it is entirely possible that way too much is revealed about celebrities' lives.

"Ernie was the ultimate politician," Brosnan said of Banks—and he did not mean politician as in running for alderman.

> He was like that right from the start. It was almost impossible to get to know Ernie Banks. He would say exactly what he was supposed to say. "It's a beautiful day. Let's play two. The friendly confines of Wrigley Field." He wouldn't say much, but what he did say was all clichés. And they weren't even funny. If he had spoken black and been a little funky it what he said, it would have been entertaining and we would have talked to him more.

"You never knew what Ernie was feeling." Brosnan said the two were at a dinner party once and Banks was asked the usual question about his great success in the game and making the Hall of Fame, but never making it to a World Series. Brosnan called "bullshit" on Banks' platitude of an answer: "'I would have loved to have done that, but I enjoyed every minute of my career with the Cubs, and if I could have played two games every day, it would have doubled my happiness.'"

Brosnan said he wished he could have gotten to know the real Ernie Banks better.[2]

Neither Brosnan nor anyone else pointed out that maybe Banks was just not comfortable being more militant. After all, the 1960s was a time of unrest, a period when the Civil Rights movement was on the front page daily, blacks in many walks of life were speaking out about injustice, and everyday citizens were marching in the streets. Dr. Martin Luther King, Jr., was leading a battle against a rigidly enforced racial status quo. America was changing, but one could still be portrayed as radical and have harm done to one's career or jeopardize financial or family security.

Brosnan was not alone in such commentary, although his words came off as fairly harsh. Ferguson Jenkins, the Hall of Fame pitcher who was a Banks teammate from 1966 to 1971 and roomed with him on the road for three years, agreed with Brosnan that Banks never talked about himself. Absolutely, Banks talked a lot, on the field, in the clubhouse, in public, but not about feelings or opinions. "He was always talking about the game," Jenkins said. "Never about himself. He was a fun guy. He was always singing, 'Chicago, my kind of town.' He sang it all the time, especially when we won. He talked to anybody, but he never talked about himself."[3]

And you know what? Nobody cared a damn. They liked Ernie Banks being Ernie Banks, the way he portrayed himself and carried himself in public. Baseball author Peter Golenbock made that very point when dissecting Banks' relationship with Cubs fans. Banks gave them what they wanted to hear.

> The fans, unlike skeptical teammates, loved that Banks always had a kind word for the inept Cubs' organization and a corny phrase or slogan for the media and fans. Even if his teammates couldn't figure out whether Ernie was sincere, the fans didn't care. The other aspect that the fans loved about Ernie Banks was that though he may have played in more losing games than any other player in the history of the game, he seemed unaffected by the losses and at the same time appeared utterly convinced that tomorrow the team would win.[4]

In those days, Wrigley Field was not an automatic sellout the way the situation became in later decades when being a Cubs fan was trendy with young people. Somehow, future generations shrugged off the constant losing and found contentment in the bleachers drinking beer, especially when all of the home games were still played in the afternoon sunshine and you could work on your tan.

13. The Strangeness of 1965

The team drew well even without performing well. Forget it when the Cubs actually became winners. Then tickets became scarce and you had to know somebody. But during the Ernie Banks era, the fans grew accustomed to losing, felt it just came with the team, maybe as a byproduct of the Billy Goat Curse or not. Fans did not need players telling them the team was awful. They read that with their own eyes. But at least the best player always seemed to have hope. He was a true believer, and Banks' spirit carried along many others. They all wanted to win. Nobody was sure the Cubs ever would, but Banks said it was so, and he was the kind of guy you could have faith in.

"Ernie Banks was a regular guy who went along in the face of adversity, just like the fans," Golenbock wrote. "He became their Moses, leading them to the Promised Land, and like Moses, never quite got there."[5] Yes, the Cubs also seemed to be wandering in the desert for 40 years.

The 1965 season was a schizophrenic one for the Cubs. Naturally, Banks was optimistic in spring training, uttering one of his poetic predictions assuring that good things were about to happen. "The Cubs will come alive in '65," was his slogan of the year. They didn't, although things were quite lively.

Banks' rhyme referred to what the Cubs' record would be like. Not accurate. But there were a number of distinguishing characteristics to the season, besides the 72–90 finish adding mightily to owner Phil Wrigley's frustration at being unable to produce a winner.

Banks was back in business and, surrounded by Billy Williams and Ron Santo, the Cubs possessed the most explosive trio of sluggers in baseball, all three of them eventually voted into the Hall of Fame. But they also reacquired George Altman, who had been with the New York Mets for two seasons, and added the young infield combination of second baseman Glenn Beckert and Don Kessinger. Those guys should have been able to win more than 72 games and finish better than eighth in the National League. Once again, the only two teams the Cubs could beat out were the expansion Mets and the Houston Astros.

The Cubs did not come close to selling out Wrigley Field on Opening Day, attracting just 19,751 fans, which meant the populace did not trust Banks' ditty. In keeping with the tenor of the season, the game ended in a 10–10 tie in 11 innings. Like many things involving the Cubs, it was pretty much an inexplicable result.

Just two days later, Chicago obtained pitcher Ted Abernathy from the Cleveland Indians. No one could explain why at the time since it did not seem as if Abernathy would bolster the staff much. He had once finished 7–2, which was the best to be said about his record, and he was 32. Out of nowhere, Abernathy became an ace reliever, appearing in a league-leading 84 games that year while saving 31. Abernathy was a revelation that season, though he did not stick around long. Anyone who saw Abernathy pitch, however, will remember his style. He was a submariner, a nearly-underhand thrower. Arm injuries had forced the right-hander to adapt and change his delivery.

Southpaw Dick Ellsworth was still around, but never came close to matching his 22–10 mark of 1963. He went 14–15 in 1965, even managing to lose a one-hitter to the Los Angeles Dodgers because the single blow was a three-run homer. The Cubs got back at LA two days later, winning 4–3 in 16 innings because of three walks and a wild pitch. Banks scored the game-winner.

The season began with Bob Kennedy as field boss, although he was still referred to by the organization as a head coach. On June 14, Lou Klein, a remnant from the College of Coaches, took over and Kennedy moved to the front office. The change of leadership did not lead the Cubs anywhere. Neither did the main group of pitchers. The Cubs still had Larry Jackson, Bob Buhl and Lindy McDaniel, but the most intriguing member of the cast was right-hander Bill Faul, who had been with the Detroit Tigers and in 1965 would have the best season of his short career with the Cubs. Faul went 6–6 with a 3.54 earned run average, but numbers were not what the fuss was about.

Faul proclaimed that as an expert in hypnosis, he put himself into a suitable trance before games he pitched, and during them he was able to hypnotize opposing batters. Much superstition has been attached to baseball over the decades, propagated by many unique characters, but if he could have produced better and longer, Faul might have demonstrated the finest act of all.

"I hypnotize myself before the game and I'm then able to hypnotize the hitters. I was really concentrating in my subconscious state on the mound," Faul reported after an August game when he shut out the Philadelphia Phillies 2–0 on two hits. Faul revealed his routine, taking himself into a corner of the clubhouse where nobody bothered him and spending another ten minutes when he "blanks out everything."[6]

At that point, Faul had pitched 26 straight scoreless innings. But whatever he was doing didn't last. Sportswriters joked that Faul put a spell on hitters. The Cubs didn't care how the job got done. To them, pitchers were somewhat like hockey goalies—hardly anyone understood their ways, but teams needed them to perform at a high level if they wanted to win.

In Faul's case, some magic fairy dust must have followed him around at least some of the time. On three different occasions during the 1965 season when he was pitching, the Cubs pulled off triple plays. That was so astonishing that some people began believing in Faul's hypnosis skills. Of course, if he was so skilled in that realm, he likely would have completed his Major League career with a record better than 12–16 and spent more than six seasons in the bigs.

During the 1965 season, Billy Williams drove in 108 runs, Banks knocked in 106, and Santo, who stroked the winning hit in the All-Star Game, collected 101 runs batted in. A vivid example of how they did so was on August 29.

13. The Strangeness of 1965

Banks and Santo belted two homers each and Williams also had a four-bagger. Chicago beat the Milwaukee Braves, 10–2, the last time the Cubs met the Braves in the Midwest before the Braves moved to Atlanta.

In 1965, left-hander Ken Holtzman was 19 years old, yet he had already earned a college degree from the University of Illinois. He was drafted by the Cubs in the fourth round of the amateur draft, the first year of the draft's existence. Outfielder Rick Monday (later a Cub) was chosen with the first overall pick by the Kansas City Athletics. A couple of other guys selected that year were future Hall of Famers Johnny Bench and Nolan Ryan.

In early summer, Holtzman was sent to Caldwell, Idaho, and then Wenatchee, Washington. Before summer's end he was working in Chicago. "My biggest thrill was when Buck O'Neil picked me up at O'Hare [International Airport] and brought me to Wrigley Field for the first time and introduced me to Banks, Williams and Santo," Holtzman said.[7] Soon enough Holtzman became a difference-maker for the Cubs, but after making his big-league debut on September 4, he finished the season 0–0 with a 2.25 earned run average in four innings spread over three games.

On September 9, one of the greatest games in baseball history was pitched in Dodger Stadium. Few would be surprised to hear that the Cubs were on the losing end. Future Hall of Fame southpaw Sandy Koufax pitched a perfect game for the Dodgers, gaining a 1–0 victory over Bob Hendley. Hendley was also a left-hander, though certainly not as accomplished as Koufax. He never won more than 11 games in a season, pitching for four teams in a seven-year Major League career that concluded with a 48–52 mark. Even in 1965, Hendley went a nothing-special 4–4 with an unsightly 5.96 ERA for the Cubs.

But on that night he was no worse than the second-best pitcher on the planet. As Koufax continued his stupendous effort, Hendley was throwing nearly as well. Into the fifth inning, Hendley was also pitching a perfect game. In that inning, the Dodgers scored when Lou Johnson walked, was sacrificed to second, stole third base and kept running when the throw was high. Johnson's double two innings later was the only hit in the game.

"In the latter part of the game [Koufax] was awesome," Hendley said. "I knew it was going to be very difficult, if not impossible, to beat him. Particularly in the last few innings, you knew he had the perfect game. As well as he was throwing and setting people down, there was very little chance of overcoming him.... This game is the most recognizable thing I've done in baseball and I came out a loser."[8]

Naturally, given the 27 men up, 27 men down, Banks was of no offensive assistance to Hendley that day. Indeed, he struck out three times as Koufax fanned 14, more than half his outs on K's. The game took 1 hour, 43 minutes to play.

Less remembered is that on September 14, the Cubs and Dodgers played again with the same starters on the mound, this time at Wrigley Field. Banks was 0-for-3 again, but this time Hendley was the winning pitcher, 2–1, throwing a four-hitter. Koufax was taken out after six innings. "We pitched against each other twice in six days," Hendley said 50 years after his September matchups with Koufax. "We both gave up two runs. We both allowed five hits. We both retired early. We both had elbow problems. He was great. I was average."[9]

Cubs fans could only have hoped for average for the team, a .500 season being a dream. Owner Wrigley was fed up. He had invented the College of Coaches as a dramatic leadership move, denigrating the value of a "dictator" manager. Now he was on the prowl for another fresh approach.

Shortly after the World Series ended (won by the Dodgers in seven games over the Minnesota Twins), Wrigley rocked the baseball world by introducing a new manager for his team for the 1966 season. The fascinating choice was Leo Durocher, the epitome of that dictator-manager Wrigley had disdained only a few years before. It was a stunning choice if only because in 1958 Wrigley had stated, "I wouldn't have him as a gift" when someone asked if Durocher was under consideration to manage the Cubs.[10]

There was nothing subtle about this hire, Durocher absolutely being one of those "my-way-or-the-highway" leaders. Sneering at the previous experiment of rotating coaches running the team, Durocher proclaimed loudly at his introductory press conference, "If no announcement has been made of what my title is," Durocher famously said, "I'm making it here and now. I'm the manager. I'm not a head coach. I'm the manager."[11]

Although he did not know it at the time, affable, genuine, friendly Banks, going on 35 for the 1966 season, was about to face the most aggravating years of his Major League career. He would be forced into coping with someone who did not care much about what he had accomplished, did not care that he was revered in Chicago, and did not even seem to think he was still a worthwhile ballplayer.

It was often said in the coming years, half in jest, half in sadness, that if Ernie Banks had never met a man he didn't like before, it was because he hadn't met Leo Durocher.

14

Ernie and Leo

By 1966, Ernie Banks was an active-duty icon for the Chicago Cubs, the mainstay of the franchise, clearly one of the greatest players who had ever adorned the roster of the club. A two-time Most Valuable Player, a perennial All-Star, and beloved for his personality and outlook, he was the ultimate symbol of the franchise.

However, he was the symbol of a perpetually losing franchise. The hardiest of fans could say, "Well, we always have Ernie Banks." Yes, they had Ernie Banks, a beacon in the darkness, in lieu of pennants and World Series experience.

In owner Phil Wrigley's mind, he had tried everything to restore winning as a habit on Chicago's North Side since the last National League pennant captured in 1945, since the imposition of the Billy Goat Curse. No one in baseball history had been more radical with a fresh approach with the advent of the College of Coaches, and all that did was earn Wrigley ridicule. So Wrigley swung the other way. It was he who had talked of the manager position as equivalent to a dictator. Now he hired one.

If Leo Durocher was one thing in the dugout, it was a dictator. Durocher was 60 years old and his resume glittered, even if his personality could be abrasive. Durocher as manager was a 180-degree shift from the College of Coaches, but on a ranking scale, Durocher's personality was also a 180-degree shift from Banks'.

Ernie Banks was everyone's friend. Durocher wasn't out to make friends in baseball. His friends were pretty much all in Hollywood. He had been married to actress Laraine Day between 1947 and 1960, and he hung out with Frank Sinatra, Dean Martin, George Raft and Jimmy Durante, among other Hollywood luminaries. One did not picture Durocher sitting around in the off-season talking strategy with Billy Southworth, Chuck Dressen and Casey Stengel, other managers of his era, so much as attending show business parties with his other set of pals reported on in the gossip columns.

Not that his baseball credentials were unsound. Durocher was a shortstop for the New York Yankees, Cincinnati Reds, St. Louis Cardinals and

Brooklyn Dodgers between 1925 and 1945. He was brash and fiery, exuding the leadership gene, a good enough fielder to be a three-time All-Star, but offering little at bat. His lifetime average was .247, and as someone who played two seasons with the Murderers Row Yankees, he was a weak link in the order. Famously, Babe Ruth called him "The All-American Out."[1] Compared to Ruth he certainly was, though that could be said about almost anyone.

Durocher played for two World Series champions, but made his mark as a manager with Brooklyn and the New York Giants. He was flamboyant, loud, and wanted to be known as a win-at-all-costs leader. Yet Durocher's humanity shone through in his unprejudiced leadership in standing up for Jackie Robinson when the rookie was enduring grief for breaking the color barrier and with a young Willie Mays on his roster whose confidence had been shaken. Durocher was known as a manager who would fight for his players, and in winning 2,008 games, he was ejected from 95.

The best-remembered saying attributed to Durocher was "nice guys finish last." Although recalled that way, Durocher did not say it that way. His wording was slightly different, but the statement was mildly edited in the retelling. The utterance occurred in 1946 when he was in charge of the Dodgers, and it referred to the arch-rival Giants. "The nice guys are all over there in seventh place. They'll finish last. Nice guys. Finish last."[2] Durocher was saying players had to have a little meanness and passion to form a winner. He liked the way sportswriters made him sound and embraced the full version of "nice guys finish last" as the title of his 1975 autobiography.

While that merged comment stands out as Durocher's contribution to *Bartlett's Quotations*, another comment Durocher made at the time of his hiring was seared into the minds of Cubs fans, at the time and forevermore, though later as an object of ridicule. "This is no eighth-place club," Durocher pronounced.[3] That's where the 1965 team had finished in the NL standings. Clearly, Durocher contemplated an upward move. When the Cubs finished tenth in 1966, the phrase haunted him: Yeah, they're a tenth-place team. The team won 13 more games in 1965 without Durocher than it did a year later with him.

Ernie Banks was 35 years old in 1966. It was not his finest season, but he was a solid contributor with 15 home runs, 75 runs batted in and a .272 average in 141 games. He was far from Durocher's biggest problem. The core of the starting lineup was first-rate with such figures as Banks, Glenn Beckert at second, Don Kessinger at short, Ron Santo at third base, and Billy Williams and George Altman in the outfield. Young Randy Hundley, officially still a rookie despite a few cameo appearances in recent seasons, was the catcher of the future.

The pitching surrendered 809 runs. Somehow, even the best pitchers on the team turned into losing pitchers that year. Dick Ellsworth, not so long

14. Ernie and Leo

before a 20-game winner, became a 20-game loser at 8–22. Ken Holtzman finished 11–16. Bill Hands was 8–13. It was too soon for future Hall of Famer Ferguson Jenkins, who finished 6–8 after coming over from the Philadelphia Phillies in a trade. Durocher was horrified and shuffled the deck. Trade after trade shipped players far and wide. Durocher concluded that the only way the Cubs would become winners was through youthful players. The team gave up Larry Jackson and Bob Buhl in the deal to obtain Jenkins, a bold move that worked out.

There were a couple of oddities that season, particularly one in light of what far-in-the-future developments would bring. Wrigley Field was the last ballpark in the majors without lights, and the Cubs were known as the only team that played all day games before lights were finally installed in 1988. In 1966, William Schlensky, not remembered for anything else in Cubs lore despite his ownership of two shares of stock, sued Phil Wrigley and the team to make the Cubs play night games. He asserted that playing all day games cost the team attendance and money. He lost his lawsuit, even if in some ways it might be said he was right all along.

A lesser oddity was the brief appearance on the scene by outfielder Ty Cline, who managed a 12-year career in the majors, but only seven games with the Cubs. He was acquired from the Milwaukee Braves and months later shipped back to the Braves when they were in Atlanta, but not before smacking five hits in one game for Chicago.

Given the core of good hitters, it seemed the Cubs of 1966 should have been better. One irritant in the clubhouse and with the fans was how Durocher began treating Banks. Banks got off to a slow start at the plate, and in April Durocher benched him. Things likely hit a low point when Durocher would not even let Banks take batting practice one day. That was a pointless insult. "I can't break out sitting down," Banks said of being confined to the dugout.[4]

It was obvious through his actions that Durocher was skeptical of Banks being part of the future. Durocher did not out and out say that Ernie was washed up, but he hinted at that when questioned by sportswriters, most of whom were in Banks' corner. In one case when asked if Banks was finished, Durocher said, "I don't know, but I do know this. He is doing things I have never seen before, things that make you wonder."[5]

Durocher was not known for being coy or shy about expressing his feelings. His nickname was "Leo the Lip," and you don't obtain a moniker like that by issuing platitudes. No matter how Durocher truly felt about Banks, however, his political instincts kicked in, and he was cautious about being too explicit about whatever doubts he had.

Banks, as always, was optimistic in spring training about the Cubs' prospects for the season. With a nod towards Durocher, he unveiled his 1966 team slogan. Admitting he had help from nephews, he sought to link it to the new era. "Shoot From The Hip With Leo The Lip" was the new motto.[6]

Even as early as March in spring training, that year held in Long Beach, California, there was speculation about how Durocher and Banks would match up since they were such different people. Stan Isaacs wrote words that seemed prescient soon after. "He [Durocher] is sure to shake things up. He might even treat Ernie Banks as something less than an institution....it would not be unreasonable to expect Banks to fret a little about the change."[7]

After hearing out Santo's analysis of Banks looking satisfied but not being pleased about representing a loser, Isaacs cornered Banks, who had interesting things to say about his mindset.

> I have always tried to keep a level head about myself. We have lost so much and so often and people ask you so often about the game that you try to adopt some kind of easy manner to handle it. No, I don't think I've ever become accustomed to losing. But it's possible that you adjust to the losing situation to the point that you do become complacent and aren't aware of it.[8]

This was very early in 1966, when players were still getting into shape, readying for exhibition games, when games played did not count in the standings. Banks expounded on how he thought Durocher would be good for the Cubs.

> I am happy Leo is here. I am delighted. I think Durocher—Leo the Lip, as they say—will shake things up. He will be able to do things that some of the others could not do. If Leo gets the Cubs going, I will be happy to play a part in helping, even if I may not be here when we eventually win a pennant. Just winning and being in the first division would be great incentive for the fellows around here. As far as I myself am concerned, when Leo was named manager, I vowed to get in the best possible shape. I want to have the best possible year for him. He is a hustling manager and I want to help him and join with him as best I can.[9]

Cubs manager Leo Durocher, the hard-bitten leader of the team in the late 1960s, who worked overtime to make an enemy out of Banks (National Baseball Hall of Fame).

14. Ernie and Leo

That was the honeymoon period. From then on, their co-existence was definitely uneasy.

Durocher put Banks on the bench in late April. After going 0-for-3 against the Los Angeles Dodgers on April 23, Banks was hitting .194. He sat out three games, came back, and was hitting .186 when sat again. On May 3, he pinch-hit against the Houston Astros and went 0-for-1, dropping his average to .182. Back to the bench for two more games and then another 0-for-1 appearance, putting his average at .178. It was not a pretty picture.

During an early-May stretch, Banks went 1-for-13. Those were tough times. Finally, against the Reds on May 14, Banks recorded a 2-for-4 game. Yet six weeks into the season, Banks was still hitting around .180, a few games with some hits offering hope the slump was dead. While he did sit out games here and there, Durocher gave Banks plenty of chances to break out.

No single game was more helpful to Banks' psyche than the June 11 contest against the Houston Astros. Banks went 3-for-5 with three runs batted in and a run scored. But they were not your average three hits. Of all things, Banks, not known as a speed demon, smacked three triples in one game, tying the Major League record (albeit shared by many players).

"Understand you tied a Major League record," Ron Santo told Banks in the locker room while shaking his hand. "That's great." Santo asked how many others had performed the feat, and when informed that Banks was the 35th man to do it, he jokingly backed off. "That many? Then I take it all back. That wasn't worth congratulations."[10]

The players laughed, Banks included. "How about that?" Banks said. "It's nice to be in the company of those speed boys. They're all fast. They can run. And this puts me them right in there with them. I guess I'm slowing down. I used to hit home runs. Now I'm down to triples."[11]

Banks reflected on his slump, letting on a bit how much it bothered him to go without big-hit games for so long. "Every night I feel like this is gonna be the night for a bunch of hits," he said after the three-triple game. "You hit the ball in the batting cage good and you say to yourself, 'I'm ready. I got it.' Then you've got to continue this through the game. About a week ago I decided not to try to pull the ball so much. Just to hit it where it is pitched. I was swinging too hard and was getting out in front of the ball. Now I'm just trying to meet the ball. That's what I did tonight."[12]

Still, even after that, there was much speculation that Banks' successor as the Cubs' first baseman was already chosen, and it would be John Boccabella. Boccabella was 25 that season. He had appeared in small numbers of games the preceding couple of seasons, hitting .391 in 23 at-bats and .333 in 12 at-bats. In mid–July of 1966, Durocher handed the first base job to Boccabella.

"Boccabella is hitting consistently and he's also doing an outstanding job in the field," Durocher said. "I believe he has a better glove than either

Banks or Lee Thomas. And, like all the other youngsters, he'll get better. The future of this team has to be with the young fellows."[13] But in 1966, when Boccabella played in 75 games, he hit just .228.

Banks showed some signs of recovering his stroke in early June, when his batting average reached .201, a rise of 20 points. From there, Banks raised his average 70 points before the end of the season. He came to the plate more than twice as often as Boccabella and out-hit him by 44 points.

These were complicated times for Banks because while he had enough to worry about just hitting the ball safely, and Durocher had enough to worry about trying to coax wins out of the team, those on the periphery watched the two interact as if they were feuding. Many years later, Banks remained reluctant to characterize the men's relationship as purely one of enmity. Banks, as was his wont, emphasized what he saw as some of Durocher's good qualities.

> He brought the energy to the organization in many ways, by excitement and creativity and fear. Most people kind of belabor the fact that he didn't like me or I didn't like him. It's a normal thing—I've learned this from my own family, and I come from a family of 12—it's a normal thing to kind of create discord between people. But I never allowed it because I learned many years ago that whoever was the boss is in charge, and I respected that. Most people thought Leo didn't like me and I didn't like him. I never met a person I disliked. That's my philosophy.[14]

Banks actually said that about never meeting someone he disliked. Banks took the high road, whether people believed him or not. Banks being known as that kind of guy always made others wonder what kind of guy Durocher was to get on a non-existent Banks bum list.

If you are the type of person who always sees the bright side, you can find good in anyone, but Banks made it sound as if he didn't have to work too hard to do that with Durocher. He said that when he didn't play, he sat next to Durocher in the dugout. Sometimes he sat next to him on the team plane. When Durocher married for a fourth time while managing the Cubs, Banks attended the wedding. Durocher may have seemed to act out intentional little cruelties, but Banks was someone who would overlook them. Durocher might be one to say that "it's just business, nothing personal," but if Banks is to be believed, likely or not, that is how he took Durocher seemingly messing with his career. "Many of the players did not quite understand my own philosophy," Banks said. "I believe in forgive and forget, and keep your mouth shut and listen to whatever somebody is trying to tell you and you can learn something. I tell my children that. But it was just misinterpreted that Leo disliked me. He made my life better. He made me a better player."[15]

Nobody was going to make Ernie Banks a better player at 35 than he had been at 25. That was no longer possible. Maybe Banks had been a little bit complacent and was being blindsided by creeping age. And just maybe,

14. Ernie and Leo

stung by Durocher shuffling him in and out of the lineup, he dove all-in to salvage his career. Maybe this, by Banks' interpretation, was making his life better, but Banks would not have been human if he did not feel some resentment towards Durocher.

When Durocher gave Boccabella the nod in July, Banks had to be surprised. He had to be more upset than he let on, although he played it straight in public with considerable grace. "As we get older, we have to make way for the younger players," Banks said. "Boccabella is getting his chance to play and he's making the most of it. He's doing a fine job out there and more power to him. I won't say it doesn't hurt, because it definitely does. However, I simply have to adjust to it, just as every player does when he gets older."[16]

Yet when Boccabella played regularly, he could not sustain his brief introductory Major League flashes. Banks did not have to say a word, but when Durocher called on him, he hit. The shaky days of the spring were in the past. Boccabella drove in 25 runs with six homers. Banks came through at 75 and 15, which seemed impossible given his start.

The great irony of Banks' horrible start and the belief that old age was encroaching was that he had come into the season in tip-top form, convinced he had learned some useful lessons about conditioning during the off-season. Banks had run into the famous sprinter and Olympic gold medalist, Jesse Owens, at a sports banquet in Saskatoon, Saskatchewan. Besides laughingly noting that they both lived in Chicago and it took a Canadian sojourn to bring them together, Owens taught him some things about fitness.

"He outlined a program for me that I have been following faithfully all spring," Banks said in April. Banks had sought the advice, he said. "I was talking to Jesse about the fact that I faded out badly the second half of the season last year. I asked him whether he thought there was any way I could build myself up physically so that I would have the strength and endurance to finish strong."[17]

So after all that, Banks started the season terribly and finished the second half strong. Did any of it really make sense other than he endured an extra-long, early-season slump? "You know, every player drops into a slump sooner or later," Banks said. "It's the ones who can snap out of it fast, within a few days, who hit .300. It's those prolonged slumps that murder you."

Many people believed Banks was never going to come out of this slump, maybe Banks included, even if he didn't say so and seemed to retain that inner faith that enabled him to bounce back over the season's last stretch. If absolutely nothing else in 1966, it was apparent that Durocher prized winning and was beholden to no players he inherited, and if Banks could not help him win, then he was dispensable.

Sportswriters believed Durocher's ego was so big he could not cope well with Banks being more popular, more entrenched with Chicago fans than his boss. But what could he expect? Ernie Banks' nickname was Mr. Cub. Durocher would become popular enough if he brought a pennant and a World Series to Chicago, but one season into his tenure he hadn't taken the Cubs anywhere except the cellar, earning ridicule for his comment about not being an eighth-place team. Durocher had ridden the Cubs directly into tenth place and humiliated Ernie Banks. These were not good ways to ingratiate himself with the fan base. He should have been hugging Banks in public in front of the TV cameras rather than suggesting that there might not be a place on the team any more for the local hero.

15

New Look Cubs

During his off-season vacation in Europe in November of 1966, Ernie Banks and his wife Eloyce met Pope Paul VI at the Vatican. As far as is known, Banks did not say, "Let's play two."

The Bankses went on a three-week European tour, visiting London, Rome, Paris and other spots, all of which featured fans who followed soccer and track and field more than baseball. Banks had done some studying, trying a bit of the language from different countries on the itinerary. Given the cramming nature of his preparation, he could only speak some basic phrases. Though he gave it a good try, it seemed as if it was always 0–2 in the count. "Just imagine," Banks said, "15 years ago I'm a kid playing on a high school field in Dallas and there I was in Vienna, eating goose liver with violin and Gypsy music in the background."[1]

Banks revealed that Vienna, Austria, had long been on his wish list as a place to visit because of his deep-rooted love of music, and this was the primary motivation for the trip. Banks was known to sing often, but this time he was thinking of the composers of the past when discussing music.

Banks brought a bottle of cognac back from France, said the shopping in Florence, Italy was fabulous, and liked the feel of having thousands of lira in his pocket because it gave him the feel of being a millionaire. If Banks had played not so many years later, he would have been a millionaire due to the salary structure changes for big-leaguers. For the 1966, 1967 and 1968 seasons, Banks made about $55,000 a year, about the height of his earning power in baseball. The exchange rate at the time between the dollar and the lira in Italy meant that an item listed as 7,000 lira was just $10.

Mightily impressed by the city of Budapest, Banks said the Hungarian monetary value was much higher yet. "I spent 100,000 florins on one purchase," Banks said. "You feel like a big shot."[2]

Probably an even bigger big shot if you gain an audience with the Pope, something arranged by a priest, Monsignor Paul Marcinkus, who was a devoted Cubs fan. Marcinkus discussed Cubs players with Banks and even brought up Ken Holtzman losing a no-hitter the season before. He heard the game on a short-wave radio. Banks had to be a little bit stunned when, after he and his wife's introduction to Pole Paul VI, the Pope said, "You are very famous."[3] The Pope seemed more impressed with Banks' reputation than Durocher did.

In the midst of his woes during the 1966 season, Banks was not ready to give up and did not see his career coming to an end, either so abruptly or any time in the immediate future. "Personally," he said, "I don't feel like my playing career is over. I believe I can play for two or three more years because I'm in sound condition."[4]

That assessment did not prevent Banks from working even harder on his body for the 1967 season. Banks turned 36 that year, and athletes of that age in all the major sports are either retired or on the downside of their careers. Unlike the 2000s, where athletes focus on staying in shape year-round and embrace new nutritional plans, workout ideas and the like to try to stay young, that was hardly a discussion point in the 1960s. Banks said he lost about seven or eight pounds to 179–180, thinking it might help his swing. He had tried playing at 185–187 and believed that was a mistake. He thought if he gained weight, he would be stronger and have more stamina, but that did not help him. So he reverted.

During the off-season, Banks consulted with his mentor Buck O'Neil, still working for the Cubs organization, but the only guy still around who really knew Banks as a younger man and could mentally compare his body types, swing, and whatever changes he had made over the years. He asked O'Neil's opinion, and it turned out that O'Neil's thinking jibed with his own about cutting weight. "I told him, 'That's just what I was thinking,'" Banks said. "So I decided to watch my diet and cut down on the calories. She's [his wife] been counting the calories ever since."[5]

During spring training, Leo Durocher still worked hard to replace Banks at first base, giving much more playing time to John Boccabella, once again a threat to start the regular season instead of Banks, and another new face, Clarence Jones. Boccabella once again had every opportunity in the world to take over the first base bag. He ended up appearing in 25 games and batting .171 that season. It was not to be. Jones got into 53 games with 155 plate appearances and did hit .252, splitting time between first base, right field and left field. But he also spent time at AAA during the summer. A year later, he saw his last Major League action in five games for the Cubs.

Banks barely even played in the exhibition games at the beginning of spring training. He sat out the first seven games and played in three out of the 19 games the Cubs engaged in during the Cactus League pre-season. When it was crunch time, when the games mattered, who was the Chicago Cubs' first baseman? Ernie Banks. Banks appeared in 151 games, all at first, in 1967.

15. New Look Cubs

Durocher was essentially running a tryout camp at first, but speaking publicly, Banks embraced the spring training rest, saying it helped him get off to a better start when the regular season began. "Leo allowed me to take my time and get myself into shape," Banks said. "If I'd been playing more, I probably would have had to push myself. It's worked out better this way."[6] Banks essentially turned an insult into a grand design for the betterment of everyone.

Banks hit seven home runs before the end of May after not hitting that many until August the season before. Certainly, Banks was a bit worried the season before when he suffered through his long slump and was shuttled back and forth to the bench. He came out swinging—and connecting—in 1967. Even he could not have known what to expect in 1967. If he started poorly again, he had to wonder if he was dead meat, going to be exiled from the team. But he didn't. He started so strongly he even fooled himself.

"You don't like to face up to it, but it's happening to you and you have the feeling that there's nothing you can do about it," Banks said of the burden of the year-old slump. "I got off to a real bad start last year and I couldn't pull the ball against any type of pitcher. But this rejuvenation, it's great. I feel like the man who couldn't walk as well as he might have thought he could and then all of a sudden began to walk better. I actually surprised myself."[7]

The Buck O'Neil conference was not the only consulting with experts Banks engaged in. He spoke to Stan Musial, the St. Louis Cardinals' Hall of Fame outfielder who had retired in 1963, and who explained how he coaxed more hits out of his bat at the end of his career. "I remembered that Stan had the same trouble toward the end of his career," Banks said. "So I went to him and asked him and he said he went to the opposite field when he got up in years. I started doing that and pretty soon I was hitting better, but I still couldn't pull the pitches I wanted to."[8]

There was another big change, too. Banks gave up his 35-inch-long, 31-ounce bat for a 36–36 bat. "That forced me to take a more rhythmic swing. I didn't swing so hard because I couldn't with the heavy bat."[9]

After the first 73 games of the 1967 season Banks had 15 homers, the same as his full-year total from 1966. He was also batting .310. "I can't remember when I hit like I'm hitting now," he said. "Maybe '61, maybe '60. I'm pulling the ball again. I'm going from first to third on singles and I'm getting to those balls [in the field] that were going past me last year. Believe me, it's a lot of fun being young again."[10]

That is precisely what it seemed like. Banks gave credit to his own desire, O'Neil, Musial, losing weight and changing bats. Apparently that equaled gulps of elixir taken from the Fountain of Youth. Another step the Cubs took helped provide Banks with more motivation, or renewed motivation, although the betting odds were that Durocher making him a player-coach was another way of easing him out of regular playing time. This way the Cubs could use Banks' talents in more than one way without bruising his feelings so much. Banks just kept fooling Durocher into playing him because he was by far the best option for first base.

Not that Banks minded the player-coach title. He enjoyed tutoring the Clarence Joneses in spring training, even if theoretically he was training his replacement. One intriguing speculation offered when the Cubs promoted Banks was that it might someday lead to his becoming the first African American manager in the majors. Looked at more closely, it appeared that Durocher was conniving to find a positive way to sit Banks more often. That was especially likely since Durocher only mentioned the idea to Banks the same morning, about two and a half hours prior to the announcement. The deal seemed less like a collaborative effort than a management directive. "Mr. Wrigley's crazy about the idea," Durocher said. "In my opinion, Banks will play a lot of baseball for us. Maybe he'll run Boccabella off first." Then, seemingly considering how that sounded, he continued, "Or put that the other way around. Boccabella's got to run Ernie off."[11]

Banks at least pretended to be crazy about the coach title. He was always the good soldier, but there was never any doubt that he wanted to keep playing full-time. "I'm very happy about it," Banks said. "I'm looking forward to working with the younger players. It's all very gratifying."[12]

Maybe not all gratifying, but it should be noted that more than 50 years ago, this made Banks just the fourth African American big-league coach. Two of the other three were Banks' good friends, O'Neil and Gene Baker. The other earlier African American coach was Jim Gilliam for the Los Angeles Dodgers. So it might well be believed that Banks was pleased by the appointment because of its semi-pioneering nature. To him, though, coaching was secondary to playing. Durocher would just have to be shown again who really belonged on first.

After losing 103 games in 1966, changes did have to be made. But the Cubs had a number of budding great position players surrounding Banks. Catcher Randy Hundley won a Gold Glove Award in 1967. Glenn Beckert had become a fixture at second base, hit .280 and also won a Gold Glove Award. Don Kessinger was a year from becoming an All-Star. And Ron Santo anchored third base and was an established star. The outfield was less settled except for future Hall of Famer Billy Williams.

The necessary off-season work was roping in more reliable pitching. Ferguson Jenkins was already on the team, acquired from the Phillies the year before, and at 24 he promptly blossomed into a 20-game winner in 1967. Ken Holtzman (9–0) was going to help. Joe Niekro may have been the lesser-known Niekro brother to Phil, who won more than 300 games and is in the Hall of Fame, but Joe won ten games in his first big-league season and 221 in all. Curt Simmons was coming to the end of his long career that included three All-Star selections, but was helpful in spots. Rich Nye was actually the second-biggest winner with 13 wins, a 2.80 earned run average, and remaining out on the mound for more than 200 innings. Chuck Hartenstein was the key reliever with a 9–5 mark and 11 unofficial saves.

Cubs fans were a hard sell, and attendance was shy of 1 million despite the 87–74 season, the team's best record since the team won 98 games and the National League pennant in 1945. There had just been one other winning season since 1946. The fans probably had no idea how to deal with such a situation.

Although Chicago was above .500 basically from the start of the season on, it took until near the end of June for the arrow to convincingly point higher than four games above. On July 3, the Cubs were 46–25 and tied for first place in the standings. They hung close to the top for most of that month, though the last time during the season the Cubs were in first place was July 24. After that they began a gradual descent, though not a collapse, and ultimately finished in third place behind the Cardinals, who won 101 games, and the San Francisco Giants. The Cubs ended 17½ games out of first. It was a good ride for a while.

This was a much better all-around team and a much more balanced one than Banks had been used to lining up with in the 1950s and throughout the 1960s to date. From catcher around to third base, the Cubs were as good as anyone in baseball.

Glenn Beckert, standing next to Banks in the field, was one of those glue guys teams need. Beckert was 6-foot-1 and 190 pounds, out of Pittsburgh, but he was in no way a power hitter. Over the course of his 11-year Major-League career, he hit just 22 home runs, with the most in a season being five. To mention Beckert's name in the same sentence as home runs was almost the beginning of a comedy monologue. He knew he had no business hitting them. "If I hit a homer," Beckert said, "it's always a surprise. I suppose you can say it's a big thrill, but when I hit 'em, they mess me up [his swing]. They can mess me up for two, maybe three weeks. I'm better off when I hit the ball on the ground. I'm dead if I hit the ball in the air. I get most of my hits when I'm hitting the ball down."[13]

Beckert typically choked up on his stick two inches, looking more like a guy who might bunt every time up than swing for the fences—and he was a very good bunter. He made swinging for the fences sound more like a disease than an aspiration. "I don't want anyone to get the idea I'm against home runs, but trying for home runs hurts a lot of fellows. The ones who can't handle it can be damaged."[14]

Although he was no fence-denter, Beckert regularly hit for average, and his lifetime mark was .283. He became a four-time All-Star. The Cubs desperately needed Beckert because he was the successor to Ken Hubbs, lost in the tragedy of that plane crash. "He's some kind of player," Durocher said of Beckert. "He's the best second baseman in the league."[15] The Cubs were fortunate to be able to say that so soon after losing Hubbs, a budding perennial All-Star.

Many years later, Beckert said he had stayed in touch with the core of that Cubs team—Jenkins, Williams, Banks and Holtzman—for decades.

Beckert and Don Kessinger made for a terrific double-play combination, though Kessinger somehow managed to hit even fewer home runs than his keystone partner. He hit just 14 during his 16 years in the big leagues. One might have thought Beckert and Kessinger were playing in the Deadball Era, spelling Johnny Evers and Joe Tinker. Kessinger grew up in Arkansas but was an All-American at the University of Mississippi in baseball and basketball. He said he was asked by several pro basketball teams whether he would play if they drafted him, but he told those clubs he was sticking with baseball. Leo Durocher turned him into a switch-hitter after he reached the majors.

"It was a great infield," Kessinger said of the group that solidified the diamond for the Cubs in the late 1960s. "The great thing was that we were able to play together for a long time, which doesn't happen in today's world so much. We were able to play together seven, eight, nine years. Oh, it was remarkable, playing with a group of guys who were all friends."[16]

For the longest time, it seemed just about everything about Ernie Banks exasperated Leo Durocher. Durocher always wanted to be the big man in town representing his team, and Banks' star eclipsed his in Chicago. Durocher had no patience for Banks' nice-guy, sunny outlook, and it seemed to drive him bonkers that the sportswriters loved Banks. He clearly wanted Banks out of the lineup, but every time he tried a new trick with a sub, Banks would emerge as the better player, and Durocher knew Banks would help him more on the field than any of the challengers. He was not so vindictive as to cost his team victories.

Durocher expounded on how everyone loved Banks. He wanted to see Banks in his rearview mirror. "His time wasn't my time," Durocher said. "Even more unfortunately, there was not a thing I could do about it. Ernie Banks owns Chicago. All the players on the Cubs said it themselves. Ernie Banks could come to bat and make a gesture telling everyone in the grandstand where they could go, and they'd rise up as a man and give him a standing ovation."[17]

Of course, Banks would never do such a thing, even under the threat of the death penalty. That was something Durocher might do, and he would bet the house he would not get a standing ovation. At one point, Durocher wanted Banks to tell the sportswriters to cease calling him Mr. Cub. Banks did not think it was his place to tell the writers what to write and said so. He was also smart enough to realize that this constant reminder in the newspapers did no harm to his standing. It was just a case of Durocher being petty.

Durocher would try to undermine Banks, and Banks would only say positive things about him. Things like "Leo can build a player's morale like no one else." Or "His one-word motto is WIN."[18]

By 1967, right-hander Ferguson Jenkins was the ace of the Cubs staff. The native of Chatham, Ontario, in Canada finished 20–13 with 20 complete games. He was a major reason why the Cubs were so far above .500. Jenkins was just beginning a career that resulted in 284 wins and a place in the Baseball Hall of Fame. He is widely considered the best Canadian player of all time.

If the Cubs were to grow beyond the accomplishment of 1967, they very much needed Jenkins to keep on winning big. Not to worry. He did so for a very long time, quite a bit of time with the Cubs, but not his entire career. However, that was the first of six straight 20-win seasons for Chicago. He was the foundation of the pitching staff.

Jenkins was not always fond of his big-league managers, but he put Durocher and his volatile personality in his own class. "When I was seven or eight years old, I got introduced to Christ through the Church, "he said. "When I was 14 years old I was baptized. And when I was 23, I finally met the devil. His name is Leo Durocher."[19]

OK, so not a compliment.

Jenkins liked Banks more than he liked Durocher and sometimes was a very interested observer as Durocher sought to run Banks off, if not from Chicago (Phil Wrigley would never trade him, proven when Durocher floated the suggestion of swapping Banks for Orlando Cepeda), than at least off the field on a regular basis. But repeatedly, Banks, merely by being his old self on the field, proved Durocher's judgment wrong. Ooh, how Durocher hated that. He always had to yield and play Banks.

Jenkins recalled each spring, Banks sidling up to him and commenting that Durocher had chosen someone else to be the starting first baseman, whether it was John Boccabella, Clarence Jones or Lee Thomas. By the end of the exhibition games, as Banks repeatedly pointed out, he had beaten out the flavor of the month and was still the Cubs' first baseman. "Leo was always giving Ernie Banks' job away. Ernie knew that Leo didn't like him," Jenkins said. "Shoot, Ernie would hit 25 home runs and Lee Thomas would be on the bench. Boccabella got traded to Montreal. One year Ernie had a bad leg and another year he had a bad hip, but he could still hit. He could flat-out hit."[20]

In 1967, Banks made the All-Star team for the first time since 1965. He hit 23 home runs and knocked in 95 runs that season while batting .276. He also received some Most Valuable Player votes for the first time since 1962.

It may be that after 1967, Durocher at least sort of resigned himself to the Ernie Banks phenomenon. He granted that Banks, a player he referred to as "grandpa," had delivered a very good season—despite his age—and said he wanted to find out what Ernie was taking to perform forever young. Durocher mentioned pharmaceuticals, but that was a joke at the time, long before baseball's steroids era.

16

Ready for a Breakthrough

Ernie Banks was not solely a perpetual optimist about the Chicago Cubs' chances in the National League, he also maintained the same outlook on his own life. It was a case of ... just ask him. Sportswriters often did so, and Banks responded in the same cheery tones as he did when mulling the Cubs' prospects for the season each spring training.

"A fellow should always be making strides, or at least think he is," Banks said. Something as minor as being asked by manager Leo Durocher to bring the team's daily lineup to the umpire at home plate made him feel good. "Makes you feel young—and feel that you're getting up in the world." For Banks, that was being classified as a player-coach, and this was the type of task a coach would perform in lieu of the manager. Banks being Banks, he spent a few extra minutes on site chatting with the New York Mets manager, Gil Hodges, whom he had played against. He told Hodges he was young enough to make a comeback since everyone was looking for .300 hitters. "I said, 'Just look young. It's not the age, it's how you look.'"[1]

Banks did look pretty young for his age, which at the beginning of the 1968 campaign was 37, a nearing-the-end number for most big-leaguers. Still, by using his famous name, Banks was building a little bit of security beyond his $55,000 salary from the Cubs. He not only had a regular, five-minute radio show, he was a key partner in a Chicago Ford dealership. He listed many ballplayers he sold cars to, including teammates Ron Santo, Ferguson Jenkins and Don Kessinger, plus opponents Art Shamsky of the Mets and future Hall of Fame pitcher Juan Marichal of the San Francisco Giants.

"It's wonderful," Banks said. "All my friends want to buy cars from us."[2]

That radio show, which featured interviews with teammates, was on the air five nights a week. This off-the-field stuff led one sportswriter to ask Banks if this was all a signal that he was contemplating retirement. Apparently, he looked surprised by the thought. "Quit? I'm not going to quit."[3]

Although that might have made Durocher's day, Banks was not thinking along those lines. The Cubs had just come off a notable winning season.

Banks had suffered through the bad times, and he wanted to live through the good times in "the Friendly Confines," whether it was one game at a time or by playing two.

If the Cubs were a symphony orchestra, the 1968 season would be considered a vamp-till-ready, continuing progress on the road to a possible pennant. The team was starting to take form, with most of the positions staffed by experienced players who could really play, and that included pitchers.

Ferguson Jenkins had emerged from the crowd in 1967, becoming a 20-game winner. If the Cubs were to improve and make a run at the NL pennant, he had to maintain that level. The Cubs were counting on him to be the ace once again, to be the leader of a mound group that included Ken Holtzman, Bill Hands and Joe Niekro. In the days of the four-man rotation, that looked like a solid group. The Cubs were still searching for bullpen help, and they found it when the Dodgers made Phil "The Vulture" Regan available. This was a major get for the Cubs.

Not that it would have mattered if Jenkins had been injured in a crazy situation in spring training of 1968. Jenkins said that when the 1967 season concluded and the Cubs were 13 games above .500, there was a pervasive sense of optimism on the team—not just Banks. The players sensed it was their time and they might be on the verge of doing something special.

"We had a feeling of, 'What's next?'" Jenkins said. "I told myself to go home, get some rest, and come back with the same type of confidence I had developed."[4] He did so, and when the team gathered in Mesa, Arizona, for spring training, the feeling was widespread. The players socialized together away from the park, and that was almost Jenkins' undoing. "Actually, I was quite lucky I got to pitch at all during the 1968 season," Jenkins said. "I had a horse riding accident that could have ruined the rest of my career."[5]

Ron Santo, Jenkins and some other players set out for a day of relaxation combining golf and a horseback ride. Joe Niekro and Rich Nye were also along, but fell behind on the trail. When Jenkins turned to look for them, his horse went nuts. Ignoring all of Jenkins' commands, the horse went into top gear and began galloping back towards the ranch. Jenkins tried to put on the brakes, to no avail. "She never stopped until she ran into Nye and his horse," Jenkins said. "I was not riding this horse. This horse was riding me." Speeding towards the stable, the horse was immune to Jenkins entreaties, and when it finally decided to stop running, it heaved Jenkins into a fence. He bounced off it and hit the ground.[6]

Riders have been killed in such accidents. Jenkins was battered. His face was bruised, one leg was bleeding from a major cut, and his right (pitching) arm was cut. The other players took Jenkins to a hospital. When Jenkins informed Durocher what happened, Durocher swore up and down for what seemed like hundreds of words. It might only be imagined how Durocher

16. Ready for a Breakthrough

would have reacted if Jenkins had been out for the season. Even always-unruffled Ernie Banks might have scowled over that. Jenkins did recover in due time and won 20 games again while starting a league-leading 40 times.

Acquiring Regan was a coup. He was the right guy at the right time for the bullpen. Regan was 31 in 1968 and had several very good years with the Dodgers on his resume, including a 14–1 summer of 1966 that included finishing a league-high 48 games accompanied by a league-high 21 saves. The closer routine as fans know it now was a far different role. If there were three-out saves, they occurred by accident rather than design. Relievers pitched several innings at a time. In 1968, Regan was 2–0 for the Dodgers when the Cubs traded Ted Savage and Jim Ellis for him and outfielder Jim Hickman, very much a slam-dunk success for Chicago. Hickman made little impact that season, but in the coming years he hit very well for the Cubs.

Regan fit in fast. Including his two wins with LA, the 6-foot-3, 200-pounder finished 12–5, and his unofficial 25 saves led the National League. By finishing 62 games, he led the NL in that category, too. His earned run average for the Cubs was 2.27. He won the "Fireman of the Year" Award.

However, Regan got in the middle of a contretemps with plate umpire Chris Pelekoudas on August 18. In a game against the Cincinnati Reds, the ump began signaling illegal pitches on Regan, three times slapping ball calls on pitches because he was suspicious of the right-hander. Twice, those gave Alex Johnson an extra chance in the box when he would have otherwise made outs. Fans—and there quite a few of them with attendance announced at more than 39,000—were furious. They booed and threw things on the field. Cubs were equally outraged, with Durocher, catcher Randy Hundley and outfielder Al Spangler all tossed from the game during arguments. When Regan was searched for "foreign substances," Pelekoudas said, "I could feel Vaseline on the inner lining of Regan's cap."[7] But that was a statement made later after Pelekoudas initially said he made the calls just because the ball swerved so dramatically. Regan denied any use of a substance to doctor the ball. Later still, a Reds player, George Culver, said he found a Vaseline tube and two slippery elm cubes near the plate. But he didn't tell Pelekoudas. This was pretty much a textbook example of a baseball brouhaha.

In early September, Regan proposed his own solution for how umpires could determine if a pitcher was fooling with the ball. If the ump suspected something, Regan said, he should yell, "OK, stop right there. Don't move!" And then the ump should march out to the mound while the pitcher was frozen in place and look at the ball before it was thrown. "I wish the umpires would do that," Regan said. "It would be fine with me."[8]

Despite this little episode, Regan was a huge plus for the Cubs. More pitching is what the team believed would lead the Cubs to the National League pennant after the significant improvement in 1967. Management thought the team must only be a couple of players away from merely topping .500 to becoming the best in the league.

By 1968, Banks, the institution of the club, had notched some serious milestones. In 1966, he collected his 2,000th big-league hit. In 1967, he surpassed Stan Hack for the second-most hits in franchise history when he hit safely for number 2,194. Adrian "Cap" Anson, a pre-1900 Hall of Famer, was still ranked first with 3,081 hits for the Cubs, essentially a mile away.

Banks was not preoccupied with his own statistics, though. He was enjoying playing for a team that won more games than it lost. Now when he uttered his little poems about the Cubs' glorious future, no one ridiculed them. Anything could happen, it seemed. Banks was no longer the only player or official at Wrigley Field with optimism. Yet the reality did not match the atmospheric conditions during the early part of the season. The Cubs were slow out of the gate, going 8–10 in April. Shades of the bad old days. It was not until May 21, when Chicago beat the Philadelphia Phillies, 6–5, to reach 20–19, that the club moved over .500. The Cubs were in fourth place at the end of the day, but no one was running away with the NL, so they were only 2½ games out of first. Banks went 1-for-4 that day and was hitting .250.

Off the field, 1968 was a terrible year for the country. The United States was in disarray. The Vietnam War was in full swing. Civil rights leader Martin Luther King, Jr., was assassinated in Memphis, Tennessee, on the balcony of his motel on April 4, 1968. This was a week prior to Opening Day. Riots followed in many cities. African Americans, disenfranchised and mistreated for generations, denied basic rights and equal opportunity, received little protection from their government or police authorities. Dr. King was the spokesman for the masses, the leader who preached peace between races and in Vietnam. His loss was a terrible waste and was felt keenly by both blacks and all right-thinking Americans.

Bob Gibson, the star hurler for the St. Louis Cardinals, was an outspoken, proud African American who was nearly crushed by Martin Luther King's murder. In the greatest modern-era pitching season, he owned 1968 like few others owned a season.

"I reeled from the impact of the assassination," Gibson said, "the cold-blooded murder of the one man in my lifetime who had been able to capture the public's attention about racial injustice, break through some of the age-old social barriers and raise the spirits and hopes of black people across the country."[9]

The soothing and inspirational words of King's speeches still resonate, from his "I Have a Dream" speech to others demanding equality. Until then, Banks' dream was to win a pennant and a World Series with the Chicago Cubs. By comparison, while a laudable aim, that seemed small after the worst of the worst kept happening.

16. Ready for a Breakthrough

Gibson conquered his emotions to pitch a spring training game on April 5. President Lyndon Baines Johnson declared a day of national mourning for King on April 7, and no exhibition games were played that day. King's funeral was conducted April 9, and Major League Baseball postponed the start of the season to April 10. Gibson was St. Louis' Opening Day starter. His earned run average of 1.12 that season was one of the most spectacular season-long feats ever by a pitcher.

Johnson's administration was shaken by the Vietnam War, and the incumbent announced that he would not seek re-election as president that fall. U.S. Senator Robert F. Kennedy jumped into the primaries as a war opponent. On June 5, just two months after Martin Luther King was assassinated, so was Kennedy, in the kitchen of a Los Angeles hotel.

Later that summer, the Democratic National Convention was conducted in Chicago at the International Amphitheatre. As Vice-President Hubert Humphrey of Minnesota accepted the ticket's nomination for president inside, outside police beat demonstrators and tear gas spoiled the air. Most considered the brutal happenings to be a police riot. There was massive tension on the streets of the country, cities roiling, black versus white standoffs. Rarely has the country been as divided as it was in the summer of 1968.

Cubs southpaw Ken Holtzman was a member of the National Guard, and his unit was called up in May to help quell unrest in the streets. He traded one uniform for another and was serving in the Guard only a short distance across town from the ballpark where he made his living. In mid–August, players for the Astros, arriving for a series against the Cubs, had to make their way past barricades to reach their Conrad Hilton Hotel while demonstrators threw stink bombs and the police fired off tear gas.

Larry Dierker was eloquent about the scene the Astros walked into. Dierker, who won 139 games in the majors and also worked as a broadcaster and a manager, was a month shy of his 22nd birthday when the incident occurred. "I was in the same age group as the people who were upset about the war," Dierker said. "I didn't feel a great kinship with the ones protesting. But once you see something like that, you don't forget it so easily. Looking back on it, that night changed me."[10]

In Chicago, not through any bold speeches, but through his personality and just being the Ernie Banks everyone knew, some credited Banks with soothing the populace as a voice of peace and reason. Long-time *Chicago Tribune* columnist John Kass was one of those who felt Banks made a unique difference, perhaps as a bridge between understanding and hatred. Calling Chicago "an angry fist" at that time, Kass wrote of Banks, "Kids needed a smile, but we didn't see a smile anywhere. Instead, there were raised voices and raised hands, and killing and looting and burning and protests. And there was also great anger in absolute silence, adults packing up the car and driving away, while their kids in the back seats looked back at their neighborhoods for the last time."[11]

It was one awful thing after another that year, some of it Chicago-centric. "There were the King riots after the assassination of Martin Luther King, Jr. in 1968, blood in our streets, and Mayor Richard J. Daley famously ordering the police to shoot to kill arsonists," Kass wrote. "And then came the Democratic National Convention and the police clubs in the air and the Yippies and the Days of Rage and old man Daley babbling and becoming an angry cartoon."[12]

Did Banks utter the Gettysburg Address? Hardly. Again, Ernie Banks' name was a simile for a smile. He was a calming man who never displayed vigorous anger. Maybe for that year, he was the only one in the entire city who behaved that way. "There was always something of a gentleman in him, a decency in his manner," Kass concluded. "He was reassuring, not like some cocky sports hero, but more like a teacher. It was that kindness that kids could see, a concern, and we could hear it in his voice. There was a steadiness to it. And we've never forgotten it."[13]

After Kennedy was killed, President Johnson declared a national day of mourning, and the scheduled game between the Cubs and the Atlanta Braves was postponed. The teams played a doubleheader, Ernie's two, the next day. For all of June, the Cubs were stuck in the mud, unable to take any long steps to free themselves, and they remained around .500, not at all the winning club of 1967. Only on that last day of July, when the Cubs defeated Houston, 6–1, with Jenkins collecting his 12th win with a three-hitter, did Chicago rise two games above .500.

Due to the surprisingly slow start for a heralded club, attendance at Wrigley Field was far from impressive by mid-summer. There were numerous games where attendance did not crack 9,000. A long-time Cubs fan might well not let go of his emotions too soon. Disappointed too often, Wrigley Field, like Missouri, was a show-me place.

Virtually out of nowhere there was a dramatic day on July 28 when it seemed as if the whole city fell in love with the Cubs all over again. Chicago played a doubleheader against the Los Angeles Dodgers and drew 42,261 fans, a standing-room-only crowd. Owner Phil Wrigley, who was not in the building but at his summer home in Wisconsin viewing on television, proclaimed the event a trifecta of victory, a "three-way perfect day for the Cubs. The weather was perfect, so were the games, as well as the attendance."[14]

That was the biggest crowd at Wrigley Field since 1948. Joe Niekro won the first game, 8–3. Ken Holtzman won the second game, 1–0, allowing four hits and striking out ten. That game was over in 2 hours, 18 minutes, prompting Banks to say it was "a great day to play three." Wrigley laughed when Banks' comment was relayed to him. "Ernie would. He's a great guy. I think

16. Ready for a Breakthrough

Ernie is revered as Mr. Cub in the same manner George Halas is as Papa Bear with Chicago sports fans."[15] Given Halas' reputation for gruffness, the stretch was probably a poor comparison other than the overarching belief in the two men fans possessed.

Holtzman was only able to pitch because after a few months away, the National Guard gave him weekend passes. He either drove to Wrigley Field to suit up or flew across the country to join the Cubs wherever they were scheduled to play. Holtzman actually missed more time in 1967 when he posted that superior 9–0 mark, but his involvement with the Guard was more noticeable in 1968 because of the violence permeating Chicago. Holtzman finished 11–14 that season, and it is easy to believe that his military time contributed to the losing record.

August was much kinder to the team. Abruptly, the Cubs began to win. Carrying over two victories from July, the Cubs won six games in a row. A week later, they won another four straight and were nine games over .500 in second place. They did not sustain the pace through the end of the month, but you would not have known that if Banks was your only source of information.

"Let's see," Banks said, "what's our magic number?" Since the Cubs were about 14 games out of first place with the St. Louis Cardinals in control, it would have taken big magic to make a serious run. "We need some help from the Braves. They've only beaten the Cards three times in 15 games. If they'd come to life in their next series.... We've got spirit—the real rah-rah spirit on this club. We're not too far out."[16]

Well, actually the Cubs were too far out and never did mount a true charge. They were OK in September and finished six games above .500, though that was after winning their last five games in a row, including Jenkins' 20th on the next-to-last day of the season. It was nice to be in the black, but it wasn't satisfying.

Of all things, those reliable hitters faltered somewhat. Banks ended up playing in 150 games. Try as he might, Leo Durocher could not keep him out of the lineup. He slugged 32 home runs and drove in 83 runs. But his batting average was only .246, Banks' lowest since his bad year of 1963. On July 17 versus the Phillies, Banks clubbed two home runs and a single to gather six runs batted in.

Billy Williams smacked 30 home runs and drove in 98 runs. He drove in nine runs in one day in a doubleheader sweep of the Braves, seven in the first game. Ron Santo belted 26 home runs, also knocked in 98 runs, and walked 96 times. Yet he also batted only .246.

Except for those averages, none of the big three could be faulted. But there was no power behind them. Outfielder Adolfo Phillips was the only other player in double figures in home runs with 13. Overall, the pitching staff permitted just 611 runs, but the hitters scored just 612 runs. Those are numbers that portend a .500 finish.

After the Cubs underachieved in 1968, Durocher wanted to make changes. The Cubs attended the winter meetings open-minded about making deals. They came home without any substantive alterations to the roster.

> We talked and we listened, and now I'll tell you why we didn't deal. I know it's the oldest game in the book, trying to swap a slice of bread for an entire loaf with a pound of sausage tossed in for good measure. I'll go along with that until they try to insult my intelligence by seeking to pawn off a lot of humpty-dumpties. That is what we were offered in exchange for some of my players. We've battled and scratched to become respectable during the last two years, and just like that, they ask for this player or that. Some of you guys would have ridden me out of town on your typewriters had I made just one of the silly deals I was offered. I know what my guys can do.[17]

Of all things, Durocher counseled patience for this team. Even if it went against his nature to stand pat, the next year he was proven right. Riding with the core of the lineup turned out to be the thing to do.

17

1969

Ernie Banks' slogan for the 1969 season was "The Cubs are gonna shine in '69." They did, not as brightly as he might have hoped, but memorably, in a feel-good season in the end characterized by "almost." Still, by Cubs standards, it was the most exciting season in a quarter-century, or since the 1945 team won the National League pennant.

The Cubs did shine, even if they did not win it all. The performance also made the team look smart for not pulling the trigger on the trade possibilities manager Leo Durocher had disdained.

At one point in mid–August, the Cubs led the National League by 8½ games. There was delirium at Wrigley Field, the sense of anticipation whetted by such a long wait. In the end, the Cubs won 92 games, unheard-of territory for a long time, but could not hold on to capture the pennant. Yet this season was one of the all-time rides in franchise history, and it was well-remembered, if not completely fondly remembered.

Banks was 38 years old during the 1969 season, at least three years into the stretch where Durocher had considered him to be washed-up. Durocher kept seeking out younger players to be the first baseman of the future, and each spring Banks beat them out by out-playing them. Such was the case in 1969, and Banks was in the lineup for 155 games that season.

Except for Durocher's preconceived notions and prejudice, Banks didn't give Durocher reasons to sit him. He didn't argue with Durocher. He didn't sneer at Durocher. He didn't go around telling sportswriters how stupid Durocher was for wanting him on the bench. Banks performed at a level where any baseball man could see he was the best candidate for the job.

Years later, Banks did admit he had a personal strategy for dealing with Durocher and people like him. It was almost too Ernie to be believed, too saintly for anyone crossed or done wrong. Yet he followed through.

> When somebody resented me, didn't like me—and that was the case with Leo—I kind of killed them with kindness. On the bench, I'd always sit beside him, on the

plane sit beside him, in the dugout sit beside him. He's always looking around seeing me. When you light a fire under my heels, it just made me better. I focused more, concentrated more, reached inside of me, and got more out of myself. Overall, he made me a better player toward the end of my career.[1]

Had that been Durocher's intent, he would have been lauded as a genius of a motivator. But it was a byproduct of his treatment of Banks, not part of his grand plan. He never would have understood that Banks was smarter than the great Durocher, the great baseball strategist. It did pay dividends for both of them, though. Banks indeed did seem to come back from the brink of the terminus of his career several times in the late 1960s.

The 1969 season was both special and unfulfilling at the same time, a special season because it involved winning quite a bit, something not associated with the Cubs of that decade. "It was the most happiness any of us had ever enjoyed in our lives," said Banks, although he may have been speaking more about himself than some of the others who became winners elsewhere. "I feel more identified with the '69 team than any of the others, even though my career was almost ended. Winning constitutes love and togetherness that lasts forever."[2]

Opening Day was April 8, and the Cubs met the Philadelphia Phillies at Wrigley Field. Attendance was 40,796. Either the pre-season hype took hold early, or fans missed the ivy on the walls over the winter. The Phillies scored a run in the first inning off Ferguson Jenkins, but the Cubs retaliated quickly with three runs. Banks hit a home run with Glenn Beckert and Ron Santo aboard. Banks hit another two-run homer in the third inning with Billy Williams on base.

Yet after the Phillies scored three runs in the ninth inning, the score was 5–5, and the game went into extra innings. Philadelphia took a 6–5 lead in the top of the 11th, and fans became morose. The thought of the same old Cubs teasing, and then disappointing, had to cross many minds. But that's not the way it played out. Banks had a chance in the bottom of the 11th but flied out. Catcher Randy Hundley singled, bringing outfielder Willie Smith to the plate.

Smith had a nine-year career. He joined the Cubs in 1968 and was a relief pitcher and pinch-hitter. He was pinch-hitting this time and swatted a two-run homer to win the game. And the fans went crazy. Someone had already counted nine standing ovations for Banks alone in this game, but this time the emotion was a mix of joy and relief, making quite a statement for a 1–0 team.

Smith brought a special flavor to his big hits, but especially to Cubs wins. "I'll always remember Willie Smith singing with that deep voice of his," Banks said. "'I've got that lovely feeling … it's gone, gone, gone.' Every time we'd win he'd sing like that."[3] And it began that day, Smith's musical accompaniment to victories.

There was extra emotion on display from the players, too, after just one game. But something about the atmosphere, the result and the way they won it, provided electricity. Smith was mobbed at home plate, almost hugged to death, and the players were slow to leave the clubhouse, slow to split up. They actually listened to a rebroadcast of game highlights together.

"We knew right there that this was the season we were going to win it," said third baseman Ron Santo, who was almost as steadily optimistic about Cubs fortunes as Banks.[4]

It's difficult to think of a first game as a turning point in a season, but this was one of them, it seemed. After the celebratory start, the Cubs went on a huge run. They tore apart April, starting 11–1 and ending the month at 16–7, in first place every day of the month. They didn't slow down there, either.

There were several highlights in April. Attendance was strong, and that was significant. The Cubs were on their way to drawing 1,674,993 fans, a tremendous increase from their recent years when they attracted hundreds of thousands fewer than a million. The fans caught the spirit early in 1969.

On April 9, the Cubs beat the Phillies, 11–3, and Williams smashed four doubles. Banks' personality, history and accomplishments loomed large over the Cubs, but Williams was also on his way to a Hall of Fame career. The 1961 NL "Rookie of the Year," Williams hit 426 home runs in his career while batting .290. For several seasons in the 1960s, he never sat out a game. In 1969, he cracked 33 homers with 95 runs batted in. Six times he was selected for the All-Star team. His nickname was "Sweet Swinging Billy Williams" because his stroke was so smooth.

On April 25, the Cubs made a significant trade. They parted with Joe Niekro (a long-term mistake), a 14-game-winner in 1968 who remained in the majors through 1988, or for 22 years, Gary Ross and Francisco Libran in a trade to the San Diego Padres, obtaining Dick Selma. The Cubs also picked up reliever Don Nottebart from Cincinnati. Selma moved into the starting rotation and went 10–8 with a 3.63 earned run average, not quite as good as Niekro had been. The Cubs already had the terrific Phil Regan in the bullpen, as well as Hank Aguirre and Ted Abernathy, whom they reacquired after three years away. Aguirre, a former Detroit Tigers starter who may have been the worst-hitting pitcher in baseball history, was nearing the end of his career at 38. His only decision that season was a win, but he made 41 appearances in relief with a 2.60 ERA. Abernathy was 36, and Regan, who went 12–6 with 17 saves that year, was 32. "They used to call the Supreme Court the nine old men," Aguirre said. "Well, just call us the three old men and I won't be offended as long as we finish as well as we started."[5]

The Cubs dealt Jim Armstrong, an infielder who never made the majors, for Nottebart, who was 33, so he fit right in with the senior citizens bullpen.

"At a time when pitching is the name of the game, I'll take the experienced pitcher every time and worry about a young infielder later," Durocher said.[6]

May was no different. The Cubs spent every day of that month in first place as well. The league took notice, the players became more enthusiastic, and management seemed all-in to win now. After Memorial Day, the Cubs were gliding along at 32–16 with a 7½-game lead in the standings. May 11–13, the Cubs won three straight shutouts behind Ken Holtzman, Jenkins and Selma. The third victory was 19–0 over the Padres. Strangely, only 5,080 people came out after 3,887 paid to see Jenkins' shutout. They missed quite the Ernie Banks show. Banks had three hits, two of them homers, scored two runs and drove in seven. That was vintage, youthful Banks reincarnated.

Three days later, the Cubs posted a ten-run inning and Holtzman threw another shutout, this time against Houston. In his next start, Holtzman shut out the Dodgers, 7–0. Holtzman was just 23 that year, still closer to the start than the finish of his career, and won 17 games.

Holtzman went on to greater glory with other teams, appearing in four World Series, but he always categorized the 1969 Cubs experience as something special, too. "And I must admit, from start to finish, that season had more excitement than did any of my seasons in Oakland or New York. Nothing compares with being in the World Series, but for a single season 1969 was something."[7]

After reaching 20 games over .500 at 36–16 on June 6, the Cubs cooled off a bit over the rest of the month. They were still sitting at 50–27 by June 30, and still led the National League by 7½ games. On June 19, Durocher got married for the fourth time, to Lynne Walker Goldblatt, at a Chicago hotel. This should have been a happy occasion, but the always grumpy Durocher did not invite all of the Cubs personnel he might have.

One story goes that with his wife along on a team bus ride, he told her he would love to have a pitcher like Bob Gibson on the Cubs. Well, who wouldn't, since he was a future Hall of Famer who had the greatest season of his career the year before? Mrs. Durocher joked, "I suppose you'd even trade me for him, wouldn't you?" Durocher replied, "No, not unless they threw in a center fielder, too."[8]

Holtzman was one of the players who could have attended the wedding, but chose not to, and anyone close enough to him understood why. Durocher had been portrayed as a civil rights paragon, sticking up for Jackie Robinson with the Dodgers in 1947 and gently soothing Willie Mays with the Giants later when he needed confidence-building. With Holtzman, the lack of sensitivity was appalling. "Hey, Jew," Durocher would yell to him. Or, "C'mon kike!" This was Durocher trying to be funny. It wasn't. It was offensive. He also called Santo "Wop" and Kessinger, who was from Arkansas, "Hillbilly."[9]

17. 1969

The 1969 Chicago Cubs, the best team Banks played on during his 19 years with the club and the one many believe should have won the National League pennant (National Baseball Hall of Fame).

Holtzman couldn't stand Durocher. He later asked owner Phil Wrigley for a trade and was accommodated, being sent to the Oakland Athletics when they were about to become the dominant team in baseball.

On June 26, the Cubs beat the Pittsburgh Pirates, 7–5. This was the kind of win a team could revel in as a good omen. Three times the Pirates built leads in the game, and the Cubs kept coming back. The game went into extra innings, and Jim Hickman hit a game-winning home run.

As he was running off the field, Santo made a gesture that became a totem of the season. He suddenly jumped in the air and clicked his heels together like a Fred Astaire dance move. Cubs fans roared, and although it had been a spur-of-the-moment reaction, Santo kept up the maneuver every time the Cubs won. It became his signature celebration. "I'm working on a double click for the World Series," he said.[10] Players on other teams hated it, but the Cubs' and Santo's attitude was pretty much "Tough luck. Deal with it."

For all the success, this seemed to be a disgruntled first-place team, one that could come apart at the seams if challenged. It was too soon to read that writing on the wall, but Durocher, who was doing his best to motivate the team, was so rough around the edges that sometimes his moves and temper became self-defeating.

One of the bitterest incidents occurred early in July, and Durocher alone was not to blame. Santo, one of the most passionate of players, a Cubs true believer regarded as a great teammate, had perhaps the worst moment of his career when he might have helped a young player. The Mets were beginning to make a run. During a July 8 game, with Jenkins carrying a one-hitter into the ninth inning, New York rallied to win, 4–3. The focal point of the defeat stemmed from an unlikely occurrence.

Don Young, just 23, was playing center field. Four years earlier, he had appeared in 11 games for the Cubs. He finally made the big club again in 1969 and got into 101 games that season. Twice in the ninth inning, he blew coverage of fly balls. Big-league outfielders don't normally make mistakes like that, but sometimes the unexpected takes place. This was an ill-timed defeat for the Cubs, whose lead in the standings dropped to 4½ games. What followed the game, however, forever imbedded the misplays into Cubs lore—unnecessarily. Instead of comforting the young player, even offering a platitude such as "We'll get them next time, boy," Durocher tore him to shreds.

"Two little fly balls," yelled Durocher as he threw a tantrum. "He watches one and let's the other one drop." Yes, Durocher threw the player under the bus. Santo compounded the rip job by saying, "Young was thinking of himself. He got his head down worrying about his batting average and not about winning the game. All right, he can keep his head down and he can keep going right out of sight for all I care. We don't need that sort of thing."[11] This lack of charity was uncharacteristic of Santo, who promptly realized his mistake and apologized the next day. But the words cut and stuck. Young was not only exiled from the Cubs in 1969, he never played another Major League game. His career had been destroyed.

However, when Santo penned an autobiography in 1993, he had a much different, more detailed and dramatic take on the entire Young matter. As team captain, Santo said he was asked by Durocher early in the season to take Young under his wing and offer encouragement because he had a tendency to get down on himself and to become moody. Santo said he gave Young pep talks. During the game in question, Santo said, Young did appear to be more concerned with his batting slump than what was happening on the field. He spoke to him during the game, Santo said, when Jim Hickman, another outfielder told him Young was mooning about his hitting. Santo said he talked to Young behind the scenes.

In the ninth inning, Santo reported, on more than one occasion when Jenkins, the pitcher, tried to wave Young over in his positioning for the hitters, he did not respond. Santo said he took over the task, but Young did not move where told to go, and the debacle followed. After the game, Santo said, he talked with some sportswriters but never blamed Young for the loss. He denied the incendiary nature of the quote that stuck and said he pretty much protected Young with his comment, "It's like anybody as a rookie. Sometimes you put your head between your legs. I've done it as a player. Those things happen." Santo said he did not give the impression that he believed Young cost the team the game. "To this day, I swear that is all I said."[12]

Such harsh assessment of a teammate did not sound like Santo, but his protestations aside, it did not seem that's how things went down. Clearly something must have been lost in translation. The next morning, newspapers had screaming headlines indicating that he had torched Young. Soon after, Santo was booed by fans at Wrigley, something that had never happened. He began getting death threats to him and his family, although he said they did not state that they were directly connected to the Young incident. It was a sloppy, frustrating loss that was magnified for a team that was still in first place, still had a solid lead on its top challenger.

The day after the Young matter flowered, the Mets' Tom Seaver was on his way to a perfect game against the Cubs when he set down the first 25 men in order. He ended up tossing a one-hitter, but the Mets did win again.

Obviously, there were some tensions in the Cubs clubhouse, but at the end of July Chicago's record was 65–41, and the Cubs still led the NL standings by 6½ games. They had been in first place every single day of the season, so there was no doubt the Cubs were playing good ball. In recognition of that, the entire Cubs infield was chosen for the National League All-Star team. That included Ernie Banks at first, Glenn Beckert at second, Don Kessinger at short, and Ron Santo at third, plus catcher Randy Hundley. That was quite the achievement.

The All-Star Game was played on July 23 in Washington, D.C., at Robert F. Kennedy Memorial Stadium, the home of the Washington Senators, and the National League won, 9–3. None of the Cubs who played had a hit. Hundley did not get into the game. That was his only All-Star Game selection. It was also Banks' last. He went 0-for-1 as a pinch-hitter.

The craziness that could surround Durocher was evident a few days after the All-Star Game. During a 3-2, 11-inning win over the Dodgers at Wrigley Field, Durocher told players and coaches he felt sick to his stomach and left the park in mid-game. He was actually pretending to be sick and skipped out on the team to accompany his new wife on a visit to her 12-year-old son Joel at summer camp, going to Eagle River, Wisconsin, by chartered plane from Meigs Field. Durocher was attempting to make this sojourn under radar, but when the plane landed, he was greeted by a banner reading, "Welcome Leo Durocher." So much for secrecy.

It was not as if the couple slipped into town unnoticed. Gossip columns on society pages wrote of their presence in the popular fishing mecca, too. It so happened that a friend of sportswriter Jim Enright had a son at the camp, as well, and witnessed the whole thing. He let Enright know, and when he wrote about it, this set off a huge controversy in Chicago. Phil Wrigley was so irate at Durocher for abandoning the club for two days during the pennant race that he nearly fired him. Wrigley was actually in Wisconsin, too, although in Lake Geneva, much closer to Chicago than Durocher. "I was told Leo was sick," Wrigley said. "I had no idea he wasn't confined to his home. I feel he owes an apology to management, players and fans. You can't run a ship without a rudder."[13]

It was somewhat amazing that Durocher got away with this escapade, but Wrigley likely tamped down his fuse with the thought that the Cubs were in first place under this man's guidance. Wrigley said he would just have to forgive Durocher this one time. As for Durocher, he was less contrite than angry at Enright for reporting the story. To compound the embarrassment, when he tried to fly back to Chicago and the team the next day, his plane was grounded because of bad weather, an additional delay.

While Banks may have born the brunt of Durocher's personality in recent years, it was becoming clearer that other players were also building grudges against him. This incident was an act of arrogance directed to the whole team, but Kessinger was another player who disliked Durocher. He avoided the wedding at the Ambassador Hotel because he didn't want to party with him.

Kessinger was liked by everyone on the team. Shortstops did not tend to be muscle-bound, but he was directed to beef up. He stood 6-foot-1 and eventually weighed 170 pounds, but not before eating his way through the off-season between 1968 and 1969.

"I'm eating a lot," he said. "I always was a good eater, but not one to gain weight. But I'm working on it. It seems that every night I'm always saying, 'Pass the potatoes,' or 'I'll take another couple of slices of bread.'"[14] Kessinger's hitting had fallen off in September of 1968, and the thinking was that if he was stronger, that would not happen again.

Kessinger had his best season in 1969. He batted .273 with 181 hits, scored 109 runs and drove in 53 while stealing 11 bases. Yet the bulking up aspect of his effort did not take. He did fall into a hitting tailspin in September. That just mirrored what was happening around him. As August turned to September, the Cubs were still in first place, 31 games over .500 with an 83–52 mark. They had resided in first place from day one in April, and when Holtzman beat the Braves on August 31, they held a 4½-game lead.

The highlight of August belonged to Holtzman, as well, and it wasn't that victory. On August 19, he pitched a no-hitter to defeat the Atlanta Braves, 3–0, at Wrigley Field. The game took just two hours flat to complete, and Holtzman faced the minimum of 27 batters, though he walked three. It was 76 degrees and sunny, and Santo drove in all three runs with a homer off future Hall of Famer Phil Niekro in the bottom of the first inning. Kessinger and Beckert scored ahead of him. Banks went 0-for-3 that day as the Cubs had only five hits.

Holtzman did not strike out a single Braves player. The closest Atlanta came to disrupting the no-hitter was a Henry Aaron shot to right field caught by Billy Williams with the wind blowing in at about 16 mph, a breeze that helped keep the ball confined inside the Friendly Confines. "The wind was blowing in and cost Henry Aaron a home run in the seventh," Holtzman admitted. "He also made the last out on a grounder to Beckert. I knew I had a no-hitter every inning after the third because the fans, who sit very close to the field, kept reminding me after each inning."[15]

When the Cubs came unglued, they fell hard and fast, almost unbelievably so. The glory times evaporated as swiftly as an ice cube left out on a 90-degree day. On September 2, when Jenkins won his 19th of the 21 he would win that season, the Cubs remained in first place, five games ahead of the Mets. They then lost eight straight games and for the first time, when they woke up on September 11, they were in second place, one game arrears of the Mets. The Cubs were in the midst of going 9–17 in September. The unkind word "choking" was applied by some.

The Mets. New York was going wild for the Mets. At the beginning of the decade, there was no National League club in New York. The Giants and Dodgers had fled to the West Coast, taking advantage of the ripe and growing California market. Stung, New York officials agitated for an expansion franchise, and the Mets came into existence for the 1962 season. For publicity reasons and to trade on his good will, the organization hired Casey Stengel to manage the team. Stengel had led the Yankees to ten pennants in 12 years between 1949 and 1960, but was fired after the 1960 season when his club lost to the Pittsburgh Pirates in the seventh game of the World Series.

The only connection between the two New York teams in the early going was the words "New York." The Yankees kept winning for a while. The Mets were the worst team in modern baseball history, debuting with a 40–120 mark. It took years to transform the lowly team, but by 1969, with an infusion of terrific young pitching, Mets management had done so. Those who dismissed the Mets as losers had an outdated perspective.

The Mets were no slugging team. It was the pitching that enabled them to win 100 games. Future Hall of Famer Tom Seaver went 25–7. Jerry Koosman was 17–9, Gary Gentry 13–12. A rookie named Nolan Ryan broke in and went 6–3 early in his own Hall of Fame career. Energetic reliever Tug McGraw was 9–3 with 12 saves.

One of the symbols of the Cubs' decline in September was the strange occasion on September 9 when the team was playing the Mets at Shea Stadium. It was Seaver against Jenkins, but it wasn't very close, a 7–1 loss for the Cubs. But the unique thing was the appearance of a black cat while Billy Williams was in the batter's box and Ron Santo was in the on-deck circle. As Santo took his warm-up swings, a black cat trotted across the field and right past him, the obvious signal of bad luck to the superstitious, and adding this sighting to the Curse of the Billy Goat provided the feeling the Cubs were doomed. There was a brief delay and the cat vanished.

"I was studying Billy Williams at the plate, when all of a sudden, a black cat jumped out of the third-base stands!" Santo said. "He ran in front of me, stopped to stare, and headed towards our dugout, where he glared at Leo, who was stooped on the front step of the dugout. Then he headed back into the stands. I don't like to walk under ladders. I throw salt over my shoulder and don't light three cigarettes on one match. I especially don't like black cats in my path."[16]

One of the unexpected heroes of the season as the Cubs sought to hang on was right-handed pitcher Bill Hands. He had come on a bit in 1968 with 16 wins, but in 1969 Hands won 20 games, the best season of his big-league career. He started 41 games, pitched 300 innings and compiled a 2.49 earned run average. He deserved all the kudos he received that season. "I was a low-ball pitcher and that helped me because the team's owner [Phil Wrigley] kept the infield grass high, which made it difficult to get ground balls through the infield. The other thing was when the wind was blowing out I was careful to keep the ball down so the hitters couldn't get the ball up into the wind."[17]

Years after the Mets passed the Cubs like a sports car passing a semi-truck, Hands was philosophical about that disappointing September. The

17. 1969

Banks was such a star with his 512 career home runs and his two Most Valuable Player Awards he often doffed his cap in response to Wrigley Field applause (National Baseball Hall of Fame).

Mets finished eight games ahead of the Cubs and won the World Series. They were referred to as "The Miracle Mets." "Basically, we just couldn't win at the end of the year and they couldn't lose," Hands said. "They just couldn't do anything wrong."[18]

There was sharp criticism of Durocher, from sportswriters, fans and players. Unlike the other teams in baseball, the Cubs still played all of their home games during the day. It was a hot and muggy summer, and many believed failure to deploy substitutes and rest regulars was costly. "I'm still convinced that playing all day games and not utilizing all 25 guys was a big Cub disadvantage against the rest of the league," Holtzman said years later.[19]

Don Kessinger wasn't as quick to blame Durocher. "Sure, it's easy to say now we should have been rested," he also said years later. "But if he had come to me in August and asked, 'Do you want a day off?' I would have said no. If he had come in July, I would have said no. I was playing great and felt good. I don't think any of us had a clue what might happen."[20]

Banks hit 23 home runs that season and drove in 106 runs. He was no drain on the offense. It was a remarkable season for someone of his age, playing in 155 games. This was the best Cubs team Banks ever played on, and he enjoyed the whole summer, right up until the time the squad faded and the Mets burst past.

Over and over again, Banks fooled Durocher, as he put it, killing him with kindness, even after Durocher referred to him as a rally killer or said he made a dumb play. Banks simply played on and hit on. During the 1969 season, Durocher, seemingly a believer at last, praised Banks. "I've retired him the last three years," he said. "I put all kinds on first base and they all fell by the wayside, and there's Ernie Banks. I wish I knew the pharmaceutical place he goes to [there's that reference about a magic pill]. I want to find it. He's 38 and young."[21]

Their personalities were direct opposites. Durocher even advertised his real self his first season in Chicago. "I'm not coming here to win popularity contests," Durocher said. "And I'm not a nice guy. I haven't mellowed. I'm still the same S.O.B. I always was. I should know. I'm the guy I'm talking about."[22]

Durocher may have said nice guys don't finish first, but he proved in 1969 that mean guys could finish second.

Of all things, Banks, the one-time radio man, joined the fraternity of sportswriters for the 1969 season. He penned a regular column for the *Chicago Tribune* (no doubt with ghost-written help). He started writing it in midseason. Lest anyone expect insider controversy, Banks heralded his approach in advance.

> It doesn't cost you anything to be happy. That's the way I'm going to write –through rose-colored glasses. There's enough troubles in the world without baseball, or sports, getting into hassles. When I come to the ballpark, I leave all the world's troubles and mine behind. I enjoy baseball so much, and the enthusiasm of the fans, that I'd be happy to stay nights in Wrigley Field if they'd roll out a cot for me near first base.
>
> Am I ever grouchy? Well, I'm not going to say I jump out of bed every morning and start putting on my Cub uniform while humming a tune. Sometimes, I give myself a pep talk as I look in the mirror in the bathroom. I tell myself I'm the luckiest guy alive. I look at Wrigley Field as my castle and I'd like to stay there. As I said, I'd even camp overnight.[23]

Banks hit well for the season, but he was as guilty as his teammates in September when he batted just .208. He was asked if he was going to retire and said no, he was already signed through the 1970 season, so he would be back.

Banks sifted through all of the reasons suggested for why the Cubs fell apart in September, but he concluded that it was mostly because Chicago hadn't been there before, had not been through the crucible of a pennant race. "Well, a lot people said we needed more rest," Banks said, "the bench, the black cat in New York, all of that stuff. But it wasn't pressure, or outside activities, or anything like that. It was fear. When you haven't won, it's scary and that's life. Dealing with the uncertainties, the unknown, and that's what I think happened to us in 1969."[24]

It was as good an explanation as any other Cubs psychoanalyst ever offered.

18

Another Highlight

Ernie Banks immediately debunked any rumors of his retirement. He was coming back for the 1970 season. Forget retirement. The Cubs may have lost out on their golden chance to capture a pennant, but there was no reason to think the team could not contend again in 1970. Banks wasn't about to quit and miss out if the Cubs' turn came. Besides, he had just driven in more than 100 runs. There was no reason to think he couldn't continue to hit.

Subdued. Morose. Depressed. Disbelieving. Pick a word to express the Chicago Cubs' mood when the 1969 season ended and they had finished eight games behind the New York Mets. Once again there would be no post-season games for the Cubs.

Few players were vocal about what went wrong during their September collapse. Manager Leo Durocher didn't say much either, although he was roughly handled in post-mortem sports stories. Many scribes were harsh in their summations of the season, blaming Durocher for letting the pennant get away, for alienating certain players, and for going AWOL during the race. Nobody hung him in effigy, but the surliness of the attitude couldn't have ruled that out.

Durocher was supposed to be the hero of this theatrical play, the man who delivered a pennant—and maybe a World Series, too—to the most downtrodden fans in the game. Instead, despite leading the team to two straight winning seasons, he was becoming the villain of the piece. Some of the criticism even surfaced by mid-season of 1969, Durocher being a somewhat easy target since he did not go out of his way to make friends with the media and reveled in his power. Even when he was about to get married again and his team was in first place, Durocher was grouchy.

A headline in the *St. Louis Post-Dispatch* read, "Leo the Lion's Feuds Are Just Ploys of Paper Tiger." Part of the story that followed by columnist Bob Broeg read: "But Leo the Lion is roaring, ripping the Chicago press at the moment when all should be as gay as the pleasure-doubling guys and dolls in a Wrigley gum commercial." He also wrote that Durocher knew he blundered by taking on Banks in his home city and underestimated his remaining abilities. Maybe, maybe not on that, though Broeg did provide the reminder that Banks "has come on like gangbusters, and now, four seasons later, is leading the league in runs batted in."[1]

That was a mild shot across the bow. In September of 1969, just as the Cubs were about to sink below the horizon, a headline in the *Pittsburgh Press* read, "Durocher vs. Chicago." The weather was about to turn, but for the moment, with the Cubs clinging to a pennant hope, he still had the fans, who serenaded him from the bleachers with "Give me that old-time Durocher; he's good enough for me" to the tune of "Old-Time Religion."[2]

After the Cubs' demise, a Los Angeles columnist made fun of Durocher's unauthorized absence in Wisconsin. The writer received an invitation from Camp Ojibwa to drop by if he was ever in the neighborhood, and he joked that he could visit with Durocher while there and they could toast marshmallows together.[3]

The irony was that Cubs owner Phil Wrigley, prior to the 1969 season, was so happy with Durocher's leadership that he tore up his existing contract and gave him a new one to manage through the 1970 season at a yearly salary of $75,000. After Durocher's infuriating road trip to Wisconsin and falling short on the field at the end of the season, it is legitimate to wonder if Wrigley would have been so generous.

The biggest blast at Durocher appeared on the newsstands in March of 1970, just in time for spring training, when the popular, widely circulated *Look* magazine contained a story with the headline "How Durocher Blew the Pennant." The lead on the story was not kind: "Leo Durocher, manager of Chicago Cubs, destroyed two of his centerfielders [Don Young and Adolfo Phillips, the latter of whom he said, "Nobody wants Phillips. You can't give him away"], and when the pennant crunch came, he had none. He called one of his players 'quitter.' [That was workhorse ace Ferguson Jenkins.] He tried to out-scramble his players to the money pot. He cultivated a broad and earnest enmity."[4] The tenor of the article did not warm up from there.

With the sudden collapse of 1969 fresh in mind, the Cubs reported to spring training for 1970. They were asked to forget all about the recent past and win it all. On paper, it could be argued, the Cubs may have been stronger. In addition to the infield group, plus Randy Hundley, all All-Stars, they added Joe Pepitone and Johnny Callison, two solid hitters who had demonstrated that they could hit home runs. Callison was just 31, but Chicago fans hoped he had at least one more productive year in him. He did. Callison slugged 19 home runs for the Cubs. In theory, Pepitone was a kindred spirit to Durocher, a man who liked to groom himself nicely, dress nicely, go out on the town and befriend celebrities. Although previously an All-Star with the Yankees, Pepitone seemed to be an old 29 when he joined the Cubs for 56 games in

1970, though he did hit 12 homers in that short time. Hurler Milt Pappas was another good add, winning ten games after joining the team in a trade.

Optimists like Ernie Banks could look at those changes and say the Cubs were still in the hunt, still going for it. Banks was 39 during the 1970 season, but coming off a reliable hitting campaign. He had to be as hurt as any Cub when the pennant got away from the team, but typical of his demeanor, he did not let it show. Whether he admitted it or not, he also had to realize that time might be running out on his career. The track record of 39-year-olds in Major League Baseball history is sketchy at best. Everyone that age is tip-toeing on the edge of a cliff. Youth is gone, wisdom and experience sometimes prevail, but everything is going to be harder.

If Banks wanted to quit, nobody would blame him. In the middle of the 1969 season, Banks was offered a job for the off-season, to manage the San Juan team in the Puerto Rican Winter League. This would have been an excellent opportunity for someone who thought of managing in his future. The experience would have been incalculably valuable. This was actually the second overture from the club after an initial approach in spring training. The team owner was clearly throwing out feelers the first time, though, because he spoke to other African American superstars such as Willie Mays and Hank Aaron, too.

The second discussion, a few months later, took place in Pittsburgh with the Cubs on a road trip. This was a firm offer, but Banks said no. He said he did so "with great reluctance" because he wanted to remain in Chicago during the off-season with his family and stay close to his business investments.[5] It was never completely clear if Banks wanted to manage in the majors after he retired as a player, even though his name was floated. In the story he wrote about Banks' flirtation with the Puerto Rico job, eminent baseball writer Jerome Holtzman referred to the player as being "most likely to become the first Negro to manage a Major League club."[6]

When Banks turned down the job, team owner Mario Navarro lamented the missed opportunity—for both sides. "He is a wonderful person," Navarro said. "The people in Puerto Rico would like him very much."[7] Probably true. It was noted as an aside that Frank Robinson, then with the Baltimore Orioles, had put in two winter seasons managing the Santurce team in the same league. As it so happened, it was Robinson who became the first African American manager in big-league history when he took over the Cleveland Indians in 1975.

About five weeks later, at his last All-Star Game, Banks was asked about managing but sounded lukewarm about the idea. "I don't have any real aspirations for managing," he said. "I like coaching much better. You can get more of a feeling with the players. You can get to the heartbeat—fielding, hitting. You can help build confidence. A coach can do things a manager can't. There is a different rapport."[8]

Banks had a little taste of coaching, but as the 1970 season began he still saw himself as a player first. The Cubs lost their first two games but by the end of April, aided by an 11-game winning streak, their record was 13–5. They had given fans a heart attack the year before, but maybe they had learned how to win from their close encounter with the pennant race.

Ken Holtzman, with 20–20 hindsight years later, believed the reason the Cubs faltered in 1969 was the newness of winning, dealing with the pressure of the pennant race, and not quite being equipped to handle everything thrown their way.

> I think that team simply wasn't ready to win. I'm telling you, there's a feeling about winning. There's a certain amount of intimidation. It's hard to explain, but it's real. The Cubs didn't have that. But the overall intimidation never existed with the Cubs. I've told the other guys this: Had we won in 1969, I would have bet my life savings we would have come back to win at least two more.[9]

In essence, what the Cubs were missing was swagger. Holtzman experienced a similar pattern with the Oakland A's, who had the swagger and who kept right on winning in the early 1970s. Teams that have never been there only think they know what it takes. Some never learn. Some acquire the necessary toughness.

That early winning streak in 1970 could have been the dividing line between learning what it takes to make a champion and the return to mediocrity. But the Cubs did not sustain that level of play. Unlike in 1969, when they held onto first place for months, they lost control of the lead by June 24, when they were in the middle of a 12-game losing streak.

When things were going swell in April and May, Ernie Banks delivered an all-time personal and team highlight. The Atlanta Braves were in town on May 12, but the crowd was weak for a Wrigley Field Tuesday afternoon game. There were just 5,264 fans in the house, not very impressive given the way the Cubs were playing. But it was an overcast day with the threat of thunderstorms, and some storms had recently passed through. In the second inning of what ultimately was a 4–3 Chicago win in 11 innings, Banks stepped to the plate against right-handed pitcher Pat Jarvis.

Banks slammed an 0–2 pitch out of the park for a solo home run. What made this blast special was that it was the 500th home run of Banks' career. Hitting 500 career home runs is still a revered accomplishment, but it was much rarer to reach that total in 1970. As of 2019, 27 players have hit at least 500 home runs. At the time Banks smashed his milestone four-bagger, just eight other players in Major League history had done so: Babe Ruth, Hank Aaron, Willie Mays, Mel Ott, Jimmie Foxx, Mickey Mantle, Eddie Mathews, and Ted Williams. This was indeed an exclusive club.

Right below its American flag on the front page with the *Chicago Tribune* name and "World's Greatest Newspaper" motto was a banner headline on

18. Another Highlight

May 13 reading "Banks Hits 500th Home Run," accompanied by a photograph of Banks swinging the bat. *Tribune* sportswriter Richard Dozer described the shot this way:

> The precious moment arrived for Ernie Banks yesterday—the precious moment in which his 500th home run reached the left-field seats in Wrigley Field. The precious moment came in the second inning with two outs and nobody on base. The dramatic home run, a low line drive which rocketed off the cement beneath the second row of plank seats in the left-field bleachers, came after Banks had taken a called strike and ball.[10]

There were some reports that talked about the count differently, but the official box score on baseball-reference.com says the count was 1-1, a ball and a strike. *The Sporting News* account, which was not printed until two weeks later, also said the count was 1-1.

When Banks crossed home plate after his jog around the bases, he tipped his cap to the fans who showed up. They made as much noise as possible in tribute as a group of 5,000 can in a park that can hold nearly 40,000. The ball bounced back from the bleachers, and Braves outfielder Rico Carty picked it up and tossed the ball to the Cubs' dugout, where it was given to Banks.

"The pitch was a fastball inside and up," Banks said. "They've been pitching me inside lately because I haven't been getting around on the ball." After the win, Banks, who acknowledged a standing ovation after taking a seat in the dugout, explained what he was thinking about once the big hit was in the books. "I was thinking about my mother and dad, about all the people in the Cubs' organization that helped me and about the wonderful Chicago fans who have come out all these years to cheer me on." In the middle of his pleasant disquisition, Banks reminded his listeners that it happened to be a Tuesday and thus the weekly Senior Citizens Day at Wrigley. "Old Man Banks hit his No. 500 on Senior Citizens Day."[11]

Even when the formal interviews were complete, Banks continued to celebrate and goof around, his joy was that strong. He helped a groundskeeper water the field and then imitated Ron Santo's 1969 signature jump in the air when he clicked his heels together. "I'm 12 years old again," Banks said. In the clubhouse, he climbed on a chair and announced to his teammates, "The riches of the game are in the thrills, not the money."[12]

Cornered again by sportswriters, Banks turned somewhat reflective, saying he still had things to accomplish in the sport. Once again, he offered no hint of impending retirement. His biggest remaining goal was the one he had chased since he broke into the majors in 1953. "To help win a pennant for the Cubs," Banks said. "And there's another thing I'd like to do—play 20 years. That would be a nice accomplishment."[13] As he spoke, Banks was in his 18th season.

The Cubs of 1970 weren't even the Cubs of 1969. A team in first place in a tight race on June 23 had a losing record and was in fourth place by June

30, 4½ games behind with a 35–37 record. The June losing streak was a killer. The one thing that saved the Cubs was that no other team ran away and hid. After the brutal slide, the Cubs reversed themselves in July and began to play good ball again. By July 31, they had staggered back to five games above .500 and were just three games out of first place. Whether or not they deserved to be within reach was another question, but that was reality. Back and forth the Cubs careened, win a few, lose one, win one, lose a couple, so by the end of August they were still five games over .500. But the complexion of the pennant race had changed. As Bill Hands won his 15th game of the season over the San Diego Padres, the Cubs rested just one game behind the Pittsburgh Pirates in the National League East Division standings.

At times the Cubs looked as if they could beat anybody in the world. In an August 19 game, Chicago beat San Diego, 12–2, by clubbing seven home runs. Jim Hickman, who recorded his best season, hit two of them and 32 for the year, plus collecting 115 runs batted in. "Gentleman Jim" also batted .315 in 1970.

Three days later, Holtzman did not give up his first hit of the game, a 15–0 victory over the San Francisco Giants, until the eighth inning. He threw a complete-game one-hitter with seven strikeouts.

As the calendar flipped to September, the Cubs felt pretty good about themselves. They crushed the Philadelphia Phillies, 17–2, on September 2 behind Milt Pappas. Banks, who had not been playing as much as he did in 1969, smacked three hits, drove in three runs, scored two and walked twice. A day later, the Cubs moved into second place, a half-game out, when Ferguson Jenkins (who won 22 games that season) beat the Phillies, 7–2. Another notable aspect of the September 3 game was that outfielder Billy Williams took the day off. He had played in 1,117 straight games since 1963. There was no injury to interfere with him being in the line-up, he merely wanted the streak to end so it would not be a distraction.

Writers did not write songs, poetry or traumatized analysis about the 1970 season, but at this juncture it almost seemed as if the Cubs had a better chance to pull out the division title or the pennant than they did in 1969. As late as September 15, the Cubs were just one game out of first place, even though they couldn't put a winning streak together. They were in second place, two games behind on September 20, on the eve of a double-header against the Cardinals in St. Louis. On that Wednesday, Bob Gibson outdueled Jenkins for a 2–1 win in the opener, and Jerry Reuss outlasted Hands, 2–1, in the nightcap.

Jenkins pitched a complete game, struck out 12 and still lost. Hands pitched seven innings, struck out eight and still lost. The Cubs had dealt for venerable knuckleball master Hoyt Wilhelm, and he pitched the last inning. But the Cubs' bats were silent. The Cubs needed to put together wins, and

18. Another Highlight

they could not. The Pirates extended their lead, and the New York Mets briefly passed them, too. The regular season ended on October 1, and the Cubs had an 84–78 record, second in the division.

Billy Williams had a monster year with 42 home runs and 129 runs batted in while batting .322. Ron Santo hit 26 more dingers and drove in 114 runs. As for Banks, this was a sign the end was in sight. He appeared in just 72 games while hitting 12 homers and driving in 44 runs.

Before the start of the 1970 season, Banks was called into the clubhouse for a meeting with general manager John Holland and told there had been threat on his life, that someone had called and said he was going to shoot Banks with a rifle. It was a stupefying moment. Banks' first reaction was to say it was probably a practical joke. Local Arizona policemen and the FBI were alerted and offered protection. Banks was shaken up. Then Ron Santo got threats. About a week later, the FBI made an arrest in Chicago. Banks said the bizarre incident made him conscious about mingling in crowds, although he never backed off from giving autographs to fans.

Shoot Ernie Banks. Imagine going after the most popular man in Chicago. The only one with a motive was Leo Durocher. It was surprising Banks didn't joke about that. Neither the threat, nor diminished playing time, sent Banks into retirement after the 1970 season. He was coming back for 1971. After all, he still had a gleam in his eye for a 20-year career.

19

Retirement

The clock ran out on Ernie Banks in 1971, a year shy of his goal of playing 20 years in the big leagues. This time manager Leo Durocher was determined to replace Banks at first base, and this time Banks' fading skills did not allow him to respond to the challenge. Since 1966, Durocher had been saying Banks was too old, and he expected him to recede into the woodwork.

But an equally determined Banks fought off benchings, showed off the talents he still retained, and proved Durocher wrong time after time. Even in 1970, he proved his usefulness as a part-time player. But it really was over for him in 1971. He was 40 years old, and his swing deserted him. When you go into a slump when you are 25, teams patiently wait for you to come out of it and regain your rhythm. When you go into a slump at 40, you're cooked. The chorus announcing that you are at the end of the line is deafening. You can't get a word in edgewise in self-defense.

Banks had no ammunition as backup. He had no proof that he could still make the big play when called upon, no statistics to show Durocher he was making a mistake. His feet moved a step slow, and his bat moved even slower. There was nothing to argue about. Over the longest Chicago summer of his life, Banks could offer no rebuttal. He played in just 39 games with 92 plate appearances, adding just three home runs to his lifetime total, and the worst thing of all was his .193 batting average. Banks made it through 19 years in the majors. Even if he wanted one more year, it's unlikely that even owner Phil Wrigley would have listened to the suggestion sympathetically.

When he was close to his final game, Banks sat in the Cubs dugout at Wrigley one day and watched as bleacher fans tossed around a balloon that resembled an extra-large baseball. "Man, that's just the way that ball used to look to me 10 years ago," he said. "I could really see it then. Right now it comes across that plate and it looks like a huge golf ball."[1] Wrong sport, but at least Banks had a gentle sense of humor about his situation.

Fans needed a sense of humor to follow the Cubs in 1971. It wasn't as if they played as badly as they had before Durocher came on the scene, but

19. Retirement

they also seemed less likely to take first place than they had in 1969. After a mediocre April, they were in fifth place in the NL East at 8–13. They stifled hope early that season. They put a move on in May and after a doubleheader on May 16, the Cubs had a record of 19–17 and were only four games out of first. Ken Holtzman beat the San Diego Padres that day, but he was just 3–4 with a high earned average. Although Holtzman was an important key to the team and he had some terrific moments that season, overall he was out of sorts in 1971. The Cubs were five games below .500 again by the end of May at 22–27, and rumors were percolating that Leo The Lip was about to be fired. It didn't happen.

In early June, the Cubs were on the right side of a memorable win. If anything might ignite the club, this one could have. Holtzman was on the mound for Chicago against the Cincinnati Reds' tough righty Gary Nolan, who won 110 big-league games. It was a night game in Riverfront Stadium with 11,751 in the stands. This was a pitchers' duel that lasted five minutes under two hours, and southpaw Holtzman, a warrior who often won the rugged games, prevailed, 1–0.

This was not just a tough-it-out win, though. Holtzman pitched the second no-hitter of his Cubs career. It was a beauty. Though he walked four, Holtzman struck out six batters. The Reds had some dangerous pop in the lineup, too, including Johnny Bench, Tony Perez and George Foster. Holtzman concluded that he was lucky both times he quelled a Major League team without allowing any hits.

> My second no-hitter in Cincinnati was also lucky, because Johnny Bench [a Hall of Fame catcher], narrowly missed getting a bunt single when it rolled foul at the last second. No-hit games are well-pitched games with a generous amount of luck thrown in. I also lost a couple of no-hitters in the ninth inning, one on a misjudged fly ball, so obviously you have to be very fortunate to complete a game like that.[2]

Chicago wasn't scoring as many runs as expected. Banks was on the bench much of the time. Newcomer Joe Pepitone, the man who may have jump-started a baseball trend with the first hair dryer in a Major League locker room, did add power. He batted .307 and hit 16 home runs with 61 runs batted in while playing in 115 games. Ron Santo, who bled Cubs colors, was still reliable, smacking 21 home runs and knocking in 88 runs. Billy Williams was still at the top of his game with 28 home runs, 93 RBI and a .301 average. After his career year, Jim Hickman dropped way off, and Johnny Callison faded to a .210 average.

Second baseman Glenn Beckert, a career .283 hitter, could do no wrong during the summer of 1971. He batted an astonishing .342, his only full season over .300. Beckert made the third of his four All-Star teams. Don Kessinger, apparently shored up by potatoes, was his usual self at shortstop and also made the All-Star team again. He had two more selections in him.

Behind the scenes, and increasingly in the open even if they spoke anonymously, Cubs players were becoming more angry and impatient with manager Leo Durocher's imperious personality, his questionable moves, and his arrogant attitude towards them. Many of the reports from the Cubs clubhouse sounded as if they were coming from disgruntled leakers inside a roiling White House.

In June of 1971, Rick Talley, one of the Cubs beat writers, saw his byline atop a story and under a headline in a sports magazine reading, "Why the Cubs Will Revolt Against Durocher." The beginning of the story offered a tell-it-like-it-is attack. "Leo's last stand," it read. "That's the status of Leo Durocher with the 1971 Chicago Cubs. He'll be fired if the Cubs don't capture the National League's eastern division championship and he may not last the month of June if they're not contending."[3]

The shine was off. Durocher had come to Chicago with the reputation of a man who could create a winner as he had done with the Brooklyn Dodgers and New York Giants. His personality grated on many, but the Cubs were no longer a last-place team, and attendance had increased to a regular turnstile count of around 1.6 million. He had not yet delivered a pennant, but the players were sick of his yelling, his insults and his grumpiness.

Talley may have been overreaching with the guarantee that Durocher was doomed if the Cubs did not finish first, but he was not far off in his other reporting of the internal goings-on. The Cubs were unhappy campers, and they were unhappier about the camp counselor than anything else. Owner Phil Wrigley was the man who hired Durocher, and he had improved the Cubs' circumstances on the field and at the box office, so Wrigley was somewhat reluctant to make a big move too quickly, just in case Durocher could come through with the kind of magic needed to lead the Cubs all the way through a strong September finish.

After the 1970 season ended, general manager John Holland had invited players to meet with him in his office and held private sessions with some of the veterans. They did not compliment Durocher. At the time, it was believed that Durocher was given a one-year ultimatum to win now or else.

Talley did quote an anonymous Cub who was clearly not a member of the Leo Durocher Fan Club. "We estimate Leo lost at least eight to 10 games for us in 1970," he said. "If he'll just leave us alone, we can win."[4] But Durocher was no laissez-faire manager. He believed in his own baseball smarts above all.

Rather remarkably, though also anonymously, a member of the front office issued a comment suggesting that the brass expected Durocher (starting his 22nd season as a big-league manager) to be a different kind of guy for the 1971 season, a kinder, gentler version. "We're hoping he'll be more of a human being," the official said.[5] Apparently, he was not familiar with the saying about a leopard never changing its spots.

The Cubs got another wake-up call from team management in June and

19. Retirement

started operating on at least six out of eight cylinders. At the end of the month, the team's record was 40–36. That was on the respectable side of the ledger, but the rest of the league had moved on without them. The Cubs were in third place, 8½ games out of first. It was not a hopeless case, but it was time to go on a serious run in order to be taken seriously. It was an intriguing thought, and indeed the Cubs finished July seven games over .500—yet farther behind in the standings.

By 1971, Durocher had overseen the overhaul of the Cubs roster many times over. Some 140 players had come and gone to keep company with nine players who had been on the team for the duration of his Chicago tenure. This was one time when the situation screamed out for a big move to energize the club heading into the last two months of the campaign.

On July 23, a secret held closely by Ron Santo for years was revealed. He told the world that he had been diagnosed with juvenile diabetes as a teenager, but had kept it quiet because he did not think people understood the illness. He feared that no team would want him. Now that he was an established and successful All-Star player, he had shown people that he could live a normal life with the disease.

As a high schooler, Santo went for hospital tests and learned he had diabetes. His first question for the doctor was whether or not he would still be able to play baseball. At a time when much less was known about the disease, the doctor said he would be able to, but would have to manage his illness and be cautious in certain ways. The scariest thing for Santo then, in the late 1950s, was reading up on the disease and discovering that some people said the life expectancy of someone suffering from it was only 25. That was a shock for someone who was 18. Santo attended a two-week course in Seattle before departing for the start of the season, quickly introduced to insulin and the need for injecting it daily.

When Santo told his story publicly, he did so because the Diabetes Association of Greater Chicago suggested he do so as a role model for others coping with problems from the disease. Originally, only road roommates Cuno Barragan (briefly in the early Sixties) and Glenn Beckert (a little bit later) knew Santo had diabetes. He quietly let the rest of the Cubs know in 1963.

Santo, who played with Barragan on the Cubs between 1961 and 1963, took him into his confidence just in case he started to look and act sickly without realizing it. "He became another set of eyes for me," Santo said. "Sometimes, coming off the field between innings, he'd say, 'Roomie, you look a little pale. Better grab a Snicker.' At least I no longer had to hide my insulin and syringes from him."[6] Santo feared suddenly passing out in public, so he was glad Barragan could keep watch.

Part if his motivation for going public in 1971 stemmed from the team throwing him a Ron Santo Day. Santo talked to GM John Holland and said that any donations that came in to honor him should go to diabetes cure research. He was a well-known professional athlete, so it was felt he could help the morale of others. Santo became a hero of sorts to members of the diabetic community.

"Think of how many diabetics you can help when they realize what you've been able to accomplish," Holland said. "It will inspire them to live life as fully as you have." Santo thought about that. "My life changed that day. I started spending more time in hospital pediatric units, visiting diabetic children. I urged them to remain positive and told them they could accomplish anything they wanted despite their disease. Kids sent me letters. So did their parents."[7]

Around age 60, Santo began having serious side-effect health problems from diabetes, and he had 15 operations in the years after, including having portions of both legs amputated because of circulatory issues.

Rather stunningly, Ron Santo Day became a source of dissension. Santo had been a Durocher supporter, but their relationship broke that day. An argument began in the clubhouse when the manager was told by players that they didn't like being criticized in the newspapers. Told he was wrong for doing so, Durocher blew up. As captain, Santo sought to intervene and make peace, but Durocher turned on him, shouting, "Well, the only f...... reason they're having a Ron Santo Day in this ballpark is because YOU asked for one!"[8]

Santo screamed back, infuriated at the suggestion, and brought Holland into the discussion to confirm that Santo had not asked for the honor. In response to Holland's comment in front of the team, Durocher yelled, "I quit!" Nearby, Ken Holtzman chimed in with "Let him go!"[9]

That illustrated the tension in the Cubs' clubhouse. Explosions could occur at any time. It was not an atmosphere conducive to rallying a team to make a charge in the standings. In between his big moments, Holtzman struggled, but Fergie Jenkins kept rolling. He was on his way to a 24-victory season with a 2.77 earned run average while throwing 325 innings. He won the National League Cy Young Award that season. If only he had had more help, but the Cubs were in disarray.

A month after the Santo scene in the dressing room, there was another blowout. Durocher verbally lashed Milt Pappas, and when players were visibly unhappy, he told them to speak their minds. Joe Pepitone did, saying to the manager, "Why are you always blaming people?" More tempers flared, and Durocher was getting it from several players. Santo even called him a liar.[10]

The happy-go-lucky Ernie Banks was caught in the middle of things. He didn't like Durocher either, but it was not his way to engage in high-powered arguments. This was the season Banks' autobiography with Chicago sportswriter Jim Enright appeared in book stores. When *The Sporting News* published a review, by the usually irascible Dick Young of the *New York Daily*

News, the headline was "Cub Star Banks Pens a Love Story." Did anyone expect anything else? Was anyone counting on a tell-all gossip book like Jim Bouton's *Ball Four*? Of course not.

> I have just read a book by a ballplayer. Nobody peeped in bedrooms with binoculars, nobody slept with somebody else's wife, no manager was made to look like a cretin, and the man who owned the ball club was not a capitalist pig forcing the author to slave at $80,000 a year. It will make a lousy movie.
>
> It is a beautiful story, simply told, because it is about beautiful people, by beautiful people. Ernie Banks, a black man, and Jim Enright, a white man, are from the same womb. They love everybody and everything and they don't go around writing it on walls. They just live it.

Enright, it was noted, once bumped into Banks in the airport in Oklahoma City and spied him hugging a statue of Will Rogers. "Here is my champion," Banks said. "He never met a man he didn't like. Neither have I. What we need in this world are more Will Rogers."[11]

As the controversy, anger and just plan junk swirled around the Cubs during the 1971 season, as they took the field every day with a smidgen of hope that they could put everything behind them, Banks played on whenever Durocher let him. Seeking to spike the poisonous atmosphere and bury rumors, on September 3 Wrigley took the extraordinary step of buying ads in four Chicago newspapers, praising the success Durocher had provided for the team, and insisted his man was not going to be fired this season. In other words, "Shut up and play ball." While the action may have soothed Durocher and took the suspense out of daily life at the ballpark, it did not light a spark in the players. The Cubs lost nine of their next 11 games.

As the Cubs staggered to the finish line, the Pittsburgh Pirates romped to the division title, winning 97 games. St. Louis came in second at 90–72. Chicago could only wave from the distance in third with its 83–79 mark. For that matter, the Cubs only tied for third with the New York Mets, both teams 14 games behind Pittsburgh.

It might be said Ernie Banks stumbled to the end of his Major League career, too. A sub-.200 average with just three home runs plus being inserted in just 39 games signaled the conclusion of his glorious, All-Star career. Banks' final home run was recorded in a 5–4 loss to the Reds at Wrigley Field on August 24. His lifetime total was 512 home runs, and his RBI total was 1,636. He had been a star as a shortstop and a star as a first baseman.

The Cubs' last home game of the 1971 season was the last game of Banks' career. The item had been reported as fact in all the papers, essentially like a carnival ad—Come See Ernie Banks Play One Last Time. Banks had not announced his retirement, and others had tried to retire him before without his approval. But things seemed different this time. You could have gotten good odds in Las Vegas that Banks wouldn't suit up for another game.

When Banks went out on the field for his pre-game workout on September 26, the early-arriving fans screamed his name. It was damp and overcast, but true to his way, Banks announced, "Isn't it a beautiful day?" Then he began singing a show tune, "On a clear day, you can see forever."[12]

Fittingly, the Cubs lost to the Philadelphia Phillies, 5–1, before going on the road for the last three games of the season—without Banks' participation. He came to the plate four times against Philadelphia, stroked a single, and walked. Each time he stepped into the box, the crowd, which was only 18,505 for the occasion, gave him a standing ovation.

Before the game, Banks signed many autographs for kids, and prior to the first pitch, he greeted first base umpire Paul Pryor. A well-wisher said the best way to go out would be to hit three home runs. Banks did not disagree. "I'm gonna start to work on that with the first pitch of the day," he said. "It's all gonna be settled once I get out there between those white lines."[13]

Ernie Banks always was happiest between the white lines at Wrigley Field. That's why they knew him as Mr. Cub.

20

A New Life Begins

Ernie Banks' final appearance in a Chicago Cubs game occurred in that September 26, 5–1 loss to the Philadelphia Phillies. As Mr. Cub, it seemed appropriate that he conclude his playing career in front of the home fans at Wrigley Field. The Cubs' season did not end that day.

The Cubs left town for a three-game road trip to Montreal to face the Expos. They lost the first two games and won the final game of the season—without Banks—to finish 83–79. Between 1953 and 1971, Ernie Banks performed brilliantly for his club. He was often a one-man team, who at his best was twice voted the most valuable player in the National League. But baseball is not a one-man sport, and for most of Banks' tenure with his favorite team he could not lift the Cubs to the pennant, or later the playoffs. It was not until the waning days of his career, when Leo Durocher took over as manager, that the Cubs rallied to record winning records. Banks never experienced the joy of participating in a World Series, winning a pennant, or even appearing in a post-season game.

Certainly, he had his glorious moments, winning two Most Valuable Player Awards. But Banks never experienced the jolt of excitement that players live for—to compete for a championship. All of his 2,528 games were played during the regular season. That is a dubious record. Banks participated in more games in his career than any other player in baseball history who did not get the chance to compete in a post-season game. In recent decades, before the Cubs turned things around in the 2000s, the team was often referred to as "The Lovable Losers." Given his popularity and image, it made more sense for Banks to be called a lovable loser.

Banks was known for his optimism, the pleasure he took in playing baseball, and always showing a friendly demeanor. How much the losing hurt him was pretty much shielded from the public. Once in a while, an insightful sportswriter would penetrate that veneer and ask pointed questions about the defeats piled high, accumulating like a supply of wood for winter.

Once, in 1961, during the dark days, when the franchise was in the midst of playing sub.-500 ball annually, Banks admitted, "You can call me 'baseball's worst loser,'" he said. "But baseball can be fun, even when you're not on a championship club." Most people would agree with that, considering baseball to be one of the most enjoyable of professions one can undertake in the United States. "Being with the Cubs has been fun for me. But, I guess there's nothing QUITE like being on a pennant winner at that. Do you know of a better way to earn a living than playing baseball?"[1]

Although Banks' outlook was supposed to be brighter than other players,' he did not view himself as much different from them. Sure, he predicted pennants in spring training, but wasn't that the time of year when everything started fresh and when the standings all read 0–0? "I'm thankful for my attitude," Banks said. "I'm not a pessimist. Every spring when I go to camp I go with the sincere feeling that we have a real chance; that we're a cinch for the first division and a contender for the pennant. It's just the way I feel. Most of these Cubs feel the same way. Did you ever hear of a baseball team that conceded the pennant in spring training?"[2]

Banks even had the answer for how he coped when things were going badly, the team was many games out of first place, and still the schedule loomed ahead with maybe 40 games to go. There were times in August or September when no player could be fooled into believing the team still had a chance for the pennant. "So then you bear down even harder," Banks said. "You spurt to prove, in the last few weeks, at least, you're better than some of the teams that took the early lead."[3]

So that's how Ernie Banks did it, this is how he provided pep talks to his inner self when the season was at its bleakest.

When Banks walked away from the Cubs roster in 1971, he was 40 years old. His estimable record included 512 home runs, 1,636 runs batted in, and there were those two MVP Award honors.

For all his trying, Durocher never found a valued replacement for Banks at first base. Banks pushed ahead of any rival handed the job, showing repeatedly, over several years even in his athletic old age, that he was better than any Durocher/Cubs alternative. At the very end, Banks knew his skills had frayed, and his body told him it was time to hang up the spikes, not Leo Durocher.

One thing Durocher pulled off was outlasting Banks with the Cubs. He was signed for the 1972 season, still convinced he could bring a pennant to the North Side. He hadn't been able to do it with Ernie Banks, so he sought to do it without Ernie Banks. After the 1966 debacle, when the Cubs showed they were not an eighth-place team and humiliated Durocher by finishing tenth, he led Chicago to five straight winning seasons. He alienated Banks and other stars while doing so, and with a personality so thoroughly the opposite of Banks,' Durocher was more scorched earth than diplomat, more abrasive than encouraging. Owner Phil Wrigley had viewed the disturbances and animosity between Durocher and the players with distaste. He must have given considerable thought to dumping Durocher. Illustrations of his concern were the firing of three coaches and the hiring of former pitcher Hank Aguirre with a peculiar role. It was conceded that Durocher and the players feuded so much that the manager needed a go-between to help communicate. That was Aguirre. He was officially a coach but put on his uniform with the players in their portion of the clubhouse.

Shortly after Banks retired as an active player, pretty much wondering what he was going to do with all his new free time in the summer, the Cubs organization came through for their main man. There was much agitating in Chicago newspapers for Banks to succeed Durocher as manager. There was no doubt he would be more popular, but was Banks a strategist of the first order? After two decades of being touted as just about the nicest man on the planet, was Banks tough enough to snap the whip and impose discipline? That seemed to be a pressing question since almost the entire roster would consist of men he had just left behind as teammates. There was no distance between Banks and most of the players.

Wrigley pretty much sidestepped those issues when he announced that he would not hire Banks as his next skipper. "Ernie has such a beautiful reputation in baseball, it would be a shame to ruin it by making him a manager," the owner said.[4] Whether that was a smokescreen covering his lack of faith in Banks' ability or a heartfelt truth was never clear. There was definitely some truth in the analysis, however. The idea of Ernie Banks as Cubs manager was appealing. But what happened as soon as the beloved Banks made a mistake on the bench leading to a Cubs defeat? Or worse, how long would it take for the nitpicking to begin if the Cubs were not winners under Banks?

"Managing is a dirty job, it doesn't last long, and it certainly isn't anything I'd wish on Banks," Wrigley added. "Ernie surely is headed to the Hall of Fame and too often you see a Hall of Famer take a job as manager, fail and then everything is spoiled because the gloss and glamour are stripped from them."[5]

Wrigley's compromise solution was to make Banks a coach for the big club after he spent the fall as a hitting coach in the Arizona Instructional League. At that time, Banks was receiving rave reviews for his advice offered to young players on their way up in the Cubs' organization, particularly future Major League outfielder Bill North.

> They tell me Ernie is doing a marvelous job with this youngster. He's wonderful working with young players. That's where he would be of greatest value. That and in public relations work. I have said many times before and I'll say it again, Ernie can have a job with the Cubs organization as long as he lives. Yes, Ernie has mentioned

being a manager a few times. But he always said he'd like to start as a coach or as a manager in the minors. But I'd still hate to see him become a big-league manager.[6]

When the 1972 season began, Durocher was still the head man, and of all things, Banks was on his staff. Durocher probably thought he had at last gotten rid of Banks when he played his final game, but here he was, still pulling on a uniform and hanging out by him in the dugout.

Outfielder Jim Hickman moved to first base—the manager still couldn't find a young heir to replace Banks—as the primary starter, making 115 appearances. Hickman hit pretty well with 17 homers and 64 runs batted in. And the rest of the All-Star infield was in place, plus catcher Randy Hundley. Glenn Beckert at second and Don Kessinger at short held their ground. Ron Santo had a special offensive year, smacking 17 home runs with 74 RBI while batting .302. That was while missing about 30 games.

Billy Williams had a tremendous season with 37 homers, 122 runs knocked in and a .333 average. On July 11, in a doubleheader against the Astros, Williams went 8-for-8 at the plate. Ten days later, he knocked in six runs in a game against the Astros. Houston needed to take out health insurance to protect the franchise against Williams' bat.

The team shored up the other outfield positions with Rick Monday and Jose Cardenal, and that was a big boost. Phil Wrigley accommodated Ken Holtzman's desire to put distance between himself and Durocher by trading him to the Oakland A's, shipping him 2,000 miles west. Cardenal was acquired for three players who were not going to start. The bench hit very poorly, though. Ferguson Jenkins remained the king of the staff with another 20-win season. Milt Pappas collected 17 wins, and Bill Hands won 11 games. Not joining the team from the minors until near the end of June, Rick Reuschel won ten with a 2.93 earned run average as a 23-year-old rookie. It was the beginning of a 19-year stay in the big leagues accompanied by 214 victories. Although his record was 11–14, Burt Hooton, a 22-year-old rookie, turned in the flashiest game on the mound, pitching a no-hitter on April 16 in just his fourth Major League start.

Before the first month of the season was even over, Durocher, 66, was resting in a Chicago hospital, missing five games due to chronic fatigue. It was a toss-up who was worse off, Durocher or 31-year-old first baseman Joe Pepitone, who not only had gastritis, but lack of interest. He stepped away from the team for 60 days and did not contribute much pop that season.

The Cubs finished 85–70. But Durocher wasn't around at the end. Under his leadership, the Cubs went 46–44. He was either pushed into a resignation or read the tea leaves and left the Cubs on July 24. While not quite saying he had fired Durocher, Wrigley offered hints. The new manager was Whitey Lockman. He was promoted from Director of Player Development. Wrigley wanted to see if the players would perform better without their despised leader—and they did. Under Lockman, the Cubs went 39–26.

20. A New Life Begins

As a player, Lockman, whose given first name was Carroll, broke into the majors as a 19-year-old with the New York Giants in 1945. He survived 15 seasons in big leagues, mostly with the Giants, but also with other National League teams. His lifetime average was .279, so he earned his keep. Lockman made one All-Star team and was part of the 1954 World Series champion Giants. He coached under Durocher and now he was succeeding him. That was the high point of Lockman's Cubs managerial tenure. He was ousted two years later when the team resumed losing.

Coach Banks was probably as relieved as anyone in the organization to see Durocher depart from Chicago. Durocher, who had turned 67, suddenly turned healthy and hired on as the new manager of the Astros barely a month after his exile from the Cubs. The best thing he could have brought to that team would have been Billy Williams. But Williams stayed in Chicago.

So did Banks. He spent the one year in uniform as coach for the 1972 season, then stayed close to the team that he did so much for and for which he did so much. When the Cubs got rid of Lockman, the debate over whether Banks should succeed him was raised in the papers again. Instead, Wrigley hired Jim Marshall this time. Of why Banks was bypassed again, Wrigley said, "He's too nice a guy. I wouldn't offer him the job. I talked about it with him and his wife, but Ernie is happy in what he is doing. He will last longer and be happier in a job he likes." Banks may have discussed things with Wrigley, but he never lobbied with sportswriters for the job, even as the crescendo was growing for Major League Baseball to hire its first African American manager. "Why would Ernie want to be a manager?" Wrigley added. "It's the next thing to being a kamikaze pilot." Wrigley made it sound as if sportswriters were making up the entire Banks-as-manager matter. "You know how writers are," he said. "They just like to sink their teeth into a controversial problem."[7]

Banks may have been Mr. Cub in lore, but he was also "Mr. Public Relations" or "Mr. Ambassador" for the Cubs and baseball. That work did not pay especially well, but he tried other things. For one thing, Banks became a good golfer. His hitting prowess with a bat translated to respectable hitting with a club, though he was hardly good enough to go on the pro tour.

Using that natural connection to people, Banks eventually signed on as a public relations man for Ravenswood Bank of Chicago and had people referring to him as a banker. That may have been a little bit overstated, but Banks did have the gift of schmoozing well, so it was easy to envision how he would be a different type of asset to the financial institution from its deposits. Actually, Banks had long before demonstrated an interest in banking and finance. In 1966, when players still needed to work in the off-season to support their families, he had worked for Seaway National Bank and took a banking correspondence course. This was typical of Banks, who throughout his life thirsted for higher education experiences and took courses at various colleges. The only college he wished to steer clear of was the old Cubs College of Coaches.

Banks also served as a member of the Chicago Cubs board of directors, which seemed logical. When the Wrigley family left the game and sold the franchise and the ballpark to the *Chicago Tribune*, Banks said his top priority was to protect his Friendly Confines' uniqueness as the only park in the majors without lights for night games. "I'm going to take a strong stand," Banks said.[8]

Of course, that was a losing battle. The change was a gradual, not a rapid one, but on August 8, 1988, lights were turned on for a game at Wrigley Field for the first time. In the 30 years since, the original low number of night games has been slowly expanded to eat up a larger portion of the schedule. However, the Cubs still play more day games than any team in the majors.

Banks always inquired about others' happiness when he met or talked with them for any length of time, especially probing how their love life was going. Banks himself, though, went through four marriages over the decades. Just as he felt about the Cubs' fortunes, he seemed perpetually upbeat about love striking.

Even before he retired, Banks' stature had grown much larger than the game of baseball in Chicago. He was a civic treasure, at least partially because he always went out of his way to be nice to fans and particularly nice to children such as those with illnesses in hospitals. In 1970, as the end of his active baseball career beckoned, Banks became a Laureate of The Lincoln Academy of Illinois and was presented the Order of Lincoln, named for President Abraham Lincoln. The non-profit, non-partisan organization bestows the award in different categories. This is the state of Illinois' highest honor, and the award is given by the governor. In Banks' case, the area he was honored for was sports. But no one doubted that much more than Banks' home run total was factored in.

Among other luminaries with Illinois roots and connections who are among the 300 notables recognized since 1965 are senator and secretary of state Hillary Clinton, football Hall of Famer Walter Payton, writer Studs Terkel, and former president Ronald Reagan. Clinton and Reagan were born in Illinois. Payton starred for the Chicago Bears. Terkel was a Chicago institution.

There are darned few people who can say they either witnessed Ernie Banks being tackled by sadness or heard him say more than his well-rehearsed patter. But yes, Banks hurt because the Cubs never won big on his watch. Many years later, he admitted how it bothered him when at gatherings his contemporary greats swapped stories about their World Series experiences, showed off their World Series rings, or spoke of the electricity they felt being with their teammates on the ultimate baseball stage.

"Sometimes I'm at a Hall of Fame reunion [they happen annually in Cooperstown, New York] and I'll look around and see I'm the only one in the room who never played in a World Series," Banks said. "I've had nightmares about it. Once, I even talked to a psychiatrist. There wasn't much he could say, just that I'd done the best I could and it wasn't meant to be."[9]

No, it wasn't. But Banks' personal achievements were not overlooked by the game. The best he could do was good enough in retirement to earn him some of the most coveted honors and rewards an athlete can receive.

21

A Hall of Famer

Ernie Banks retired from baseball after 19 years on the roster of the Chicago Cubs at the end of the 1971 season. There is a five-year post-retirement waiting period before a player can be considered on the ballot for induction into the Baseball Hall of Fame in Cooperstown, New York.

For a time, it seemed, it was a point of pride amongst voters not to enshrine people in their first year of eligibility. That attitude eventually loosened up, and more players have been elected early in recent years than in the 1980s and 1990s.

The former Cubs shortstop and first baseman's name was put before the voters in 1977, and he was elected that year and inducted into the Hall of Fame later that summer. Under the rules, players must receive 75 percent of the vote to be elected. The results were announced on January 19. Banks, a first-timer, was named on 321 ballots, or 83.8 percent.

That year he was the only player elected by the Baseball Writers' Association of America. Second in the voting was slugging Braves third baseman Eddie Mathews with 62.4 percent of the vote. Mathews, whose vote-getting improved by 13.7 percent that year, was eventually voted into the Hall.

Gil Hodges was third, and Enos Slaughter (another future choice) fourth. Then came a spate of Dodgers, Duke Snider, Don Drysdale and PeeWee Reese, all of whom were ultimately enshrined. They were followed by Nellie Fox, Jim Bunning, George Kell, Richie Ashburn and Red Schoendienst. All have been elected. Farther down the balloting list were very fine players like Roger Maris, Lew Burdette, Alvin Dark, Don Newcombe, Ted Kluszewski, Mickey Vernon and Elston Howard. More than 40 years later, none of them have been elected.

Although none of those stalwarts were voted into the Hall with Banks, the Veterans Committee chose Al Lopez, Amos Rusie and Joe Sewell. The Negro Leagues Committee chose Martin Dihigo and John Henry Lloyd. That group then disbanded.

Some insinuated that New York sports columnist Dick Young may have

21. A Hall of Famer

been the most cynical of journalists, but he was full of unabashed praise when it came to Ernie Banks. Upon the revelation of Banks' choice for the Hall of Fame at the Hotel Americana in New York, Young picked up his pen.

It was not as if Young had never met Banks before, watched him play, or heard him talk baseball. But those sessions came in small doses because Young was not a Chicago Cubs beat writer following the team around the nation. His visits with the club were intermittent. So even though he thought he had a grasp on Banks' character, this event was a reminder, and Young essentially was pinching himself because he thought Banks was too good to be true.

"He's not real. He can't be," Young thought.[1] Then he wrote:

> But he is. In this time of materialism, amidst the money-grabbing athletes, the money-squeezing owners, the money-demanding agents, in this time of bitching and griping and coveting and envying, stands Ernie Banks, a towering Gibraltar.
>
> There are greater ballplayers in there [the Hall of Fame]. There is no finer person. You cannot get Ernie Banks to say a bad word about anyone. He loves everyone. He loves sportswriters. A baseball player who loves sportswriters. Ernie Banks is a saint.[2]

Young said the writers present lunged and probed, almost like a boxer looking for a weakness in his foe's defense, but nothing they asked, nothing they said, made a dent in Banks' mood or caused him to say anything negative about anyone he came into contact with during his years in baseball, or maybe anywhere ever.

Banks recounted a story of his youth, when he was seven years old and accompanied his mother Essie to a market in Texas, but they couldn't afford to buy all of the luscious things on display that he wanted to eat. He was way too young to be a wage earner, the man of the house, or the financial supporter of his large family. He told his mom that he wanted to do something for her, that he wanted to amount to something in life.

"Don't worry, Ernest, you will," she said. "Just remember, always look at the bright side of things. We are doing fine. We have so much more than so many other people in the world."[3]

All those years later, it was evident Banks had followed his mother's advice in how he lived his life. He was definitely a man who looked on the bright side.

It was no particular surprise that Banks, the face of the Chicago Cubs franchise, with credentials like his large number of home runs and two National League Most Valuable Awards, was supported by the voters early in the process. In the *Peanuts* comic strip, Linus, one of the little-boy characters, walks around in a cloud of dust, kicking up dirt all around him. Banks was pretty much followed by a halo of sunshine wherever he went.

Certainly, everyone who attended the Hall of Fame induction ceremony on August 8, 1977, knew a smiling Ernie Banks would be on display to receive the greatest honor a baseball player can obtain. Banks had a built-in smiley face, so he definitely wasn't going to be frowning on this day. Mr. Cub was 46 years old. Banks' main responsibility during his few-day visit to upstate New York was to talk. He was very good at doing that in informal settings, but his acceptance speech would be delivered before a crowd of thousands while he stood behind a podium. It was different from expounding on baseball while standing next to his locker in the clubhouse.

"I once read that success depends on talents God gave you, and also on the people who believe in you," Banks said. "The honor belongs to those people who believed in me—my parents, my wife and children, and those individuals such as Monte Irvin and 'Cool Papa' Bell, who helped teach me. And then, of course, there are the fans."[4]

It was a good time for Banks to reflect on growing up in Dallas with few advantages, that his large family, supportive parents and many siblings did aid him, and that he played softball more than baseball as a young boy.

Banks was the ninth player to top 500 home runs in a career, and few players in history were as respected and admired for gentlemanly character away from the field. Banks made his teammates, fans and the sportswriters who covered him all happy, and this was baseball's reciprocation, making Ernie Banks happy.

The fans who journeyed to Cooperstown from Chicago—and Cubs fans from elsewhere—came prepared to fete their hero. A banner in the crowd read, "America Loves Ernie Banks." Banks saw the sign lifted by his personal fan club on the premises and smiled. He promptly thanked "thousands of Cubs fans." He glanced at the sky and continued, "There's sunshine, fresh air, and the team is behind us. Let's play two."[5]

Indeed, as Banks often appended onto that comment, it was a beautiful day for baseball.

By the time Banks was enshrined, Cubs owner Philip K. Wrigley had passed away. Otherwise, he surely would have been present to watch his favorite player have the game's greatest recognition bestowed upon him. Wrigley died at 82 on April 12, 1977, between the announcement of Banks' selection and the induction. Wrigley was actually watching the Cubs on television when he passed away. In recent decades, he had chosen not to attend games at the ballpark that bore his family name because he drew too much attention. Perhaps, given that reasoning, he might not have shown up in Cooperstown. Banks made a point of noting Wrigley's absence and his own desire to have seen Wrigley at the Hall for the occasion. Banks called Wrigley "one of the finest gentlemen ever and a man who gave me a lot of confidence. I only wish he were with me."[6]

As the most recent active player selected by the writers, and the only one in 1977, Banks was the center of attention even more than he might have

21. A Hall of Famer

been if he was one of perhaps four chosen in that manner. Three of the others, Dihigo (1971), Rusie (1942), and Lloyd (1964) were unable to attend because they were long dead. The others in attendance who spoke for themselves were Sewell, then 78, a remarkable contact hitter who practically never struck out, and catcher Al Lopez, who in the 1950s managed two American League teams to the World Series and was just shy of his 69th birthday. "It's certainly nice to be here in person," Sewell joked about the good fortune of his longevity.[7]

Banks wore a dark suit, a white shirt, and a tie of more than one color but dominated by red. He was introduced at the podium for the outdoor induction ceremony by Commissioner Bowie Kuhn. While saying he was "deeply honored and grateful" to become a member of the Hall of Fame, in his four-minute speech Banks said this was the happiest day of his life and it always would be.[8]

While Banks was no longer an active player, he stayed close to the game. There was a certain irony when in February of 1978 he was elected to the Cubs' board of directors by stockholders, since he was chosen to fill the seat vacated by Phil Wrigley' death. As so many other corporations did due to the state's friendly business regulations, the Chicago Cubs were actually registered in Delaware, and the meeting took place in Wilmington. That year there was an attempt to move the annual meeting to Chicago for 1979, but it did not pass.

Banks also remained in demand for public appearances, though more so in the Chicago area than in Delaware. However, he fielded invitations for speeches in many places around the country. Being a Hall of Famer enhanced his national standing even more. Anyone who sought Banks as a speaker could pretty much bet on an upbeat talk. It would have been a shock to hear Banks suddenly talk harshly about his days in baseball or to utter discouraging words to young people. When Banks came to your town, the odds were remarkably high against him making news of a negative sort that would play out on the national wire services like the Associated Press or United Press International. One of the nation's best-known optimists was not going to change in his late forties.

Whether the location was coincidental or not, being in upstate New York not far from Cooperstown, in March of 1978, just as spring training was gearing up, Banks visited a golf and tennis club in Syracuse as a keynote speaker for General Electric. Banks was basically a salesman for life, a man who brought cheer wherever he traveled. His optimistic demeanor played well even with audiences not involved with baseball, who may only have known his name as a famous baseball player.

A sample of Banks' material from answers to questions posed by the audience is just so Ernie. He was quizzed on who was going to win the pennant that year, 1978. "Why, the Cubs. Who else?" He may have been in another part of the country, but Banks said, "Chicago is the greatest city in the world." As a man who showed his concern about others' love-life happiness, he said, "Marriage is the greatest institution in the world."[9]

Interestingly, on a stop in this part of the world, it seemed that Banks credited his father for his outlook on life, a diversionary comment that replaced the story told to Dick Young about his mother. "I never have looked on the negative side of things," Banks said. "I guess I took after my father. As I look back on his life, I can see that he was always happy. I came from a large family—seven boys and five girls—and I remember that our house was always a fun place to be."[10]

Banks said that when he joined the Cubs in 1953 after his stay with the Kansas City Monarchs, the veterans welcomed him and treated him well. They did not haze the younger man, but instead helped him.

> I remember a lot of the veterans were nice to me, especially Hank Sauer. Here I was, a scared, nervous kid in the clubhouse and Hank came up to me right off and said, "How ya doin', kid? If you ever need anything, don't be afraid to ask me." He used to stand around the batting cage with me and say, "I'm going to get two hits tonight." That's the kind of people I've always tried to be with—confident, optimistic people.[11]

At times in such talks, Banks could be exceedingly self-effacing. He was not only an aw-shucks guy, but almost belittled his own talent. Seven years into his retirement, Banks discussed the modern game as if he had been playing during the Deadball Era. "I doubt if I could even hardly play now," he said. "I'd be happy just to be on the Cubs team." He talked about the speed of current shortstops and how marvelously strong their arms were. "Strength and quickness wasn't my game."[12]

Nobody was going to accuse Banks of getting a swelled head because he had been elected to the Hall of Fame. Of course, he was forgetting what set Hall of Famers apart from the other thousands of Major League players: They were designated as all-time greats of the game. When he took his comments to such extremes, it actually sounded silly. He should have left a message for Davey Concepcion to call him back when he hit 500 home runs.

In 1981, Banks wrote a sports opinion column for the *Chicago Tribune*. An explanatory box accompanying the story said he was helping to establish a Black Baseball Hall of History in Ashland, Kentucky. The column itself was Banks' suggestion for the creation of a black baseball Hall of Fame.

When Boston Red Sox star Ted Williams was inducted into the Hall of Fame in 1966, part of his acceptance speech focused on making a case for African American stars of the past years who had been shut out of the majors because of racial discrimination. "I hope that some day the names of Satchel Paige and Josh Gibson in some way could be added as a symbol of the great Negro players that are not here only because they were not given the chance," Williams said.[13]

21. A Hall of Famer

Ernie at bat. Banks hit well enough to be voted into the Baseball Hall of Fame in 1977 (National Baseball Hall of Fame/Osvaldo Salas).

In 1971, under Commissioner Kuhn's initiative, a system was put into place to induct some of those overlooked players. At first those elected were to be honored in some kind of separate-but-equal wing like public schools, but that was soon scotched.

Between 1971 and 1977, before it was disbanded with the class that joined Banks in the Hall, a special committee voted to induct Paige, Gibson, Buck Leonard, Monte Irvin, Cool Papa Bell, Judy Johnson, Oscar Charleston, Martin Dihigo, and John Henry Lloyd. Once the initial work was accomplished, the responsibility for adding any more Negro Leagues players was turned over to the Veterans Committee. In 2006, another special committee was formed to investigate contributions made by other Negro Leagues players and owners, and 17 more people were added to the Hall.

There was much talk among old Negro Leagues stars about who might be chosen. Word was out that a committee was meeting. As Buck O'Neil made his own rounds of the game, helping kids, attending ballgames, visiting with former players, and lobbying on behalf of some of them such as Turkey Stearnes, Hilton Smith and Willie Wells, people would approach him on the topic. "Buck, are you going into the Hall of Fame this year?" was the query of one autograph seeker. "I don't know," O'Neil replied. "That's what they're saying." The man added, "I'm pulling for you."[14]

To fans like that—and many others—the biggest shock when the 17 names were announced was that O'Neil's name was not on the list. The omission of Buck O'Neil, Banks' mentor, coach and advocate, seemed like a colossal mistake. Many baseball fans were stunned that the independent committee chose not to honor him. After that occurred, Hall officials took matters into their own hands. In 2008, the Hall established the Buck O'Neil Lifetime Achievement Award. To further recognize O'Neil, the Hall erected a large bronze statue of him—it is on display on the first floor.

In that 1981 column, Banks spoke of the debt he owed to the players like O'Neil and Bell, who encouraged him when he was on the cusp of making the majors with the Cubs. "I would look at someone like Cool Papa Bell," Banks said, as a younger man then-innocent of the reasons barring Bell from the top level of the game, "who to me had more ability and think, 'Well, you're not in the majors and you're better than me.'"[15] At first he did not realize that Bell was urging him on because he had missed out, born too soon, and now it was Banks' turn.

Just by remaining visible in his retirement, especially in Chicago, by working in the Cubs' front office, Banks found himself honored in several ways he never imagined. Teams in the major professional sports leagues in the United States approach retiring numbers differently, with some practically never retiring a player's number and others retiring so many there are huge gaps in available numbers for new players to wear.

One example in professional basketball is the Boston Celtics. There are so many retired numbers waving in the rafters of the TD Garden, it almost looks like high-class laundry. Not that those players are not worthy, especially with such a storied franchise that has won so many championships. Likewise, one of the Cubs' neighbors in Chicago, albeit representing the National Football League, also has honored many players. The Chicago Bears have sometimes nearly run out of available numbers because of the rules governing how pro football teams must distribute them, with quarterbacks and running backs displaying one of a selected group of numbers, and the same applying to linemen and the like.

Major League Baseball also predates NFL football, the NBA and the National Hockey League, so in theory many early greats could jam the metaphorical rafters with retired numbers. However, until the 1920s players did not wear numbers on their uniform jerseys. The National League was founded in 1876, but it was not until 1929 that teams wore uniform numbers. The New York Yankees and the Cleveland Indians began the trend. The Indians had actually experimented with player numbers on sleeves during the 1916 and 1917 seasons, but didn't continue.

What this meant is that early stars, even Hall of Famers, were never identified with a number the way modern players are. Joe Tinker, Johnny

21. A Hall of Famer

Evers and Frank Chance, the Cubs' early great double-play combination, did not wear numbers. The Cubs did not have any retired numbers at all. In 1982, the team took Banks' No. 14 out of circulation for all time, the first jersey number the Cubs retired. After that, the team retired Ron Santo's No. 10, Ryne Sandberg's 23, the 26 worn by Billy Williams, and the 31 worn by both Ferguson Jenkins and Greg Maddux (on the same day, when the team ran one 31 up a flag pole in right field and one in left field).

Once again, Banks was the trailblazer, recording a first for the Chicago Cubs organization.

22

Living to the Fullest

The way Ernie Banks handled himself in public, combined with the achievements recorded on the diamond, meant he had built up enormous reservoirs of goodwill anywhere he traveled, but most particularly in Chicago, where he was a living legend.

For most, being the face of a franchise with the iconic nickname Mr. Cub, a perennial All-Star, one of the best ever to play baseball and with an on-field career immortalized and validated by induction into the Baseball Hall of Fame, would be enough. In the decades following his retirement from baseball, however, Banks displayed his inquisitive mind in many ways as he explored facets of the world not contained by the Friendly Confines of Wrigley Field.

It was well into the 2000s when Banks began talking up his desire to do something so special and important for the world that he would win the Nobel Prize. When it comes to lifetime achievement awards, having a Nobel Prize bestowed on you probably tops the Baseball Hall of Fame. Generally, people do not set out with a specific goal of winning the Nobel Prize for Peace, for Literature, or for anything else. It is like baseball in that sense. They begin at the bottom and spend years developing a contribution. Eventually, it may be noticed and regarded as a special contribution, and that academy hanging out in Sweden and Norway retreats behind closed doors and takes a vote to grant an award to someone on the planet who has achieved something that has significantly helped that planet.

During a National Public Radio interview, Banks revealed that he first thought of winning the Nobel Prize for Peace when he was 15 years old. "I think about that a lot," Banks said. "I dream about it. I see myself in Stockholm. That has been my journey. I mean I've been chasing the footsteps of my life to do something worthwhile. I haven't done anything yet."[1]

He did mean off the baseball field. Banks' heart was in the right place. He wanted to find a cause to support that would be embraced and implemented for the common good, something that would help millions lead better lives. His thoughts pretty much zeroed in on the homeless and poor.

22. Living to the Fullest

Long removed from his playing career, Banks actually moved to Marina del Rey in Southern California for a spell. His three children, the twin boys and his daughter, were grown and worked in professional capacities in the West. Banks keenly followed baseball and frequently golfed, but his mind was always wandering to the problems of the world and how he could make a difference. It was not as if he had forgotten his own financially limited upbringing in Dallas. He was well aware there were people, many, many of them children, living in far worse circumstances than he encountered. Baseball led Banks into a life of comparative luxury, financial security and fame, where he did not want for money. He was the focal point of a constituency that loved and admired him. "Sometimes I say this to my closest friends," Banks said. "'I don't believe I suffered enough in my life.' I see people in other parts of the world, they have no shoes, sleep on the floor, no food. That's real suffering. When I see some people struggling, I have empathy for them."[2]

Banks admitted these gigantic problems sometimes kept him awake at night pondering solutions. He did not know if he had the clout, or a famous enough name, to organize other well-known and well-off athletes and entertainers to band together, each throw $100,000 into a kitty, and use the money for good. He believed he and Oprah Winfrey could do major things together. "I look at my life and I don't think I've done anything," Banks said more than once. "I want to do more at 74."[3]

Banks chose the whimsical phrase about his age to echo the old days when he rhymed sentences about the Cubs' chances of winning the pennant in a particular season. Maybe Banks became more introspective as he aged— or he never revealed that side of himself when he was young and concentrating on getting his next base hit.

After Phil Wrigley died and the Cubs were sold to the *Chicago Tribune* company, Banks' relationship with the team changed somewhat. For years, though, the club maintained a personal services contract with him, a sort of ambassador-on-call role. There was never any schism between Banks and the Cubs. He was always out there talking up the Cubs, giving speeches, representing the team where necessary. But he was also working on his financial portfolio, and when he turned 55 he received a payment of more than $4 million from the Cubs. That traced to his decision to take Philip Wrigley on a long-ago offer to put half of his salary aside over several years.

Those who have money contribute to charities in varying ways. Some do so quietly with cash donations. Some do so in a splashy manner by funding a new school or capital project that is named for them or a relative. Banks wanted to solve all of the world's poverty ills in one swoop. "I know my life is like seeing the world through rose-colored glasses," he said, "and I don't see the world like the general public sees it. Sometimes I feel like an alien."[4]

Certainly he was an alien with good intentions, or maybe an alien because of those good intentions. He met Nobel laureate Nelson Mandela of South Africa and asked him questions about poverty. He met Hillary Clinton, a former First Lady and Secretary of State, as well as a U.S. Senator, and discussed world peace. He took college courses as an ad hoc student and was proud when Missouri Valley College bestowed an honorary doctorate on him. He had the right to call himself "Dr. Banks."

Even as a much older man, traveling in circles with other famous athletes and well-known Americans, Banks retained the somewhat starry-eyed, still somewhat unbelievable life he had come to lead. One day, he was golfing at Augusta National, the esteemed course where the Masters Golf Tournament is conducted each April, and the foursome included Bill Gates and Warren Buffett, two of the richest men in the world. "I golfed with half of the U.S. economy at Augusta National!" Banks exclaimed.[5]

When he was an active player, even during the Civil Rights Movement, Banks steered away from making what may have been perceived as controversial political statements. He was not even a controversial candidate when he briefly dipped his toe into politics and ran for alderman. That changed later in life. He did not hold back so much. If he felt something was right, he supported it.

In May of 1999, Banks came out as a backer of organ and tissue donation. Granted, this was more of a personal choice than a strongly debated political stand. But when Banks decided it sounded like a good idea, he signed an organ donor card alongside Illinois Secretary of State Jesse White at a press conference. This was not a fleeting thing. Banks' image was placed on posters to be distributed to doctors around the country as part of a "Give So Others Can Live" program.

The issue had become personal to Banks. Walter Payton, the great Chicago Bears running back, was engaged in a public fight against a rare liver disease and was hoping for a liver transplant to save his life. Payton died a few months later.

> The one thing that really highlighted all of our lives is our good friend Walter Payton. It just hit me so hard because there are only about 5,000 professional athletes in the United States. When something happens to one of us, it affects all of us. We really feel it. We're concerned about it. I was totally hurt about a great friend. Athletes are human beings. They get sick, too.[6]

Also, Banks' old teammate and friend, Gene Baker, was awaiting a kidney transplant. So this was no abstract issue for him.

> I didn't get a chance to play in the World Series. That's OK. But all my life I have always prayed one day I'm going to have an opportunity to do something to help somebody else, to make a difference in someone's life. I'm really proud and happy to be associated with this tremendous program. Maybe the little things I can do might

22. Living to the Fullest 171

not be that great, but I do know one person can change a lot of things. One person can make a difference. I want to be that one person—working with all of you on the team—to make a difference, to help somebody's life, to change their lives, to extend their lives.

When Banks urged people to "step up at the plate and donate," he was working baseball into his talk, but he couldn't come up with a rhyme.[7]

Some years later, Banks did embrace a more controversial cause, one simultaneously endorsed by the Cubs, too. In 2010, the Cubs announced that they would take part in Chicago's Gay Pride Parade and that Banks was going to ride on the team float, waving to the crowd. In an earlier era, such a stand by the Cubs and Banks would have been political poison. Such a position in 2010 was removed from the darkest of Neanderthal days, though the time had been reached in American society when it was difficult to foresee fans boycotting the purchase of Cubs tickets en masse. At the time, fans were lucky to be able to obtain tickets for individual games. And after his decades as Mr. Cub, it was difficult to imagine much backlash against Banks.

Still, this combined gesture impressed a *Sports Illustrated* writer sufficiently to say that if the United States was really a courageous and passionate country, then the Cubs should be America's Team for supporting the gay and lesbian movement. Those who wrote for publications oriented towards gay and lesbian readership praised the Cubs for taking such a stand and were further surprised when it was announced that Banks would be part of the parade. That was a showstopper and an even more important statement of support because Banks' was the biggest name of all connected to the club.

As it so happened, Brent Sopel, who skated for the Chicago Blackhawks' Stanley Cup-winning National Hockey League team, was also committed to riding on a different float, accompanied by the Stanley Cup. Sopel, a married father of three, was doing so to honor the son of one of his former general managers, who had come out of the closet and been killed in an automobile accident only months later.

A writer for *Outsports*, said these were significant developments. "This is huge," he wrote. "First the Stanley Cup, now a Hall of Fame Baseball Player? Wow. Ernie Banks was the Cubs' first black player. Fitting that he would be a part of this historic event."[8]

It was just additional evidence that Banks' popularity crossed all lines.

In the late 1990s, when Banks was busy gadding about trying to save the world and make a difference in it, it was revealed that he was suffering from hypertension, or high blood pressure. Since some people associated the long-term illness only with stress, they thought it impossible that such an easy-going guy like Banks could have contracted it and had to cope with it on a daily basis. The diagnosis was made in 1997, though knowledge of it became more widespread in 1999.

Banks pinned the development on the drastic way he had to change his life when he retired from baseball. Instead of going to Wrigley Field at the same time every day to report for work, or to hook up with teammates at the airport regularly to fly to work, he was on a whole new schedule. Change meant stress to him.

> When I got out of baseball, I was like brain dead. I said, "Gosh, I don't know anything, and I don't know anybody out of baseball, and I don't have any skills." My kids were going to college, my income went down, so I had to find a job to support my family. This is not crying. It just changes what I'm talking about. Lifestyle changes that happen to all of us. I wasn't used to change. I'm the only professional athlete who played his entire career in one city, with one team, one owner, one park, one life. So when I had to deal with change, it affected my immune system.[9]

Sure enough, when Banks had a sit-down with his doctor, he was told he had to lose weight, work out daily, change his eating habits and take medication. The same message gets delivered to millions of Americans every year for one ailment or another, including commonly for high blood pressure. Banks took the doctor's words seriously. "The disease of hypertension pushed me over to reality," Banks said. "It's not about a 3-and-2 count and trying to hit a home run for the Cubs. That's not pressure. That's not reality. Reality is a stroke, diabetes, kidney failure, all the things that come from high blood pressure. And the thing is, a lot of people have it and don't even know they have it."[10]

Words of wisdom from Dr. Banks.

It finally happened. In the 1990s and early 2000s, along came a fresh Cubs slugger who hit more home runs than Banks, who engaged with the fans and became hugely popular. This coincided with a period of Major League Baseball when the home run was a grander weapon than ever, when everyone seemed to be a slugger, and for the first time in more than 35 years, bashers threatened Roger Maris' 1961 home run mark of 61 in a season.

Sammy Sosa, an outfielder from the Dominican Republic, broke into the majors at 20 with the Texas Rangers. He did not play much and moved to the Chicago White Sox. In 1992, the two Chicago teams cut a deal. The Cubs swapped George Bell for Sosa's potential. In 1993, Sosa began blossoming and thriving with the Cubs, bashing 33 home runs and driving in 93 runs while also stealing 36 bases. He was young, fleet, and powerful.

Sosa began making All-Star teams in 1995, and his production kept expanding. In 1998, he led the NL in runs with 134 and runs batted in with 158. That season, Sosa and Mark McGwire of the St. Louis Cardinals engaged in a riveting home run battle in pursuit of Maris' record. Baseball's image had been severely tarnished when a players-owners feud led to a strike in 1994 and the cancellation of the World Series. Fed-up fans swore off the game, and attendance dropped when play resumed in 1995. That pall hung over the sport for a few years.

22. Living to the Fullest 173

However, the McGwire-Sosa duel generated so much energy, excitement, and attention that fans once again filled parks just hoping they might see one of the big two slam a home run. On September 8, McGwire belted his 62nd homer to surpass Maris. Sosa soon tied him, and they both put the former New York Yankee in their rearview mirror. At the end of the chase, McGwire's new record was 70 home runs and Sosa collected 66, at the time the two top totals in big-league history.

Over the next several years, twice Sosa again exceeded 60 home runs and closed in on Banks' lifetime Cubs mark, eventually passing him. Banks, as was to be expected, was gracious in discussing Sosa's prowess, his stature as a Cub, and bypassing Banks on the all-time homer list. Sosa finished his career with 609.

"I just knew it was coming," Banks said when Sosa surpassed his 512 homers. "There is no finer person I would have liked to have seen break it other than Sammy. I could see Sammy's ability when he first came to the Cubs." Banks said he had once visited Sosa in the Dominican, where they played golf and talked baseball. "He is just a cordial, smart young man. He's like my son. I wish I had learned Spanish when I was younger so I could communicate with him a little bit more. To me, he always has had the ability to be one of the greatest power hitters who ever played. Sammy can hit the ball to all fields with power."[11]

But then it all frayed around the edges. The feel-good McGwire-Sosa rivalry unraveled. As Congress, the courts, and Major League investigators became involved, it was shown that much of baseball's power surge in home runs may have been attributable to the use of illegal, performance-enhancing drugs, from steroids to other substances. McGwire later admitted to using such drugs. Sosa's reputation was tainted when his name showed up on a list of alleged users. He has never admitted taking any performance-enhancing supplements, and testifying under oath, he said he never broke the law or failed a drug test. However, McGwire and Sosa remain linked together in the eyes of many, and neither has made much headway in being elected to the Baseball Hall of Fame, once thought to be a lock for both.

Later, not ignoring the Sosa reports, Banks, in his own diplomatic way, urged Sosa to tell the truth about everything that happened, one way or another. "I would say just what Mark McGwire did," Banks said. "You know, come clean with it. Explain it to them. You know he will have fans in the Dominican. Just say, 'This is what happened.' Just admit it and live with it and understand it. I am sure a lot of people will forgive him."[12]

Sosa has made no statements about steroids in recent years and does not make appearances in Chicago. There seems to be no connection between him and the Cubs, at least for now.

In 2011, Banks was chosen as a recipient of the Beacon Award, presented to individuals "whose lives have been emblematic of the spirit of the Civil Rights Movement." He was honored along with actor Morgan Freeman and musician Carlos Santana at the Civil Rights Game between the Philadelphia Phillies and host Atlanta Braves at Turner Field in May of that year. Banks was cited as the Beacon Of Life winner for establishing his "Ernie Banks Live Above and Beyond Foundation." The organization's aim is to improve the lives of underprivileged children and senior citizens by building stronger neighborhoods and working to eliminate age and race discrimination.

The connection between Ernie Banks and the world seemed to expand continuously. In 2013, President Barack Obama summoned Banks to the White House to present him with the Presidential Medal of Freedom, the highest civilian honor the United States can bestow. It was created in 1963 by President John F. Kennedy, and over the decades several baseball stars had been honored, including Jackie Robinson, Roberto Clemente and Banks' close friend Buck O'Neil, as well as Henry Aaron, Joe DiMaggio, Frank Robinson, Stan Musial and Ted Williams.

Also in sports, Jesse Owens, Paul "Bear" Bryant, Muhammad Ali, Arthur Ashe, Pat Summit and Billie Jean King are among those who have been recognized. Numerous Americans from all walks of life have been honored. There were 16 honorees in Banks' group, including former President Bill Clinton, astronaut Sally Ride, Oprah Winfrey, and feminist Gloria Steinem. Cubs owner Tom Ricketts and former Banks teammates Billy Williams and Ferguson Jenkins attended.

Obama, a Chicago resident and a White Sox fan, teased Banks by saying, "Let's play two." He added, "That's Mr. Cub—the man who came up through the Negro Leagues making $7 a day, and became the first black player to suit up for the Cubs, and one of the greatest hitters of all time. He is just a wonderful man and a great icon of my hometown."[13]

Banks was 82 and still seemed bewildered that he had done so much despite starting out with the odds stacked against him. Each honor that came his way seemed to surprise him all the more.

"I look at my life and any of my 11 brothers or sisters could have done this, too, so why me?" Banks said of the Medal of Freedom. When Banks received the call from the White House informing him of the honor, he said, "'Wow, are you kidding? The same award as Buck O'Neil?' I've got to settle into the idea that 'Ernie, this is it. This is the pinnacle of what you've accomplished for the way you've led your life.'" When the Chicago sportswriter interviewing him said maybe this was going to be his highest honor of all and he might not get that Nobel Peace Prize, Banks added, "I said I haven't done that ... yet."[14]

23

The End

Ernie Banks never seemed to be at a loss for words. He might, on occasion, choose not to say very much, or choose his words carefully, but he usually had something to say about almost anything.

On the day the Chicago Cubs unveiled a statue of their great slugger, though, Banks seemed almost overcome by the honor of gazing upon himself in bronze outside Wrigley Field. Dazzled and joyful, pleased at the depiction and reflective about what it meant, when Banks looked at this image of the young Ernie at bat, he said, "Is that me?" Well, yes, it was. He repeated that thought, "Is that me?"[1]

That was Banks' visceral reaction at the March 2008 festivities when he was feted in a special ceremony outside the ballpark he loved. It was a fitting tribute to and for Mr. Cub, immortalized in the same form in which he stood in the batter's box, his upright, right-handed stance poised to pounce on a pitched ball and maybe launch it beyond the ivy for one of those 512 home runs.

Wearing a Cubs cap and a coat, because it was raining and not nice enough in Wrigleyville to play two that day, Banks picked up a bat and emulated his old form. Banks referred to the erection of the statue as a "miracle." Some Cubs fans defied the lousy weather to be on hand, and they struck up a chant of "Ernie! Ernie!"[2]

Actually, the idea of constructing a Banks statue had been floating around for some time. In the latter stages of getting it designed and sculpted, the Reverend Jesse Jackson and Chicago's WSCR-AM 670 radio talk show figures Mike North and Mike Murphy lobbied for the work. Sculptor Lou Cella of nearby Highwood, Illinois, was hired to shape it.

"This should have happened 10 or 15 years ago," said Henry Aaron, one of Banks' contemporary Hall of Fame competitors from his playing days.[3] Aaron, Billy Williams, Ferguson Jenkins and Ron Santo, three of Banks' most significant teammates, were also present to honor Banks. Banks, always identified by a trademark smile, was also smiling in the statue, no accidental depiction. "It's the best," Banks said of the statue. "This is the epitome of American life to be able to have this honor bestowed upon me. Think about that. Just me. And when I'm no longer here, I'll still be here. It's amazing. This is amazing to me."[4]

Although the weather was shaky, the Cubs did squeeze in their particularly early Opening Day game against the Milwaukee Brewers, losing 4–3 before 41,089 fans inside Wrigley. During the seventh-inning stretch, Banks led the crowd in the traditional singing of "Take Me Out to the Ballgame." Manager Lou Piniella wondered how the Cubs could not win on such a day with Banks, Williams, Jenkins and Santo in the house. It was a day when many people said nice things about Banks, including Aaron, the man who first broke Babe Ruth's home run record before yielding it to Barry Bonds, and who as another African American player in the 1950s faced his own discriminatory forces. "You were the greatest ambassador for baseball and you still are a great ambassador," Aaron said to Banks.[5]

Of all the late-in-life honors Banks received, the statue was the most obvious and visible one to his fans and Cubs fans. It was on proud display year-round, all seasons. There did not even have to be a game played for fans to stop and admire it. On game days, many paused before entering Wrigley to take their seats and took pictures standing in front of it.

Certainly, the Presidential Medal of Freedom was special. But the medal was draped around Banks' neck and then left public view. The statue was always there, the constant Banks reminder.

In the time between Banks' receipt of the Medal in November of 2013 and early 2015, his health began to fail. In old age, he was as slender as he had been as an active player—apparently the doctor's message took about exercise and watching his diet. As a young man and well into his forties, Banks still looked young, with few wrinkles. Some of those became apparent when he was an older man, but although he did wear glasses later in life, he was not thoroughly wizened.

Near the end of his life, Banks became estranged from his fourth wife, Liz, and moved back to Chicago. All of his immediate family was in California. A woman helped look after him, but in the months before his death from a heart attack on January 23, 2015, Banks often complained about being lonely.

For several years, well-known former Chicago sportswriter Ron Rapaport had been trying to get Banks to complete a more authoritative and detailed autobiography of his life and career than existed. They would have many stops and starts, according to Rapaport, but despite a signed contract from a publisher, he could never get Banks to complete it. After Banks' death, Rapaport wrote about these lengthy back-and-forth contacts and some previously unveiled sadnesses of Banks' life in his last days. He noted that Banks' autopsy cited dementia, something which might have explained some of his

23. The End

problems relating to old friends and close family. Rapaport believed Banks was profoundly lonely, but when he spoke to his caretaker and wife, it seemed, they seemed ready and willing to help him at any time, that it was he who pushed them away, or talked gloom and doom.

Rapaport did not dispute the public vision of Banks, only wrote that there was more to the man and he was more complicated beneath the many human layers of personality than most knew. "What was it about him?" Rapaport wondered. "Why was Ernie, virtually alone among the great players of his generation such an idealized, one-dimensional fantasy? But Ernie escapes all context. He is nothing but sunshine and smiles. Just as he was defined by his image, so was he imprisoned by it."[6]

Rapaport's was a far more melancholy portrait of Banks than others'. But perhaps Banks had changed and lost his long-held smile as he faded and passed away a week shy of his 84th birthday. But when Banks died and the tributes to him poured in, they all addressed his magnificent baseball abilities and his public image as a man, as one of the friendliest, most open guys in the world, who never met a man he didn't like except for Leo Durocher, and the person who brought such brightness into the lives of so many.

The once-so-strong athlete had taken some falls in his Chicago apartment, always a menace to the elderly who don't catch themselves before hitting the floor. Banks was actually traveling in an ambulance to a hospital when he died.

Thomas Ricketts, the Cubs chairman and the front man for the family that owns the Cubs, was the first to offer praise of Banks. "He was one of the greatest players of all time," Ricketts said. "He was a pioneer in the major leagues. And more importantly, he was the warmest and most sincere person I've ever known."[7]

It was natural that people with Cubs connections led the way with tributes and comments mourning Banks, but the rest of Chicago chimed in, many online. The Chicago Bears stated, "Bears send deepest condolences to Chicago Cubs on passing of legendary Hall of Famer Ernie Banks: Mr. Cub." "Mr. Cub, What you have done for the game of baseball and the city of Chicago and everyone you have ever touched will never be forgotten. RIP."— From Cubs present player Anthony Rizzo. "I'm so sorry to hear the passing of Mr. Ernie Banks! What a Special Man! Always put a smile on my face when seeing him! God bless you."—Hall of Famer Frank Thomas. "The legend, the Chicago icon, passes away ERNIE BANKS, may be the best man I ever met in baseball. RIP. Let's play 2. Condolences to his family."—Former manager Ozzie Guillen.[8]

President Obama and First Lady Michelle Obama issued a statement that included the observation that Michelle Obama watched Cubs games on TV with her dad when Ernie played. "Somewhere, the sun is shining, the air is fresh, his team's behind him, and Mr. Class—'Mr. Cub'—is ready to play two," said the president of the United States.[9]

A public visitation was scheduled for Banks in his casket at Chicago's Fourth Presbyterian Church for January 30 and January 31, the second day what would have been Banks' 84th birthday. The memorial service also took place there and was televised on local station WGN, the Cubs' own online site, and other sports sites.

The Rev. Jesse Jackson and Chicago Mayor Rahm Emanuel, who called Banks "a humble hero," spoke at the memorial service. So did ex-teammates Ferguson Jenkins, Banks' road roommate at the end of his career, Randy Hundley, George Altman and Billy Williams, and Hall of Famers Henry Aaron, Reggie Jackson, Andre Dawson and Lou Brock. Jackson pulled out a surprise. He exhorted the congregation to stand and applaud as a birthday wish for Banks. Joel Banks, one of Ernie's twin sons, wished him a happy birthday during his own eulogy.[10]

Williams, who knew Banks for more than a half a century, said the loss of Banks was significant, and he was slowly processing his death. "People not only here in Chicago, but people around the world recognize the type of individual he was," Williams said. "It's beginning to sink in now. I've lost a great friend. You've lost a great friend." Williams said he had tried to touch base with Banks on the phone to talk only a few days before he died, but could not reach him. When Banks' kids were young, Williams actually babysat some of the time. Now that their father was gone, he thanked them "for lending me your father that many years."[11]

The fans who lined up for the viewing saw a casket draped with a Cubs No. 14 jersey and a picture of Banks behind it. Some of them wore Banks jerseys themselves.

Jenkins always got a chuckle at how Banks was a non-stop chatterer during their playing days together, whether he was manning first base and the action was live, in the Cubs' dugout or clubhouse, on road trips or elsewhere. Sometimes he rode with Williams and Banks to games, and in the car Banks also was always talking away. Jenkins said Banks was like "AM and FM. He was like a radio. You couldn't turn him off."[12]

Although many cried and sadness was in the atmosphere, most called this memorial service a celebration of life, and if Ernie Banks' life was to be celebrated there were going to be many smiles. Jerry Banks said, "We've heard countless stories of interactions with fans. It makes our mourning his passing easier. For every tear we shed comes 10 stories of laughter, followed by, 'That sounds like dad.'" Jerry recalled his father often said, "I feel like I can fly."[13]

Ricketts, the owner, mingled with some Cubs fans who turned out for this final goodbye to Banks and said many shared Ernie stories with him. "Ernie Banks is not 'Mr. Cub' because we loved him," Ricketts said. "Ernie

23. The End

Banks became 'Mr. Cub' because he loved us back. As it turns out, Ernie became 'Mr. Cub' through no more magic than just being himself."[14]

Oh, it seemed as if the stories about Ernie Banks, the man and ballplayer, would never stop that day. Mayor Emanuel called Banks "summer personified." Williams said Banks "never did have a mean streak in his body." Jerome Banks said Buck O'Neil turned his father from "a caterpillar into a butterfly," with the shift from the Kansas City Monarchs to the Chicago Cubs.[15]

Following the memorial service, which lasted nearly two hours, a procession drove through Chicago streets, passing Wrigley Field (under reconstruction at the time) and beneath the famous ballpark marquee announcing the Cubs' schedule. There had been some discussion that Banks might have wanted to be cremated, but he was buried in Graceland Cemetery. The actual burial did not take place until February 6, after Liz Banks went to court to prevent cremation.[16]

Soon after, there emerged some disputes over Banks' last wishes and his final will. Banks had sometimes said publicly he would like his ashes to be spread at Wrigley Field. He and his wife were going through a divorce at the time of his death, but she made sure he was buried in Chicago. Regina Rice, Banks' caretaker near the end of his life, took the other viewpoint.

A few weeks after the memorial service, Liz Banks and Banks' children protested a will dated October 17, 2014, turning over power of attorney, a health-care statement and his worldly goods to Rice and leaving them nothing. The Bankses said they knew nothing of a substitute will. When Ron Rapaport interviewed members of the Banks family and Rice, they presented opposing views of what was going on over the final months of Banks' life. The Bankses said she prevented them from talking to Ernie. Rice said Banks frequently told her to change his phone number so family members couldn't reach them. She claimed she changed the numbers, as directed, but texted them to the family. Liz Banks asserted that Rice made Banks change the numbers and "isolated" him. As for money, Rice said Banks' estate was valued at only about $16,000.[17] However, in later court documents, as Rice continued to manage the estate, some of Banks' memorabilia was placed at auction, and it was valued at $250,000.

At one point, it was said in court that in 2013, once Banks and Liz had decided to divorce, he had sent a cease and desist letter to his wife in terms of her representing him in his business or financial dealings.

In September of 2016, the Banks family and Rice nearly came to a settlement. Then attorneys representing Liz Banks pulled out, and that deal was scuttled. The presiding judge then retired, further setting back resolution.

Young Ernie Banks would have abhorred this messy argument over his remains and his intentions. If it was in his power, he would have tried to make everyone happy, Regina Rice, Liz Banks, and his boys. That would have been most like the Ernie Banks everyone thought they knew. Maybe this was the conflict Banks was supposed to resolve to obtain that Nobel Peace Prize recognition.

This posthumous warfare was unseemly, but that is not how Banks will be remembered. He will be remembered as a great and marvelous baseball player of both grace and power, someone who was considered a civic treasure in Chicago, and as a man who lit up a room when he entered it the way few people ever could. Whether he hid certain problems from the world or not made him no different from the rest of humanity who saw no need to hang dirty laundry in public. Banks probably would have regretted this dispute going public. Otherwise, his only public regret was playing 2,528 games without competing in the post-season. Wouldn't you know it, in 2016, not long after he died, the Cubs actually won their first World Series since 1908. Banks not only didn't play in one, he didn't live long enough to see the Cubs play in one. He would have loved to witness that triumph.

Somewhere along the way, it was instilled in Ernie Banks that whether through dramatic actions like hitting a home run, simply signing his name for youngsters who looked up to him, or touching millions of people with his smile, his words and his spirit, that it was his responsibility to help make planet Earth a happier place. Few would argue that he did not succeed.

It seemed so appropriate that when the mourners filled her church for Banks' memorial service that January day, presiding the Reverend Shannon Kershner said, "We have come here to thank God for Ernie Banks."[18]

Chapter Notes

Introduction

1. Lew Freedman, *Cubs Essential: Everything You Need to Know to Be a Real Fan* (Chicago: Triumph Books, 2006), 50.
2. Paul White, "Ernie Banks' Legacy Extends Far Beyond Mr. Cub Status," *USA Today*, January 24, 2015.
3. Phil Rogers, *Ernie Banks: Mr. Cub and the Summer of '69* (Chicago: Triumph Books, 2011), 4.

Chapter 1

1. Jerome Holtzman, "Banks, Honored by 20,000, Thankful He's an American," *The Sporting News*, August 29, 1964.
2. Holtzman.
3. Holtzman.
4. Lew Freedman, *Cubs Essential: Everything You Need to Know to Be a Real Fan* (Chicago: Triumph Books, 2006), 56.
5. Holtzman.
6. Holtzman.

Chapter 2

1. Ernie Banks and Jim Enright, *"Mr. Cub"* (Chicago: Rutledge Books, 1971), 23.
2. Banks and Enright, 24.
3. Banks and Enright, 28.
4. James Enright, "Ernie's Only Race Problem: To Beat Throw to First Base," *The Sporting News*, August 22, 1964.
5. James Enright, "Family Fought Losing Battle with Window, Pop Recalls," *The Sporting News*, February 17, 1960.
6. Enright.
7. Enright.
8. Enright.
9. Ernie Banks, "Ernie Didn't Dream of Big League Role in His Early Teens," *Chicago Tribune*, June 23, 1969.
10. Banks.
11. Ron Santo and Phil Pepe, *Few and Chosen: Defining Cubs Greatness Across the Eras* (Chicago: Triumph Books 2005), 14.

Chapter 3

1. Bob Broeg, "Cool Papa to Swell with Pride as Ernie Enters Shrine," *St. Louis Post-Dispatch*, August 7, 1977.
2. Broeg.
3. Broeg.
4. Buck O'Neil, Steve Wulf, and David Conrads, *I Was Right on Time* (New York: Simon & Schuster, 1996), 189.
5. O'Neil, Wulf and Conrads, 189–190.
6. O'Neil, Wulf and Conrads, 30.
7. O'Neil, Wulf and Conrads, 33.
8. Ernie Banks and Jim Enright, *"Mr. Cub"* (Chicago: Rutledge Books, 1971), 43.
9. Banks and Enright, 44.
10. O'Neil, Wulf and Conrads, 190.
11. Bob Smith, "O'Neil Gave Banks to Cubs," *Chicago Daily News*, June 9, 1962.
12. Banks and Enright, 45.
13. Banks and Enright, 47.
14. Banks and Enright, 51.

Chapter 4

1. Art Rust, Jr., *Get That Nigger Off the Field: An Informal History of the Black Man in Baseball*, (New York: Delacorte Press, 1976), 137.
2. Rust, 137.
3. Bob Smith, "O'Neil Gave Banks to Cubs," *Chicago Daily News*, June 9, 1962.
4. Smith.
5. Buck O'Neil, Steve Wulf, and David

Conrads, *I Was Right on Time*, (New York: Simon & Schuster, 1996), 190–191.
 6. O'Neil, Wulf, and Conrads, 191.
 7. O'Neil, Wulf, and Conrads, 192.
 8. James Enright, "Cubs Sign Banks, Negro Star," *Chicago American*, September 8, 1953.
 9. Enright.

Chapter 5

 1. Ernie Banks and Jim Enright, *"Mr. Cub"* (Chicago: Rutledge Books, 1971), 67.
 2. Charles F. Faber, "Gene Baker," Society of American Baseball Research Bio Project (no date).
 3. James Enright, "Coast Pilots Say Yes," *Chicago American* (Baseball Hall of Fame Archives, August 1953, date missing).
 4. Enright.
 5. Wendell Smith, "Can't Hurt L.A," *Chicago American* (Baseball Hall of Fame Archives, August 1953, date missing).
 6. Howard Roberts, "Cubs Claim Baker Made Banks," *Chicago Daily News*, March 8, 1956.
 7. Roberts.
 8. Roberts.
 9. Banks and Enright, 56.
 10. Peter Golenbock, *Wrigleyville: A Magical History Tour of the Chicago Cubs*, (New York: St. Martin's Press, 1996), 350.

Chapter 6

 1. Gordon Edes, "George Digby and Willie Mays, the One That Got Away," *ESPN.com*, May 3, 2014.
 2. Edes.
 3. John Klima, "When the Yankees Were Not Ready for Willie Mays," *New York Times*, September 12, 2009.
 4. Klima.
 5. James Enright, "At Last! Matthews to Bring Up Baker," *Chicago American*, September 1, 1953.
 6. Lew Freedman, *Game of My Life: Chicago Cubs*, (Champaign, IL: Sports Publishing, 2007), 108.
 7. Lew Freedman, *Cubs Essential*, (Chicago: Triumph Books, 2006), 51.
 8. Ernie Banks and Jim Enright, *"Mr. Cub"* (Chicago: Rutledge Books, 1971), 80.
 9. Banks and Enright, 81.
 10. Banks and Enright, 81.
 11. Banks and Enright, 82.
 12. Banks and Enright, 83.
 13. Charles F. Faber, "Gene Baker," Society of American Baseball Research Bio Project (no date).
 14. Banks and Enright, 84.
 15. Banks and Enright, 85.
 16. Banks and Enright, 85.

Chapter 7

 1. John Snyder, *Cubs Journal*, (Cincinnati: Emmis Books, 2005), 378.
 2. Snyder, 378.
 3. Ernie Banks and Jim Enright, *Mr. Cub*, (Chicago: Rutledge Books, 1971), 87.
 4. Carrie Muskat, *Banks to Sandberg to Grace* (Lincolnwood, IL: Contemporary Books, 2001), 40.
 5. Janice Petterchak, *Jack Brickhouse: A Voice for All Seasons* (Chicago: Contemporary Books, 1996), 117.
 6. John C. Hoffman, *Hank Sauer* (New York: A.S Barnes & Co., 1953), 20.
 7. Muskat, 46.

Chapter 8

 1. Ernie Banks, and Jim Enright, *"Mr. Cub,"* (Chicago: Rutledge Books, 1971), 93.
 2. James Enright, "Banks in Grand Slam Record," *Chicago American*, September 20, 1955.
 3. Enright.
 4. Phil Rogers, *Ernie Banks: Mr. Cub and the Summer of '69* (Chicago: Triumph Books, 2011), 83.
 5. Rogers, 59.
 6. Rogers, 59.
 7. Rogers, 103.
 8. Rogers, 103.
 9. Ed Prell, "Cubs Sign Banks' Brother Ben," *Chicago Tribune*, February 10, 1956.
 10. Banks and Enright, 93.
 11. Banks and Enright, 94.
 12. No byline, "Baker Named Bucs Farm Aide," *Pittsburgh Press*, May 29, 1959.
 13. David Condon, "In the Wake of the News," *Chicago Tribune*, July 5, 1961.
 14. Condon.

Chapter 9

 1. Ernie Banks and Jim Enright, *"Mr. Cub"* (Chicago: Rutledge Books, 1971), 19–20.
 2. Carlos Mendez, "Mr. Cub Anoints A-Rod as Best Ever," *Fort Worth Star-Telegram*, September 26, 2002.
 3. Banks and Enright, 21.
 4. Phil Rogers, *Ernie Banks: Mr. Cub and the Summer of '69* (Chicago: Triumph Books, 2011), 122.
 5. Rogers, 123.
 6. Rogers, 126.
 7. Peter Golenbock, *Wrigleyville: A Magi-*

cal History Tour of the Chicago Cubs (New York: St. Martin's Press, 1996), 348.
   8. Banks and Enright, 138.
   9. Banks and Enright, 94–95.
   10. Mendez.
   11. Edgar Munzel, "Banks Season 'Greatest Ever' by a Shortstop," The Sporting News, September 11, 1959.
   12. Banks and Enright, 96.

Chapter 10

   1. Lew Freedman, Cubs Game of My Life (Champaign, IL: Sports Publishing, 2007), 85.
   2. Freedman, 89.
   3. Freedman, 89.
   4. Freedman, 89–90.
   5. Ron Santo and Phil Pepe: Few and Chosen, Defining Cubs Greatness Across the Eras (Chicago: Triumph Books, 2005), ix.
   6. Santo and Pepe, ibid., ix.
   7. George Altman and Lew Freedman, George Altman: My Baseball Journey from the Negro Leagues to the Majors and Beyond (Jefferson, NC: McFarland, 2013), 91.
   8. Altman and Freedman, 93.
   9. Santo and Pepe, 13.
   10. Santo and Pepe, 14.
   11. Milton Gross, North American Newspaper Alliance, April 1, 1960.
   12. Gross.

Chapter 11

   1. Buck O'Neil, Steve Wulf, and David Conrads, I Was Right on Time (New York: Simon & Schuster, 1996), 199–200.
   2. O'Neil, Wulf and Conrads, 201.
   3. O'Neil, Wulf, and Conrads, 202–203.
   4. O'Neil, Wulf, and Conrads, 205.
   5. Edward Prell, "No Manager for Cubs in '61—Wrigley," Chicago Tribune, January 13, 1961.
   6. O'Neil, Wulf and Conrads, 213–214.
   7. Jerome Holtzman, "Were the Cubs' College of Coaches a Complete Failure? To a Degree…" Chicago Tribune, December 21, 1986.
   8. Zack Helfand, "Diminished Power of Managers in Baseball Echoes Cubs' Early '60s College of Coaches," Los Angeles Times, November 4, 2015.
   9. Lew Freedman, Cubs Essential, (Chicago: Triumph Books, 2006), 76.
   10. Ron Kantowski, "Cubs' College of Coaches Wasn't So Dumb," Las Vegas Review-Journal, March 14, 2015.
   11. Billy Williams and Fred Mitchell, Billy Williams: My Sweet-Swinging Lifetime with the Cubs (Chicago: Triumph Books, 2008), 1.
   12. Williams and Mitchell, 74.

   13. Williams and Mitchell, 74.
   14. No byline, "Some Ernie Quotes You Can Bank On," Chicago Tribune, January 24, 2015.
   15. Williams and Mitchell, 75.
   16. Lew Freedman, personal interview, 2005.

Chapter 12

   1. Charles Cleveland, "Ernie Banks to Run for Alderman in 8th," Chicago Daily News, December 20, 1962.
   2. Ben Joravsky, "The Time Mr. Cub Ran for Alderman," The Chicago Reader, January 28, 2015.
   3. Joravsky.
   4. Edgar Munzel, "Banks Learning Quickly in New Job at Gateway," Chicago Tribune, March 14, 1962.
   5. Arthur Daley, "Sports of the Times, Rookie First Baseman," New York Times, May 18, 1962.
   6. Jerome Holtzman, "Bruins Worry Over Banks, Vet Slugger Fights Dismal Slump," Chicago Sun-Times, June 8, 1963.
   7. Holtzman.
   8. Ernie Banks and Jim Enright, "Mr. Cub" (Chicago: Rutledge Books, 1971), 136.
   9. Ron Santo and Randy Minkoff, For Love of Ivy (Chicago: Bonus Books, 1993), 46.
   10. Santo and Minkhoff, 46.
   11. Santo and Minkhoff, 48.
   12. R. Lincoln Harris, "Cubs of the 1960s: Lou Brock," Wrigleyvillenation.com, July 13, 2014.
   13. Phil Rogers, Ernie Banks: Mr. Cub and the Summer of '69 (Chicago: Triumph Books, 2011), 159.
   14. Rogers, 160.
   15. Jerome Holtzman, "Banks, Honored by 20,000, Thankful He's an American," The Sporting News, August 29, 1964.
   16. Holtzman.

Chapter 13

   1. Paul White, "Ernie Banks' Legacy Extends Far Beyond Mr. Cub Status," USA Today, January 24, 2015.
   2. Peter Golenbock, Wrigleyville: A Magical History Tour of the Chicago Cubs (New York: St. Martin's Press, 1996), 352.
   3. Lew Freedman, personal interview, April 2018.
   4. Golenbock, 353.
   5. Golenbock, 353.
   6. Hal Bock, "Cub Hurler Says He Can Hypnotize the Hitters," Associated Press/Park City (Utah) News, August 4, 1965.
   7. Lew Freedman, personal interview, 2006.

8. Marty Noble, "The Day Hendley Allowed Just One, Koufax Was Perfect," *MLB.com*, September 9, 2015.
9. Noble.
10. John Snyder, *Cubs Journal* (Cincinnati: Emmis Books, 2005), 435.
11. Snyder, 435.

Chapter 14

1. Joe Niese, *Burleigh Grimes: Baseball's Last Legal Spitballer* (Jefferson, NC: McFarland, 2013), 189.
2. Frank Graham, "Leo Doesn't Like Nice Guys," *New York Journal-American*, July 6, 1946; Leo Durocher, "Nice Guys Finish Last," *Cosmopolitan*, April 1948.
3. John Snyder, *Cubs Journal* (Cincinnati: Emmis Books, 2005), 436.
4. Paul Dickson, *Leo Durocher: Baseball's Prodigal Son* (New York: Bloomsbury, 2017), 248.
5. Dickson, 248.
6. Stan Isaacs, "Banks Shoots from the Hip for Leo the Lip," *Newsday*, March 3, 1966.
7. Isaacs.
8. Isaacs.
9. Isaacs.
10. No byline, "Ernie Banks' Three Triples in One Game Ties Record," *Houston Post*, June 12, 1966.
11. *Houston Post*, ibid.
12. *Houston Post*, ibid.
13. Edgar Munzel, "End of the Line for Vet Banks? Ernie Loses Post to Boccabella," *The Sporting News*, July 16, 1966.
14. Carrie Muskat, *Banks to Sandberg to Grace* (Lincolnwood, IL: Contemporary Books, 2001), 41.
15. Muskat, 42–43.
16. Munzel.
17. Edgar Munzel, "Sprinter Owens' Tips Put Banks in Tip-Top Shape," *Chicago Tribune*, April 9, 1966.

Chapter 15

1. Jerome Holtzman, "Europe's Cities Fascinate Cubs' Traveler Banks," *Chicago Sun-Times*, November 19, 1966.
2. Holtzman.
3. Holtzman.
4. Edgar Munzel, "End of the Line for Vet Banks? Ernie Loses Post to Boccabella," *The Sporting News*, July 16, 1966.
5. Jerome Holtzman, "Banks Trims Pounds, Puts TNT in Mace," *The Sporting News*, June 3, 1967.
6. Holtzman.
7. Bob Wolf, "Even Banks Is Surprised at Remarkable Comeback," *Milwaukee Journal*, July 2, 1967.
8. Wolf.
9. Wolf.
10. Wolf.
11. Jerome Holtzman, "A Dual Role for Banks—Professor-Performer," *Chicago Sun-Times*, March 18, 1967.
12. Holtzman.
13. Jerome Holtzman, "Beckert Modern Star with Old-Time Style," *The Sporting News*, August 10, 1968.
14. Holtzman.
15. Holtzman.
16. Lew Freedman, *Cubs Essential: Everything You Need to Know to Be a Real Fan* (Chicago: Triumph Books, 2006), 82 and 85.
17. Phil Rogers, *Ernie Banks: Mr. Cub and the Summer of '69* (Chicago: Triumph Books, 2011), 138.
18. Ernie Banks and Jim Enright, *"Mr. Cub"* (Chicago: Rutledge Books, 1971), 151 and 152.
19. Ferguson Jenkins and Dorothy Turcotte, *The Game Is Easy, Life Is Hard*, (Grimsby, ON: The Ferguson Jenkins Foundation, 2002), 63.
20. Rogers, 215.

Chapter 16

1. Jerome Holtzman, "At 37, Banks Hits, Sells Cars and Has His Own Air Show," *Chicago Sun-Times*, July 27, 1968.
2. Holtzman.
3. Holtzman.
4. Ferguson Jenkins, and Lew Freedman, *Fergie: My Life from the Cubs to Cooperstown* (Chicago: Triumph Books, 2009), 81.
5. Jenkins and Freedman, 83.
6. Jenkins and Freedman, 83.
7. Jerome Holtzman, "Regan Guilty? Bruins Raging at Pelekoudas," *Chicago Sun-Times*, August 31, 1968.
8. Jerome Holtzman, "Regan Tells Umpires How to Trap Cheating Hurler," *The Sporting News*, September 7, 1968.
9. No byline, "Bob Gibson Put Aside Grief to Pitch While Mourning MLK," *Retrosimba, St. Louis Cardinals' History*, March 29, 2013.
10. Joe Distelheim, "A Not-So Golden Anniversary," *The Hardball Times*, February 14, 2018.
11. John Kass, "Ernie Banks Gave Chicago Something to Smile About in the Turbulent '60s," *Chicago Tribune*, January 24, 2015.
12. Kass.
13. Kass.
14. No byline, "Cub SRO Game 'Three-Way Perfect Day' to Wrigley," *Chicago Tribune*, August 10, 1968.
15. *Chicago Tribune*.

16. No byline, "Banks Inquires—'What's Cubs' Magic Number?'" *Chicago Tribune*, August 24, 1968.
17. Jerome Holtzman, "Lippy 'Insulted' by the Crumbs Rivals Offered," *Chicago Sun-Times*, December 21, 1968.

Chapter 17

1. Phil Rogers, *Ernie Banks: Mr. Cub and the Summer of '69* (Chicago: Triumph Books, 2011), 15.
2. Rick Talley, *The Cubs of '69* (Chicago: Contemporary Books, 1989), 28.
3. Talley, 28.
4. Rogers, 78.
5. James Enright, "Strong Cub Bullpen Manned by A.L. Rejects," *Chicago American*, May 24, 1969.
6. Enright.
7. Talley, 54.
8. Tom Fitzpatrick, "Win or Lose, Leo Breeds Fear and Dislike," *The Sporting News*, November 1, 1969.
9. William Barry Furlong, "How Durocher Blew the Pennant," *Look*, March 10, 1970.
10. John Snyder, *Cubs Journal* (Cincinnati: Emmis Books, 2005), 457.
11. Snyder, 457.
12. Ron Santo and Randy Minkoff, *Ron Santo: For Love of Ivy* (Chicago: Bonus Books, 1993), 93–94.
13. Paul Dickson, *Leo Durocher: Baseball's Prodigal Son* (New York: Bloomsbury, 2017), 262.
14. Jerome Holtzman, "Skinny Kessinger Stuffing Himself—'Potatoes, Please,'" *Chicago Sun-Times*, December 28, 1968.
15. Lew Freedman, personal interview, July 25, 2006.
16. Santo and Minkoff, 83.
17. Fluffy Saccucci, "Bill Hands Won 20 in That Historic Year of 1969," *Sports Collectors Digest*, April 7, 1995.
18. Saccucci.
19. Freedman, personal interview.
20. Talley, 199.
21. Jimmy Cannon, "An Original," New York syndicated column, May 1, 1969.
22. Fitzpatrick.
23. No byline, "Try a Little Happiness: Banks to Write for Tribune," *Chicago Tribune*, June 10, 1969.
24. Talley, 29.

Chapter 18

1. Bob Broeg, "Leo the Lion's Feuds Are Just Ploys of Paper Tiger," *St. Louis Post-Dispatch*, June 4, 1969.
2. Bill Christine, "The Sports Beat: Durocher Vs. Chicago," *Pittsburgh Press*, September 8, 1969.
3. Melvin Durslag, "It Was a Time for No Lip," *Los Angeles Herald-Examiner* (date missing, National Baseball Hall of Fame Library).
4. William Barry Furlong, "How Durocher Blew the Pennant," *Look*, March 10, 1970.
5. Jerome Holtzman, "Ernie Turns Down Latin Pilot's Post," *Chicago Sun-Times*, June 5, 1969.
6. Holtzman.
7. Holtzman.
8. No byline, "Banks Just Hopeful He'll Get to Pinch Hit," *Washington Star*, July 23, 1969.
9. Rick Talley, *The Cubs of '69* (Chicago: Contemporary Books, 1989), 55–56.
10. Richard Dozer, "Banks Hits 500th Home Run: Cub Joins Elite," *Chicago Tribune*, May 13, 1970.
11. Edgar Munzel, "Banks on 500th, Thought of Mom and Dad," *The Sporting News*, May 30, 1970.
12. Munzel.
13. Munzel.

Chapter 19

1. No byline, "Nostalgia Gets Up 'At Bat' in Ernie's Last Home Game," *Newark Star-Ledger*, September 28, 1971.
2. Lew Freedman, personal interview, July 26, 2009.
3. Rick Talley, "Why the Cubs Will Revolt Against Durocher," *Sports Today*, June 1971.
4. Talley.
5. Ron Santo and Randy Minkoff, *Ron Santo: for Love of Ivy* (Chicago: Bonus Books, 1993), 13.
6. Ron Santo, "Ron Santo's Secret on the Field," *Guideposts*, October 24, 2008.
7. Santo.
8. Santo and Minkoff, 111.
9. Santo and Minkoff, 112.
10. John Snyder, *Cubs Journal* (Cincinnati: Emmis Books, 2005), 476.
11. Dick Young, "Cub Star Banks Pens a Love Story," *The Sporting News*, May 29, 1971.
12. Paul Hemphill, "The Last Days of Ernie Banks," *Sport*, December 1971.
13. *Newark Star-Ledger*.

Chapter 20

1. David Condon, "Baseball's Hardest Loser," *Chicago Tribune* magazine, April 2, 1961.
2. Condon.
3. Condon.
4. Edgar Munzel, "Cubs Open Spot for Banks as Coach," *The Sporting News*, November 27, 1971.

5. Munzel.
6. Munzel.
7. James C. Mullen, "'Banks Too Nice' to Manage: Wrigley," *Chicago Sun-Times*, August 1, 1974.
8. Dick Shippy, "A Banker Who Really Can Swing," *Akron Beacon-Journal*, August 25, 1981.
9. Ron Rapoport, "The Last Years of Ernie Banks," *Chicago Magazine*, October 2015.

Chapter 21

1. Dick Young, "Great Player, a Greater Man," *New York Daily News*, January 20, 1977.
2. Young.
3. Young.
4. Michael Strauss, "Humor and Emotion Prevail as Cooperstown Inducts 6," *New York Times*, August 9, 1977.
5. Bob Broeg, "Banks Is Mr. Big at Hall of Fame Induction," *The Sporting News*, August 20, 1977.
6. Broeg.
7. Broeg.
8. Ernie Banks Hall of Fame induction speech, August 8, 1977. *YouTube*.
9. Bud Poliquin, "Everything's Great with Banks," *Syracuse Post-Standard*, March 9, 1978.
10. Poliquin.
11. Poliquin.
12. Poliquin.
13. Hayden Bird, "Ted Williams Used His Hall of Fame Speech to Advocate for African-American Players," *Boston.com* sports, July 25, 2017.
14. Joe Posnanski, *The Soul of Baseball: A Road Trip Through Buck O'Neil's America* (New York: William Morrow, 2007), 183.
15. Ernie Banks, "Baseball Could Use a Black Hall of Fame," *Chicago Tribune*, February 8, 1981.

Chapter 22

1. Ernie Banks and Steve Inskeep, "Ernie Banks Still Swinging for Worthwhile Life," National Public Radio, October 13, 2009.
2. David Haugh, "Mr. Cub Takes on the World," *Chicago Tribune*, July 24, 2005.
3. Haugh.
4. Haugh.
5. Haugh.
6. Elliott Harris, "Quick Hits: Banks Backs Organ Donation," *Chicago Sun-Times*, May 19, 1999.

7. Harris.
8. Cyd Zeigler, "HOFer Ernie Banks in Gay Pride Parade," *Outsports*, June 25, 2010.
9. Dave Cunningham, "Not-So-Funny Ernie Banks," *Orlando Sentinel*, March 12, 1999.
10. Cunningham.
11. Fred Mitchell, "Q&A: Ernie Banks," *Chicago Tribune*, April 21, 2004.
12. Fred Mitchell, "Mr. Cub to Mr. Sosa: Come Clean," *Chicago Tribune*, January 25, 2010.
13. Carrie Muskat, "Banks Receives Presidential Medal of Freedom," *MLB.com*, November 20, 2013.
14. David Haugh, "Presidential Honor Has Mr. Cub Singing a Happy Tune," *Chicago Tribune*, August 13, 2013.

Chapter 23

1. Fred Mitchell, "As He Gazes at His Statue, Joyful Banks Asks, 'Is It Me?'" *Chicago Tribune*, March 31, 2008.
2. Mitchell.
3. Mitchell.
4. No Byline, "Cubs Legend Banks Honored with Statue Outside Wrigley Field," Associated Press, March 31, 2008.
5. Associated Press.
6. Ron Rappaport, "The Last Years of Ernie Banks," *Chicago Magazine*, October 2015.
7. No byline, "Chicago Cubs Hall of Famer Ernie Banks Dead at 83," Reuters, January 24, 2015.
8. No byline, "Sports World Mourns Passing of Ernie Banks," *Chicago Tribune*, January 24, 2015.
9. Mark Townsend, "President Obama Says Goodbye to Cubs Legend Ernie Banks," Yahoosports.com, January 24, 2015.
10. "Cubs Legend Banks Remembered," Associated Press, January 31, 2015.
11. Associated Press.
12. Associated Press.
13. Carrie Muskat, "Banks Honored at Emotional Memorial Service," *MLB.com*, February 1, 2015.
14. Muskat.
15. Phil Rogers, "Banks Got Better, Never Bitter, in Face of Adversity," *MLB.com*, February 1, 2015.
16. No byline, "Suitability of Banks' Caretaker Faulted," Associated Press, February 17, 2015.
17. Rappaport.
18. Muskat.

Bibliography

Books

Altman, George, and Lew Freedman. *George Altman: My Baseball Journey from the Negro Leagues to the Majors and Beyond.* Jefferson, NC: McFarland, 2013.
Banks, Ernie, and Jim Enright. *Mr. Cub.* Chicago: Rutledge Books, 1971.
Dickson, Paul. *Leo Durocher: Baseball's Prodigal Son.* New York: Bloomsbury, 2017.
Freedman, Lew. *Cubs Essential: Everything You Need to Know to Be a Real Fan.* Chicago: Triumph Books, 2006.
Freedman, Lew. *Game of My Life: Chicago Cubs.* Champaign, IL: Sports Publishing, 2007.
Golenbock, Peter. *Wrigleyville: A Magical History Tour of the Chicago Cubs.* New York: St. Martin's Press, 1996.
Hoffman, John C. *Hank Sauer.* New York: A. S. Barnes, 1953.
Jenkins, Ferguson, and Lew Freedman. *Fergie: My Life from the Cubs to Cooperstown.* Chicago: Triumph Books, 2009.
Jenkins, Ferguson, and Dorothy Turcotte. *The Game Is Easy, Life Is Hard.* Grimsby, ON: Ferguson Jenkins Foundation, 2002.
Muskat, Carrie. *Banks to Sandberg to Grace.* Lincolnwood, IL: Contemporary Books, 2001.
Niese, Joe. *Burleigh Grimes: Baseball's Last Legal Spitballer.* Jefferson, NC: McFarland, 2013.
O'Neil, Buck, Steve Wulf, and David Conrads. *I Was Right on Time.* New York: Simon & Schuster, 1996.
Petterchak, Janice. *Jack Brickhouse: A Voice for All Seasons.* Chicago: Contemporary Books, 1996.
Posnanski, Joe. *The Soul of Baseball: A Road Trip Through Buck O'Neil's America.* New York: William Morrow, 2007.
Rogers, Phil. *Ernie Banks: Mr. Cub and the Summer of '69.* Chicago: Triumph Books, 2011.
Rust, Art, Jr. *Get That Nigger Off the Field: An Informal History of the Black Man in Baseball.* New York: Delacorte Press, 1976.
Santo, Ron, and Randy Minkoff. *For Love of Ivy.* Chicago: Bonus Books, 1993.
Santo, Ron, and Phil Pepe. *Few and Chosen: Defining Cubs Greatness Across the Eras.* Chicago: Triumph Books 2005.
Snyder, John. *Cubs Journal.* Cincinnati: Emmis Books, 2005.
Talley, Rick. *The Cubs of '69.* Chicago: Contemporary Books, 1989.
Williams, Billy, and Fred Mitchell. *Billy Williams: My Sweet-Swinging Lifetime with the Cubs.* Chicago: Triumph Books, 2008.

Bibliography

Periodicals/Magazines

Chicago Magazine
Cosmopolitan
Guideposts
The Hardball Times
Look
Outsports
Sport
The Sporting News
Sports Collector's Digest
Sports Today

Newspapers

Akron Beacon-Journal
Chicago American
Chicago Daily News
Chicago Reader
Chicago Sun-Times
Chicago Tribune
Fort Worth Star-Telegram
Houston Post
Las Vegas Review-Journal
Los Angeles Herald-Examiner
Los Angeles Times
Milwaukee Journal
Newark Star-Ledger
Newsday
New York Journal-American
New York Times
Orlando Sentinel
Pittsburgh Press
St. Louis Post-Dispatch
Syracuse Post-Standard
USA Today
Washington Star

Internet and News Services

Associated Press
Boston.com/sports
ESPN.com
MLB.com
National Public Radio
North American Newspaper Alliance
Retrosimba/St. Louis Cardinals
Reuters
Society of American Baseball Research
Syndicated Column
Wrigleyvillenation.com
Yahoosports.com
YouTube.com

Personal Interviews

George Altman
Ernie Banks
Glenn Beckert
Ken Holtzman
Ferguson Jenkins
Don Kessinger
Ron Santo
Billy Williams

Index

Aaron, Hank 23, 27, 53, 54, 69, 70, 71, 135, 141, 142, 174, 175, 176, 178
Abernathy, Ted 99, 129
Adams, Bobby 81
Aguirre, Hank 129, 155
Air Force Academy 83
Alabama 41, 49, 83
Albuquerque 68
Ali, Muhammad 174
Altman, George 29, 77, 81, 94, 99, 104, 178
Amarillo Colts (Detroit Colts) 15, 16, 18, 19, 23, 24, 43
Ambassador Hotel (Chicago) 134
American Basketball League 36
American Communist Party 40
American Football League 12
American League 9, 21, 26, 37, 67, 68, 70, 74, 78, 163
Anderson, Bob 71
Anson, Adrian (Cap) 122
Arizona 62, 145
Arizona Instructional League 155
Arkansas 130
Armstrong, Jim 129
Ashburn, Richie 69, 76, 77, 160
Ashe, Arthur 174
Ashland, Kentucky 164
Associated Press 163
Astaire, Fred 132
Atlanta Braves 101, 105, 124, 125, 135, 142, 174
Augusta National (golf course) 170

Baird, Tom 29, 42
Baker, Gene 19, 22, 26, 29, 31, 32, 33, 34, 35, 36, 38, 42, 43, 44, 45, 46, 49, 50, 52, 54, 55, 59, 60, 61, 62, 63, 64, 114, 170
Baker, Eugene 46
Ball Four (book) 151
Baltimore 36
Baltimore Elite Giants 24
Baltimore Orioles 22
Bankhead, Dan 22, 27
Banks, Benjamin 62

Banks, Eddie 8, 10, 11, 13, 14
Banks, Eloyce 8, 94, 111
Banks, Ernie 1, 2, 3, 4, 5, 7, 8, 9, 10, 11, 12, 13, 14, 15, 16, 17, 18, 19, 20, 21, 22, 23, 24, 25, 26, 27, 28, 29, 30, 31, 32, 33, 34, 35, 36, 37, 38, 39, 42, 43, 44, 45, 46, 47, 48, 49, 50, 51, 52, 53, 54, 55, 57, 58, 59, 60, 61, 62, 63, 64, 65, 66, 67, 68, 69, 70, 71, 72, 73, 74, 76, 77, 78, 79, 80, 82, 83, 84, 85, 86, 87, 88, 89, 90, 91, 94, 95, 96, 97, 99, 100, 101, 102, 103, 104, 105, 106, 107, 108, 109, 110, 111, 112, 113, 114, 115, 116, 117, 118, 119, 120, 121, 122, 123, 124, 125, 127, 128, 130, 133, 134, 135, 137, 138, 139, 141, 142, 143, 144, 145, 146, 147, 150, 151, 152, 153, 154, 155, 157, 158, 159, 160, 161, 162, 163, 164, 165, 166, 167, 168, 169, 170, 171, 172, 173, 174, 175, 176, 177, 178, 179, 180
Banks, Essie 10, 11, 14, 16, 161
Banks, Jerome 8, 94, 178
Banks, Joel 8, 94, 178
Banks, Liz 176, 179
Barragan, Cuno 149
Bartlett's Quotations 104
Baseball Hall of Fame 5, 15, 18, 22, 29, 33, 40, 41, 58, 59, 76, 78, 79, 81, 82, 84, 86, 90, 93, 98, 99, 101, 105, 113, 114, 117, 119, 122, 130, 135, 136, 147, 155, 159, 160, 161, 163, 164, 165, 166, 168, 171, 177
Baseball Writers Association of America 69, 160
Baseballreference.com 143
Batavia, New York 63, 64
Baton Rouge, Louisiana 46
Beacon Award 174
Beacon of Life 174
Beaumont, Texas 45
Beckert, Glenn 75, 99, 104, 114, 115, 116, 128, 133, 135, 147, 149, 156
Bell, Cool Papa (James Thomas) 9, 10, 18, 19, 20, 40, 60, 162, 165, 166
Bell, George 172
Bench, Johnny 101, 147
Billy Goat Curse 57, 99, 103, 136

Index

Billy Goat Tavern 57
Birmingham Black Barons 24, 41
Black Baseball History Museum 164
Black Sheepherders (San Antonio/San Angelo) 19
Blair, Bill 15, 18, 20
Blues Stadium 23
Board of Aldermen (Chicago) 88
Boccabella, John 107, 109, 112, 114, 117
Bonds, Barry 176
Booker T. Washington High School (Texas) 12, 14, 15, 21
Boston 55
Boston Braves 41, 42
Boston Celtics 53, 166
Boston Red Sox 22, 37, 41, 58, 164
Boudreau, Lou 72, 77
Bouton, Jim 151
Bragan, Bobby 33, 34
Brickhouse, Jack 8, 53
Brock, Lou 81, 83, 86, 91, 92, 93, 94, 178
Broeg, Bob 139, 140
Broglio, Ernie 93, 94
Brooklyn Dodgers 9, 15, 22, 35, 39, 40, 41, 42, 54, 58, 66, 104, 135, 148
Brosnan, Jim 69, 97
Brown, Joe 63, 64
Brown, Willard 22
Brown University 40
Brown vs. Board of Education 47
Bryant, Paul "Bear" 174
Buck O'Neil Lifetime Achievement Award 166
Budapest 111
Buffett, Warren 170
Buhl, Bob 91, 100, 105
Bunning, Jim 160
Burdette, Lew 58, 160
Burgess, Smoky 75
Burns, Ken 20
Burns (George) and Allen (Gracie) 61
Burton, Ellis 91
Busch Stadium 37
Buzhardt, John 77

Cactus League 112
Caldwell, Idaho 101
California 1, 88, 135, 176
Callison, Johnny 140
Camp Ojibwa 140
Campanella, Roy 22, 25, 27, 29, 96
Canada 117
Cardenal, Jose 156
Cardwell, Don 77
Carrabelle, Florida 20
Carrasquel, Chico 37
Carter, Johnny 15
Carty, Rico 143
Cavarretta, Phil 43, 44, 51, 54, 55, 56
Cedar Rapids, Iowa 30
Cella, Lou

Cepeda, Orlando 117
Chance, Frank 167
Charleston, Oscar 165
Chase Hotel 44
Chatham, Ontario 117
Chicago 4, 7, 8, 9, 13, 23, 28, 35, 36, 37, 38, 48, 50, 54, 60, 62, 73, 78, 79, 88, 91, 96, 97, 101, 102, 103, 109, 110, 117, 123, 124, 125, 130, 134, 138, 139, 140, 145, 146, 150, 151, 155, 156, 157, 158, 162, 163, 164, 166, 168, 171, 173, 175, 176, 177, 178, 179, 180
Chicago American 11, 35, 43
Chicago American Giants 24
Chicago Bears 53, 158, 166, 170, 177
Chicago Blackhawks 171
Chicago Bulls 53
Chicago Cubs 1, 2, 3, 4, 7, 8, 9, 10, 16, 20, 28, 29, 31, 32, 33, 34, 35, 37, 38, 40, 42, 43, 45, 46, 47, 48, 49, 50, 51, 52, 53, 54, 55, 56, 57, 58, 59, 60, 61, 62, 63, 64, 65, 66, 67, 68, 71, 73, 74, 75, 76, 77, 79, 80, 81, 82, 83, 84, 86, 87, 88, 89, 92, 93, 94, 95, 97, 98, 99, 100, 101, 102, 103, 104, 105, 106, 111, 112, 113, 114, 115, 116, 117, 119, 120, 121, 122, 123, 124, 125, 126, 127, 128, 129, 130, 132, 133, 134, 135, 136, 137, 138, 139, 140, 141, 142, 144, 145, 147, 148, 149, 151, 152, 153, 154, 156, 158, 160, 161, 162, 163, 164, 167, 169, 171, 172, 173, 175, 176, 177, 180
Chicago Defender 27
Chicago Today 11
Chicago Tribune 1, 15, 123, 138, 142, 143, 158, 164, 169
Chicago White Sox 29, 36, 42, 53, 55, 77, 172
Cincinnati 33, 147
Cincinnati Reds 54, 55, 64, 66, 74, 86, 103, 107, 121, 129, 147, 151
Civil Rights Game 174
Civil Rights Movement 38, 46, 47, 98, 170, 174
Civil War 12, 39
Clarke, Philip R. 8
Clemens, Doug 93
Clemente, Roberto 8, 174
Cleveland Buckeyes 24
Cleveland Indians 21, 22, 36, 40, 42, 64, 72, 74, 99, 141, 166
Cline, Ty 105
Clinton, Bill 174
Clinton, Hillary 158, 170
Cobb, Ty 18
Cole, Dick 81
College of Coaches 81, 82, 84, 89, 102, 103, 158
Collins, Rip 81
Comiskey Park 28
Concepcion, Davey 164
Confederacy 12
Congress 173
Conley, Gene 53, 54
Conrad Hilton Hotel 123

Index

Cooperstown, New York 5, 59, 159, 160, 162, 163
County Stadium 61
Craft, Harry 81
Cricket 39
Cronin, Joe 41
Crosley Field 33
Culver, George 121

The Daily Worker 40, 41
Dallas, Texas 3, 9, 10, 12, 13, 15, 18, 20, 21, 23, 25, 26, 43, 50, 62, 111, 162, 169
Dallas Black Giants 13, 14
Dallas Cowboys 12
Dallas Green Monarchs 14
Dallas Morning News 12, 13
Dallas Texans 12
Dallas Times-Herald 13
Daley, Richard J. 8, 123, 124
Dark, Alvin 37, 71, 77, 160
Davenport, Iowa 33, 46
Davenport High School (Iowa) 46
Dawson, Andre 67, 178
Day, Laraine 103
Days of Rage 124
Deadball Era 164
Delaware 163
Delmore, Vic 71
Democratic National Convention 123, 125
Denver (minor league baseball) 84
Desautel, Gene 34
Des Moines, Iowa 33, 46
Detroit Tigers 41, 56, 57, 100
Diabetes Association of Greater Chicago 149
Dickey, Bill (catcher) 30
Dickey, Bill (pitcher) 28, 30, 33
Dierker, Larry 123
Digby, George 41
Dihigo, Martin 160, 163, 165
DiMaggio, Joe 59, 71, 174
Dirksen, Everett (U.S. Senator) 88
Doby, Larry 21, 22, 23, 25, 29, 40
Dodger Stadium 101
Dominican Republic 172, 173
Dozer, Richard 143
Drabowsky, Moe 63, 64
Dressen, Chuck 103
Drott, Dick 63
Drysdale, Don 78, 160
Durante, Jimmy 103
Durocher, Leo (Leo the Lip) 102, 103, 104, 105, 106, 107, 108, 109, 110, 112, 113, 114, 116, 117, 118, 119, 120, 121, 125, 126, 127, 128, 130, 132, 133, 134, 137, 138, 139, 140, 145, 146, 147, 148, 149, 150, 151, 153, 154, 155, 156, 157
Dykes, Jimmie 68

Eagle River, Wisconsin 134
Easter, Luke 22
Ellis, Jim 121
Ellsworth, Dick 91, 100, 104

El Paso, Texas 36
Elston, Don 63, 82
Emanuel, Rahm 178, 179
Enright, Jim 11, 30, 34, 42, 43, 75, 134, 150, 151
Ernie Banks Life Above and Beyond Foundation 174
Evangline League 62
Evers, Johnny 116, 166

Faul, Bill 100
FBI 145
Fenway Park 55
Fitzsimmons, Fred 63
Florence, Italy 111
Florida 20
Fondy, Dee 63
Forbes Field 52, 74
Ford (automobiles) 119
Fort Bliss 36
Foster, George 147
Fourth Presbyterian Church 178
Fox, Nellie 160
Foxx, Jimmie 59, 142
France 111
Freeman, Morgan 174
Friend, Bob 58, 74, 75

Gallagher, Jim 43
Gamble, Oscar 80
Garciaparra, Nomar 67
Gates, Bill 170
Gay Pride Parade 171
Gehrig, Lou 59
General Electric 163
Geneva, Wisconsin 134
Gentry, Gary 136
Germany 27, 40
Gettysburg Address 97, 124
Gibson, Bob 122, 130, 145
Gibson, Josh 9, 10, 40, 164, 165
Giles, Warren 8,
Gilliam, Jim 114
Goldblatt, Joel 134
Goldblatt, Lynne Walker 130
Golenbock, Peter 98, 99
Gottlieb, Eddie 18
Graceland Cemetery 179
Great Depression 11, 12,
Green, Pumpsie 22
Grimm, Charlie 8, 71, 72, 77, 81
Guillen, Ozzie 177
Gypsy 111

Hack, Stan 35, 51, 54, 63, 122
Halas, George 125
Hands, Bill 105, 120, 136, 144, 145, 156
Harlem Globetrotters 36
Hartenstein, Chuck 115
Hartnett, Gabby 78
Hatton, Grady 83

Haynes, Marques 36
Hayward, Buster 25
Hemus, Solly 37
Hendley, Bob 101, 102
Henderson, Rickey 93
Highwood, Illinois 175
Hickman, Jim 132, 133, 144, 147, 156
Hillman, Dave 63
Himsl, Vedie 62, 81
Hobbie, Glen 77
Hodges, Gil 119, 160
Holland, John 63, 71, 83, 93, 94, 148, 149, 150
Hollywood 103
Hollywood Stars 33
Holt, Goldie 81
Holtzman, Jerome 90, 141
Holtzman, Ken 101, 105, 112, 114, 116, 123, 124, 125, 130, 132, 135, 137, 142, 144, 147, 150, 156
"Home on the Range" (song) 44
Homestead Grays 18
Hooton, Burt 156
Hotel Americana 161
Houston Eagles 24
Houston 45s/Astros 84, 99, 107, 123, 124, 130, 155, 157
Howard, Elston 22, 23, 25, 29, 41, 160
Hubbs, Ken 83, 86, 91, 92, 93, 116
Humphrey, Hubert 123
Hundley, Randy 104, 114, 121, 128, 134, 140, 156, 178
Hungary 111
Hurwitz, Hy 69

Illinois 158
Indianapolis Clowns 23, 25
Inserra, Bob 8
International Amphitheatre (Chicago) 123
International League 46
Irvin, Monte 22, 52, 69, 162, 165
Isaacs, Stan 106
Italy 40

Jackie Robinson All-Star Team 25
Jackson, the Rev. Jesse 175, 178
Jackson, Larry 91, 100, 105
Jackson, Reggie 178
Jacksonville, Florida 25
Japan 29, 40, 77
Jarvis, Pat 142
Jenkins, Ferguson 98, 105, 114, 116, 119, 120, 121, 124, 128, 130, 132, 133, 135, 136, 145, 156, 167, 174, 175, 178
Jeter, Derek 67
Jethroe, Sam 41
Jim Crow 3
Johnson, Alex 121
Johnson, Connie 22, 26
Johnson, Judy 9, 165
Johnson, Lou 29, 101
Johnson, Lyndon Baines 123, 124

Johnson, Roy 44
Jones, Clarence 112, 114, 117
Jones, Sam 22, 59

Kaiser, Don 63
Kansas 15
Kansas City 20, 21, 22, 23, 24, 25, 80
Kansas City Monarchs 9, 18, 19, 20, 21, 22, 23, 24, 25, 26, 27, 28, 29, 30, 33, 34, 36, 42, 44, 46, 50, 58, 62, 77, 80, 93, 164, 179
Kass, John 123, 124
Keeler, "Wee" Willie 18
Kell, George 160
Kennedy, Bob 7, 100
Kennedy, John F. 91, 174
Kennedy, Robert F. 123, 124
Kershner, the Rev. Shannon 180
Kessinger, Don 99, 104, 114, 116, 119, 130, 133, 134, 135, 137, 147, 156
Kiner, Ralph 52, 54, 69, 90
King, Billie Jean 174
King, Martin Luther, Jr. 48, 98, 122, 123, 124
Klein, Lou 81, 100
Kluszewski, Ted 160
Koosman, Jerry 136
Korean War 27
Koufax, Sandy 90, 101, 102
Ku Klux Klan 12, 13, 42
Kuenn, Harvey 37
Kuhn, Bowie 165

Lafayette, Louisiana 62
Landis, Kenesaw Mountain 40
Lasorda, Tommy 82
Las Vegas 151
Law, Vern 74, 75
Lawing, Gene 44
Leonard, Buck 40, 165
Lewis, Jerry 62
Lews, Bob 44
Libran, Francisco 129
Lincoln, Abraham 158
Lincoln Academy of Illinois 158
Lindbergh, Charles 92
Linus (comic strip character) 161
Little Monarchs 19
Lloyd, John Henry 160, 163, 165
Lockman, Whitey 156, 157
Logan, Johnny 37
London 111
Long, Dale 63, 72
Long Beach, California 106
Lopez, Al 160, 163
Los Angeles 140
Los Angeles Angels (AAA) 31, 32, 33, 34, 35, 42, 46
Los Angeles Dodgers 66, 77, 78, 82, 90, 96, 100, 101, 102, 107, 120, 121, 124, 130, 134
Look Magazine 140
Lown, Turk 63

Maddux, Greg 167
Maglie, Sal 58
Major League Baseball 12, 15, 23, 66, 67, 90, 92, 95, 123, 151, 157, 166, 172
Mandela, Nelson 170
Mantle, Mickey 41, 70, 142
Marcinkus, Paul 111
Marichal, Juan 119
Marina Del Rey, California 169
Maris, Roger 160, 172, 173
Marshall, Jim 157
Martin, Dean 62, 103
Martin, Fred 81
Martin, Dr. J.B. 28
Martinsville 7, 46
Masters Golf Tournament 170
Mathews, Eddie 71, 142, 160
Matthews, Wid 29, 32, 35, 36, 42, 43, 55, 62, 63, 80
Mattingly, Don 59
Mays, Willie 7, 22, 27, 29, 41, 52, 69, 104, 130, 141, 142
McDaniel, Lindy 8, 59, 61, 91, 100
McGraw, Tug 136
McGwire, Mark 172, 173
Meigs Field 134
Memorial Coliseum, Los Angeles 66
Memphis, Tennessee 122
Memphis Red Sox 24, 28
Mesa, Arizona 79, 120
Mexico 41
Meyer, Russ 58
Milwaukee 61
Milwaukee Braves 33, 37, 53, 60, 63, 66, 86, 101, 105, 160
Milwaukee Brewers 176
Minner, Paul 54
Minnesota Twins 102
Minoso, Minnie 22, 42
Miracle Mets 137
Mississippi River 46
Missouri 124
Missouri Valley College 170
Mr. Cub 2, 5, 11, 30, 75, 76, 78, 94, 96, 110, 125, 152, 153, 157, 162, 168, 174, 175, 177, 178
Mobile, Alabama 44, 45, 83
Moline, Illinois 46
Monday, Rick 101, 156
Montgomery, Alabama 80
Montreal 117
Montreal Expos 153
Montreal Royals 40
Moon, Wally 54, 71
Mota, Manny 8
Moton High (Virginia) 46
Moyrn, Walt 72
Municipal Stadium (Kansas City) 78
Murderers Row 104
Murphy (Billy goat) 57
Murphy, Mike 175
Musial, Stan 71, 113, 174

National Basketball Association 12, 18, 53, 166
National Football League 12, 39, 91, 166
National Guard 123, 125
National Hockey League 12, 166, 171
National League 3, 8, 9, 26, 30, 32, 36, 37, 41, 53, 54, 57, 60, 61, 65, 66, 67, 68, 69, 70, 71, 74, 76, 78, 83, 89, 90, 93, 94, 96, 99, 103, 119, 120, 121, 122, 127, 130, 133, 134, 135, 144, 147, 148, 150, 153, 157, 161, 166, 172
National Pastime 39
National Public Radio 168
Native Americans 39
Navarro, Mario 141
Nebraska 15
Negro Leagues 9, 18, 20, 21, 22, 23, 24, 26, 28, 29, 40, 41, 42, 44, 77, 85
Negro Leagues Committee (Baseball Hall of Fame) 160
Negro Leagues Museum 20
New Mexico 15
New Orleans 44
New York (state) 162, 163
New York City 49, 138
New York Cubans 24
New York Daily News 150
New York Giants 22, 41, 42, 55, 66, 104, 135, 157
New York Mets 3, 54, 56, 84, 86, 99, 119, 132, 133, 135, 136, 137, 139, 145, 151
New York-Pennsylvania League 64
New York Yankees 22, 23, 41, 42, 74, 103, 130, 136, 140, 166, 173
Newcombe, Don 22, 25, 29, 58, 61, 160
Niekro, Joe 114, 120, 129
Niekro, Phil 114, 135
Nobel Prize 5, 88, 168, 174, 180
Nolan, Gary 147
North, Bill 155
North, Mike 175
Notre Dame (university) 92
Nottebart, Don 129
Nye, Rich 115, 120

Oakland 35, 130
Oakland Athletics 130, 132, 142, 156
Obama, Barack 4, 97, 174, 177
Obama, Michelle 177
O'Doul, Lefty 34
O'Hare International Airport 101
Oklahoma 15,
Oklahoma City 151
Old West 12, 23
Olive Hotel 44
O'Neil, Buck (John) 18, 19, 20, 21, 22, 23, 24, 25, 26, 27, 28, 29, 42, 43, 44, 53, 62, 77, 80, 81, 82, 83, 84, 86, 92, 93, 94, 101, 112, 113, 114, 165, 166, 174, 179
Order of Lincoln 158
Ott, Mel 142
Outsports 171

Owens, Jesse 109, 174

Pacific Coast League 33, 34, 42, 46, 55, 68, 73
Paige, Satchel 9, 10, 18, 20, 21, 22, 27, 29, 40, 164
Pappas, Milt 141, 144, 150, 156
Paris 111
Payton, Walter 158, 170
Peanuts (comic strip) 161
Pelekoudas, Chris 121
Peoria, Illinois 53
Pepitone, Joe 140, 147, 150, 156
Perez, Tony 147
Perranoski, Ron 77
Pershing Hotel 28
Petrocelli, Rico 64
Philadelphia 18, 44
Philadelphia Athletics 42
Philadelphia Phillies 22, 32, 41, 67, 69, 86, 100, 105, 114, 122, 125, 128, 129, 144, 152, 153, 174
Philadelphia Stars 24
Phillips, Adolfo 140
Pieper, Pat 71
Pignatano, Joe 87
Piniella, Lou 176
Pittsburgh 115, 141
Pittsburgh Courier 27
Pittsburgh Pirates 8, 22, 26, 41, 52, 54, 59, 63, 64, 67, 74, 86, 94, 132, 136, 144, 145, 151
Pittsburgh Press 140
Pope Paul VI 111, 112
Presidential Medal of Freedom 4, 174, 176
Providence Grays 40
Pryor, Paul 152
Puerto Rican Winter League 141

Quad Cities 46

Raft, George 103
Rapaport, Ron 176, 177, 179
Ravenswood Bank 157
Reagan, Ronald 158
Reese, Pee Wee 33, 37, 160
Regan, Phil 120, 121, 129
Rehabilitation Institute of Chicago 9, 94
Reuschel, Rick 156
Reuss, Jerry 144
Rice, Del 53
Rice, Hal 52
Rice, Regina 179
Richmond, Virginia 46
Ricketts, Tom 174, 177, 178
Rickey, Branch 15, 26, 27, 35, 40, 41, 45
Ride, Sally 174
Ripken, Cal, Jr. 67
Riverfront Stadium 147
Rizzo, Anthony 177
Robert F. Kennedy Memorial Stadium 134
Roberts, Curt 22, 24, 26
Roberts, Robin 58

Robinson, Frank 63, 64, 81, 141, 174
Robinson, Jackie 9, 15, 18, 22, 23, 26, 27, 35, 38, 39, 40, 41, 45, 52, 69, 104, 174
Robinson, Rachel 45
Rodgers, Andre 91
Rodriguez, Alex 64, 67, 68, 69
Rogers, Will 151
Rome 111
Ron Santo Walk to Cure Diabetes 75
Roosevelt, Franklin D. 11,
Roosevelt, Theodore 52
Rose, Pete 66
Ross, Gary 129
Rounders 39
Rozelle, Pete 92
Rush, Bob 63
Rusie, Amos 160, 163
Ruth, Babe 49, 56, 59, 68, 104, 142, 176
Ryan, Nolan 101, 136

St. Louis 18, 44, 144
St. Louis Browns 19, 21, 36, 42
St. Louis Cardinals 29, 33, 37, 54, 58, 60, 61, 64, 71, 77, 81, 93, 103, 113, 115, 122, 125, 144, 151, 172
St. Louis Post-Dispatch 139
Salt Lake City 92
San Antonio (minor league baseball) 83, 84, 85
San Diego Padres 129, 130, 144, 147
San Francisco Giants 7, 66, 78, 85, 86, 90, 115, 144, 148
San Juan, Puerto Rico 141
Sandberg, Ryne 167
Sanford, Jack 85
Santana, Carlos 174
Santo, Ron 16, 73, 74, 75, 76, 77, 78, 83, 91, 92, 97, 99, 100, 101, 104, 107, 114, 119, 120, 125, 128, 129, 132, 133, 134, 135, 136, 143, 145, 147, 149, 150, 156, 167, 175, 176
Saperstein, Abe 36
Saskatoon, Saskatchewan 109
Sauer, Hank 52, 54, 55, 164
Savage, Ted 121
Scheffing, Bob 63, 71, 72
Schlensky, William 105
Schoendienst, Red 160
Seattle 73, 92, 149
Seattle Mariners 73
Seattle Pilots 73
Seattle Rainiers (Angels, Indians) 73
Seaver, Tom 133, 136
Seaway National Bank 157
Selma, Dick 129, 130
Sewell, Joe 160, 163
Shamsky, Art 119
Shantz, Bobby 93
Shea Stadium 136
Siannis, William 57, 58
Simmons, Curt 58, 115
Sinatra, Frank 103

Slaughter, Enos 160
Smalley, Roy 33
Smith, Hilton 165
Smith, Wendell 35, 45
Smith, Willie 128, 129
Snider, Duke 160
Sopel, Brent 171
The Sopranos 37
Sorrell, Barney 26
Sosa, Sammy 78, 172, 173
South Africa 170
Southern University 81, 92
Southworth, Billy 103
Spahn, Warren 58, 68, 69
Spangler, Al 121
The Sporting News 8, 94, 143, 150
Spring, Jack 93
Springfield, Illinois 46
Springfield, Massachusetts 33
Staley, Gerry 37
Stanley Cup 171
Starkville, Mississippi 18
Stearnes, Turkey 165
Steinham, Gloria 174
Stengel, Casey 103, 136
Stephens, Vern 37, 58
Stockholm 168
Summit, Pat 174
Sweden 168
Syracuse, New York 163

"Take Me Out to the Ballgame" (song) 176
Talbot, Bob 51, 55
Talley, Rick 148
Tappe, Elvin 81
Tatum, Goose 36
Taylor, Sammy 71
Taylor, Tony 72
TD Garden 166
Terkel, Studs 158
Texas 12, 15, 20, 161
Texas Rangers 68, 172
Thomas, Frank (1950s) 77
Thomas, Frank (2000s) 77, 177
Thomas, Lee 108, 117
Thompson, Hank 22, 29, 69
Thomson, Bobby 72
Three-I League 30
Tinker, Joe 116, 166
Toledo Blue Stockings 40
Toth, Paul 93
Trice, Bob 42
Turner Field 174

UCLA 92
United Press International 163
U.S. Army 26, 27, 32, 36, 62
U.S. Constitution 60
U.S. Marines 53
U.S. Navy 46

U.S. Supreme Court 47
University of Illinois 101

Vatican 111
Veeck, Bill 21, 22, 23, 36, 37, 40
Venezuela 37, 41
Vernon, Mickey 160
Vienna 111
Vietnam War 122, 123
Virginia 46

Walker, Moses Fleetwood 40
Walker, Verlon 81
Walker, Weldy 40
Walls, Lee 63, 66
Ward, Preston 52
Washington, D.C. 134
Wells, Willie 165
Wenatchee, Washington 101
WGN Broadcasting 94, 178
Whistler, Alabama 79
White, Jesse 170
White, William Edward 40
White House 148, 174
Whitlow, Robert 83
Wilhelm, Hoyt 144
Williams, Billy 78, 79, 83, 84, 85, 91, 97, 99,
  100, 101, 114, 125, 128, 129, 135, 136, 144, 145,
  147, 156, 157, 167, 174, 175, 176, 178, 179
Williams, Marvin 41
Williams, Ted 41, 142, 164, 174
Wilmington, Delaware 163
Wilson, Hack 50
Winfrey, Oprah 169, 174
Wisconsin 124, 140
Wooden, John 92
Works Progress Administration 11,
World Series 3, 21, 53, 57, 66, 72, 74, 93, 98,
  102, 104, 110, 122, 130, 132, 136, 137, 139, 153,
  158, 159, 163, 170, 172, 180
World War II 14, 27, 39, 40
Wrigley, Philip K. 9, 51, 59, 60, 77, 81, 82, 88,
  99, 102, 103, 105, 117, 124, 132, 134, 136, 140,
  148, 151, 155, 156, 157, 158, 162, 163, 169
Wrigley Field (Friendly Confines) 1, 4, 5, 7,
  8, 16, 28, 29, 32, 38, 52, 54, 55, 57, 58, 59,
  63, 66, 71, 73, 78, 85, 86, 88, 94, 95, 96, 97,
  98, 101, 102, 105, 114, 120, 122, 124, 125, 127,
  128, 133, 134, 135, 138, 142, 143, 146, 151, 152,
  153, 158, 168, 172, 175, 176, 179
Wrigleyville 58, 175
WSCR-AM 670 (radio) 175

Yawkey, Tom 41
Yippies 124
YMCA 11, 15
Young, Dick 150, 160, 161, 164
Young, Don 132, 133, 140

Zimmer, Don 77

www.ingramcontent.com/pod-product-compliance
Ingram Content Group UK Ltd.
Pitfield, Milton Keynes, MK11 3LW, UK
UKHW042010140426
5217IPUK00015B/1092